Teaching International Content
Curriculum Resources
for Social Work Education

Edited by Rosemary J. Link and Lynne M. Healy

CSWE
PRESS

Council on Social Work Education | Alexandria, VA

ISBN 0-87293-115-3

Printed in the United States of America on acid-free paper that meets the American National Standards Institute Z39-48 Standard.

Council on Social Work Education, Inc.
1725 Duke Street, Suite 500
Alexandria, VA 22314-3457
www.cswe.org

Contents

MODULES
Policy

Practice/Policy

Ethics

Racism/Oppression

HBSE/Practice/Diversity

Travel Study

RESOURCES FOR CURRICULUM AND FACULTY DEVELOPMENT

CONTRIBUTORS

Introduction to the Collection

Rosemary J. Link and Lynne M. Healy

This timely volume is intended to support programs in their implementation of the Council on Social Work Education's (CSWE, 2001) Educational Policy and Accreditation Standards. It will provide readers with a guide to the required international elements of the standards and offer resources in order to achieve the expectation that programs *prepare social workers to recognize the global context of social work practice* (Educational Policy, 1.2). At the 2003 CSWE Annual Program Meeting, Frank Baskind, president, asked "What are the key points of entry that we can use to help our students to understand that social work practice occurs in a global context?" In this collection readers will see "points of entry" that are natural and can be easily adapted for existing courses; they will also see innovative approaches to syllabus and curriculum building that reflect the deepening awareness of social work as an international profession. The numerous references and sample assignments provided will allow educators to make international content more explicit in their own teaching. In order to establish a context for these materials our introduction is in five parts:

- The impact of globalization on the social work profession;
- The basis for our conceptual understanding of international and global issues as integral to our curriculum;
- International perspectives in the CSWE EPAS;
- Specific introduction of the syllabi and modules in the volume;
- Acknowledgments

THE IMPACT OF GLOBALIZATION ON SOCIAL WORK

Globalization is a potent force shaping the social and economic environment of the early 21st century. An article in *Foreign Policy* noted that even the "least globalized" countries "are being drawn together by new forces beyond their ability to control, whether it is global warming, the spread of infectious disease, or the rise of transnational crime" (Measuring Globalization, 2001, p. 8). In addition to the widely recognized world economy, globalization includes social, political, health, and environmental dimensions and offers new arenas for social action (Healy, 2001). As Ife (2000) cautioned, social forces must be emphasized along with the economic in order to promote effective action at the global level. The more negative effects of globalization are often emphasized, but social work educators must also recognize the opportunities for positive change in the increasingly interconnected world. Kofi Annan, Secretary General of the United Nations, provided an important perspective for social work in noting that "while globalization creates opportunities for economic exploitation and exacerbates some problems, it also provides chances for confronting many of the world's most pressing issues" (Asamoah, 2003, p. 2).

The material in this volume demonstrates that international content is not a separate field targeted at the few, but part of all our professional journeys. Family pathways often begin and end in different communities, regions and countries, so that crossing and recrossing borders is a norm. Almost all students will practice with people who are of a different culture and national origin to their own, requiring a broad and more global understanding of diversity. Integrating international content into the curriculum is not in tension with an emphasis on cultural diversity and the need to challenge discrimination in our local communities, rather it is all of a piece. When students can recognize the dangers and desperation that cause people to leave their familiar surroundings and seek work elsewhere, even across national borders, they can combat discrimination and identify oppressive practices more assertively. When students pause to realize their own and their clients' interdependence with other countries of the world, they become more respectful of initiatives and resources in locations beyond their own experience. As noted in a speech to the 2001 Conference of Caribbean and International Social Work Educators by Vishanthie Sewpaul, a South African social work educator, internationalizing the curriculum will allow social work educators to transcend parochialism, understand similarities and differences among nations, and prepare students for "emancipatory practice" as they gain new understanding of global inequalities.

Recent trends and events have brought new attention to global interdependence. The population of the United States is changing in ways that significantly affect social work practice, especially as a result of the movement of people to escape poverty and war. The Census Bureau reports that "One in five Americans speaks a language other than English at home . . . and 11.9 million people live in linguistically isolated homes, meaning nobody in the home 14 or older knew English very well, up 54% from 1990" (U.S. Bureau of the Census, 2003). It is cautiously estimated that 11.5% of the U.S. population are foreign born, although figures concerning illegal immigration are considered to be underestimates (U.S. Bureau of the Census, 2003). Social work agencies work with refugees, migrant workers, international adoptees, victims of torture, transnational families, and people suffering the effects of racism and discrimination. With the immigrant population at its highest level since the 1920s, it is almost certain that every social worker will be doing cross-cultural work in the course of her (or his) career and doing so in hospitals, schools, child welfare and mental health agencies, not only in specialized services (U.S. Bureau of the Census, 2003).

Globalization, as noted earlier, brings both tensions and opportunities. Social workers are practicing in communities where families are struggling to keep jobs above minimum wage and many people experience ambivalence about transnational corporations moving their work force from country to country. Very few of us, with the exception of ascetics and perhaps followers of Mahatma Gandhi (who spun his own clothes from Indian-grown cotton) get through our day without relying on products from a variety of nations. Few students pause, however, to recognize their interdependence with the rest of the world and to think where their coffee beans or tea bushes grow or to research the source of their rubber-soled shoes. It is encouraging that the social impact of international economic changes is reported daily in U.S. media while a decade ago most newspapers relegated international concerns to a special back section. Students may however come to class with biases about the impact of increasing interdependence and it is important to include a variety of entry points in dialogue and resources. Some of the ways people are becoming aware of the complexities of globalization as it affects their lives include the arrival of migrant workers and refugees in their neighborhoods, reporting of offshore employment, more stringent requirements for immigrant employees; cautions about travel to certain parts of the world, and questioning of the impact of transnational corporations (Shiva, 2002). While the state of California debates permission for illegal immigrants to hold driving licenses, a North Carolina editorial claims that: "State's workers suffer in a global economy—the price of progress a future that looks worse than the past" (The Sunday News & Observer, 2004, State's workers suffer in a global economy. p. 1A). More posivitively, reports are beginning to recognize that U.S. citizens have long relied on immigrant labor and are only now seeing this vital contribution to our social and economic relationships (Blevins, 2002). Also, awareness is growing of the increasing cooperation in health programs and medical research. The World Health Organization has been able to reduce the impact of diseases that know no borders (such as SARS) and are increasing collective efforts to share innovations in cancer treatments and to attack the AIDS pandemic in Africa and elsewhere (www.who.int/csr/sars/en/).

There is no room for ignorance of the rest of the world because we are so closely intertwined. Even as we realize that U.S. systems of education have left college students with little knowledge of geography we know we have to help them with new demands because social work has become international in its responsibilities. In a spring 2004 classroom quiz conducted by one of the editors in her Global Peace and Development course, none of the students could list all six countries bordering Iraq even though some of their family members were involved in combat there; few knew that AT&T service engineers for their telephones are in Bangalore, India, and several expressed resentment at offshore employment even as they benefit from less expensive goods and labor. These gaps in knowledge are indicators of needed curriculum changes and increased preparation for fieldwork.

As soon as social work students put a foot into their agencies they grapple with international issues. When Baskind refers to "points of entry" for students into international work, he invites us to connect students' practice experience to global realities. The following illustrations are examples of a service at the crossroads of international tensions. Recently the Seattle International Adoption agency was closed due to concerns about protocols with their international partners; it was discovered that some of the "orphans" adopted in the United States from Cambodia actually had parents living in their homeland (Shukovsky, 2003). As the authors write this introduction, Jane Jeong Trenka's memoir *The Language of Blood* criticizes the lack of preparation of adoptive parents of children from other countries by social service agencies in the Midwest. In a list of questions Trenka (2003, p.188) raises global awareness issues for social workers and parents: What kind of training was provided for the adoption social workers? What kind of information was provided to adoptive parents about international/interracial adoption? Were there mandatory classes for prospective parents? What kind of follow-up took place? For this young woman the path has been a hard one: "The way I think about myself these days is with the word that best describes me: exile. I hadn't thought of myself as an exile or immigrant before—just a lucky adoptee. But now, I see that "exile" is the word that fits me best" (p.188, 199). To answer the questions posed helps students recognize the subtleties of language as they seek to communicate effectively with clients of different culture and experience, and strengthens service, in this example in relation to international adoptions.

Another "point of entry" to use to increase students' global awareness is the impact of the "war on terror" declared by the Bush administration. Sensitivity to the impact of international events on the United States has been heightened by the terrorist attacks on the World Trade Center and the Pentagon on September 11, 2001, and by the military operations in Afghanistan and Iraq, and the focus on "homeland security" that followed. The homeland security elements of the "war on terrorism" have emphasized increased surveillance, tightened border and immigration restrictions, and increased scrutiny of people from countries identified as "likely" sources of terrorists. After discussion of the impact of the Bush administration "war on terrorism" on diverse populations, the CSWE International Commission issued a statement in September 2003, which has been approved by the board of directors as the following resolution:

> We, the members of the International Commission, recognize and are deeply concerned about the after-effects of September 11, 2001. This tragedy changed all our lives and our communities. The impact of the events of this day has been particularly severe on Arab Americans, and South Asian Americans of all religions, that is, Muslims, Sikhs, Hindus and Christians. They have been subjected to ongoing racial profiling in airports, hotels, restaurants, border crossings, schools, jobs and every other aspect of life. They have also been victims of hate crimes. We believe that the after-effects of September 11, 2001 have implications as to what we should be teaching to our students. In this regard, we would like to remind colleagues of the opportunities afforded by the Social Work curriculum to advance students' awareness of human rights and civil liberties through attention to: (a) provision of culturally appropriate services to all victims of oppression and to include victims of the current times; and (b) utilization of social work interventions to effectively evaluate and challenge legislation, and to influence policies that conflict with human rights.

Educators will find the examples of international adoptions and the "war on terrorism" and resulting profiling of foreigners to be among many "points of entry" for inclusion of international content in the social work curriculum. Such examples are particularly useful because they clearly link domestic and international concerns in social work practice. There are a broad range of global policy instruments that can assist social workers in preparing themselves and their service users and clients for global realities. These range from the Universal Declaration of Human Rights to policies with specific focus such as the United Nations Convention on the Rights of the Child. The social worker implementing an international perspective expects to gather ideas for intervention from a wide array of international organizations and many of these resources are referenced later in this volume.

While globalization is creating tensions for social workers, it is also offering a wider lens with which to experience creativity and new solutions to old problems in the profession. Innovations and opportunities in working with people, be they prospective adoptive parents, recent immigrants, people in exile, or those in need of a child-friendly city, can be discovered with this wide global perspective on the profession and its resources. In this context, child friendly refers to a community that seeks to establish an environment that enhances children's well-being and fulfills the expectations of the United Nations Convention on the Rights of the Child (UNICEF, 2002). For example, the 2004 video titled *The Children of Italy* gives a glimpse of a unique urban place for children. The video shows part of a project to offer a "child friendly city" in Pistoia in northern Italy. All adults and agencies are involved, from the police chief to the kindergarten to the mayor.

A similarly encouraging project relevant for social workers is the increased attention given to "micro lending" and savings accounts based on the Grameen Bank model in Bangladesh. For many people experiencing poverty, it is hard to obtain credit. In the Grameen model people may apply for small loans and collectively fund projects without the Western expectation of collateral. This model has been so successful that it is now being imported to Kentucky and the Midwest through the Full Circle Fund in Chicago (Elliott and Mayadas, 1999). The syllabi in this volume offer many more instances of initiatives and innovations that enhance social work practice across the globe.

THE BASIS FOR OUR CONCEPTUAL UNDERSTANDING OF INTERNATIONAL AND GLOBAL ISSUES AS INTEGRAL TO THE SOCIAL WORK CURRICULUM

The conceptual underpinning of this collection's approach to internationalizing curriculum is a broad one that invites students to look beyond national borders. We interpret global and international content as an extension of existing material and experience, rather than a radical departure and daunting new area to fit into our packed programs. The global content identified here reflects the concept of interdependence and opportunity. As stated by President Clinton (1993) in his first inaugural address, "There is no longer a clear division between what is foreign and what is domestic. The world economy, the world environment, the world AIDS crisis, the world arms race—they affect us all" (p. A15). Similarly, we believe it is impossible to practice social work without becoming involved with global issues.

Sometimes social work curriculum has focused on the immediate locality and micro-level skill building and has treated international issues as a separate area of knowledge. The syllabi in this volume indicate that there is a place in the curriculum for both infusion of international content in foundation and concentration courses and the offering of specialized courses on international topics. Ensuring that students see the international as connected to their professional responsibilities is essential, and the infusion of content is necessary to ensure exposure for all students. As suggested by Jones and Kumssa (1999),

> It is a mistake to compartmentalize international education excessively. In fact, it is necessary that cosmopolitan issues be considered in regular social policy classes, that child welfare include mention of child labor and the rights of the child, that human growth and the social environment make reference to other cultures (those close to our borders and further afield), that direct and indirect practice courses routinely consider immigrants and refugees, and so on. (p. 212)

The following overview of international elements in the EPAS reflects this expectation that social work programs take responsibility for ensuring that all students are exposed to international perspectives and that graduates are prepared to be responsible professionals who can competently advocate for just social policies and human rights.

INTERNATIONAL PERSPECTIVES IN THE COUNCIL ON SOCIAL WORK EDUCATION EDUCATIONAL POLICY AND ACCREDITATION STANDARDS (EPAS)

International Requirements in the Standards

The adoption of the 2001 Educational Policy and Accreditation Standards (EPAS) represents a major advance in expanding international perspectives in social work education. The Educational Policy section of EPAS replaces the 1992 Curriculum Policy Statement that contained only a brief reference to the importance of worldwide professional cooperation in its preamble, but no mention of international content in the body of the standards. The new standards give significant recognition to the importance of a global perspective and require international content in several components of the curriculum, as will be detailed below.

Following a preamble that acknowledges social work's concern for human rights and for "social and economic justice worldwide," EPAS states that "professional social workers are leaders in a variety of organizational settings and service delivery systems within a global context" (Educational Policy 1.0). Furthermore, the Educational Policy 1.2 states that programs achieve the purposes of social work education in a variety of ways including helping students recognize the "global context of social work practice." The sections of EPAS that are most relevant to this volume are specific references to international content in the requirements for foundation curriculum in the social justice and social policy areas.

In Educational Policy 4.2, Populations at Risk and Social and Economic Justice, there is direct reference to the requirement that the curriculum address the "global interconnections of oppression" as well as human rights. Specifically, the policy requires that programs: "integrate social and economic justice content grounded in an understanding of distributive justice, human and civil rights, and the global interconnections of oppression."

In Educational Policy 4.4, Social Welfare Policy and Services, students are required to consider the interaction between systems of all sizes, a familiar concept from their practice interventions. Further, they are expected to acquire the knowledge and skills "to analyze organizational, local, state, national and international issues in social welfare policy and service delivery."

Although the words international and global do not appear in them, Educational Policies 4.1 on Diversity and 4.3 on Human Behavior and the Social Environment are also important in developing and teaching international content, as they give considerable emphasis to the importance of culture and cultural diversity. Diversity content (Educational Policy 4.1) "emphasizes the interlocking and complex nature of culture and personal identity. It ensures that social services meet the needs of groups served and are culturally relevant." As more than one in every nine people in the United States is foreign born, knowledge of world cultures and the human migration experience is increasingly an essential part of cultural competence.

Implications of EPAS for Curriculum Building in International Social Work

The inclusion of international content in standards for the foundation curriculum means that all students must receive this content, either through infusion or through specific required courses. Thus EPAS supports the premises identified earlier in this introduction that the international/global and the local/domestic are increasingly difficult to separate and that such separation is antithetical to understanding the global practice context. For many social work programs, infusion of international content will be selected as the most reasonable means of addressing EPAS. The ideas shared below are beginning suggestions from the editors for infusion of required international content.

Global Content on Practice and Oppression/Justice

The social work curriculum provides many opportunities to alert students to the extent of social and economic oppression in the world and new global realities of everyday practice settings, for example, in child protection, refugee resettlement, employment relocation, migrant services, health services settings and health issues such as AIDS and SARS, cross-national adoptions, and school social work. Students may be introduced to the concept of interdependence early in their programs and may relate it to the simple reality of depending on the rest of the world for their daily coffee, clothes, and shoes. From interdependence it is a short step to consider that while we are dependent on the economic production of many countries of the world, income and resources are unevenly distributed, leaving millions living on less than $1 per day in the developing world (United Nations Development Programme, 2003). Relevant content under this standard includes introductory information on economic interdependence and exploitation, the interaction of global systems of privilege, and acquiescence in discrimination against women, racism, and persecution of immigrants. Issues such as the HIV/AIDS pandemic, or international migration can be used to illustrate the complexities and realities of forces of oppression that operate on the global scale.

The concept of human rights is relatively new in American social work education but of growing importance in social work internationally (International Federation of Social Workers, 1988; United Nations Centre for Human Rights, 1994). Inclusion of international human rights laws, the United Nations human rights machinery, civil society human rights action, and application of human rights principles to social work practice and ethics are recommended.

Social Welfare Policy

International issues are increasingly intertwined with and inseparable from domestic social issues. The use of the term "international issues" in EPAS suggests a departure from the standard comparative social welfare approach often used in the past to introduce limited international content. Instead, programs are encouraged to introduce students to social issues at the global level. Both foundation social policy and child welfare courses, for example, could address international adoption as a policy dilemma, or consider optimal approaches to ensuring children's rights. The AIDS pandemic and the crisis of AIDS orphans; trafficking in women, children, and migrants; and immigration policy are just a few of many critical international issues for social work consideration in the policy curriculum. Coverage of the impact of U.S. policies on the well-being of people in other parts of the world should be considered. The syllabi and modules in the volume suggest rich resource material on the issues and on the existing international organizations and structures that can contribute to policy solutions.

Cultural Diversity and Human Behavior and the Social Environment (HBSE)

If EPAS is considered in the context of globalization, the implications for the curriculum in cultural diversity and HBSE suggest increased attention to cultures of origin of the growing foreign-born population and the now 20% of families in the United States that include at least one foreign-born parent. Attention must be paid in both classroom and field placements to developing knowledge and skills in cross-cultural communication, cultural sensitivity, and learning how to learn about diverse cultures. The migration process is for many a life-altering experience and one that must be addressed by social service and mental health providers. Preparation for these practice roles must begin in professional education.

GUIDE TO THE COLLECTION

The course outlines and modules in this volume illustrate the variety of approaches to inclusion of international content in social work curricula. Models range from infusion of international content in foundation and concentration courses to specialized electives on international social work or social development. A few of the courses in the volume are part of concentrations or elective specializations with significant international focus.

Because EPAS requires reaching all students with international content, we begin the volume with the infusion models. Section I contains outlines that demonstrate infusion of significant international content and perspectives into foundation courses. Included are three outlines that model different approaches to social welfare policy and services (SWPS). The outline for Global Perspectives on Human Need, submitted by Robin Wingo, meets a general education requirement for BSW students at Mankato University. The outline developed by Vanmala Hiranandani, building on the work of Katherine van Wormer, is a required BSW course in social policy at the University of Northern Iowa. Social Welfare Policy and Services II, taught by Charles Guzzetta, is one of several topical offerings that meet the MSW requirement for a second policy course at Hunter Colllege. Human Behavior in the Social Environment as developed by Rosemary Link of Augsburg College provides a model for a required MSW HBSE course richly infused with international content. The final selection in the section is a required foundation community practice course in Monmouth University's MSW program in which Robin Mama demonstrates the local–global connection.

Specialized courses on international social work or international social development are grouped in section II. These contain rich and comprehensive materials for adaptation, either to develop specialized courses for the reader's own program, or for inclusion in modules in foundation or concentration courses. The selections include an MSW elective course developed by David Engstrom at San Diego State University, a doctoral elective from Catholic University taught by Frederick Ahearn, a course on International Social Development taught by Richard Estes as a required course in the graduate program at Washington University and as an elective at the University of Pennsylvania MSW program, a course on Social and Economic Development taught by Margaret Sherraden and Shirley Porterfield and required for students in several MSW macro concentrations at the University of Missouri–St. Louis and Washington University, and an elective BSW course on International Social Work submitted by Maria Bartlett of Humboldt State University.

The next series of syllabi approach international content with a focus on a specific topic. The series begins with two outlines that emphasize a human rights approach to teaching international content. International Social Work and Human Rights is an elective course in the MSW program at Springfield College, developed by Joseph Wronka. Human Rights in Global Perspective, developed by Diane Falk, is an elective intended for second- and third-year undergraduates at Richard Stockton College. Readers will note that EPAS now includes human rights as an important concept for social work and will find many useful resources in the outlines in this section and in the module on women's human rights in the final grouping.

Readers with a special interest in content on the social problems and practice/policy issues of women are directed to the next two syllabi. These courses, one with a focus on women and development submitted by Beth Cagan from the BSW program at Cleveland State University, and one emphasizing violence against women, submitted by Barbara Turnage of the University of Central Florida, provide global perspectives on oppression as well as a wealth of examples for inclusion in social policy courses. Readers should note that Cagan's course meets university general education requirements for both Writing Across the Curriculum and Non-Western Culture and Civilization, and Turnage's course is available to both graduate and undergraduate social work students.

Two additional specialized courses address topics of growing significance to social work. Golam Mathbor's course, an elective in the MSW program at Monmouth University, emphasizes civil society and the role of nongovernmental organizations, both at home and globally. Globalization and Sweatshops, an elective at the University at Albany, State University of New York, taught by William Roth and Katharine Briar-Lawson, focuses on sweatshops as a problematic component of globalization. While organized as full courses, both syllabi contain materials that can be adapted for inclusion in other parts of the curriculum.

The final section of the volume contains a set of modules that can be adapted for a variety of courses. The first three modules present alternative models for addressing EPAS-mandated content in the area of Social Welfare Policy and Services. These are two-session modules developed by Beth Cagan of Cleveland State University to introduce international content into the introductory social work course; a module on social exclusion developed by Suzanne McDevitt of Edinboro University of Pennsylvania, with content that could be used in courses on social policy and in courses on oppression and social justice; and a unit used by M. C. "Terry" Hokenstad of Case Western Reserve University as part of the required foundation SWPS course in the MSW program.

A three-session module on sustainable development developed by Dorothy Gamble of the University of North Carolina at Chapel Hill, where it is taught as part of a comprehensive course on the topic, provides numerous resources for adaptation. Judith Gordon's comprehensive module on women's human rights, taught at the College of New Rochelle also as part of a full course on the topic, includes innovative class assignments.

The next three modules address topics not covered elsewhere in the volume. The first is a module on international perspectives on ethics, developed by Lynne Healy of the University of Connecticut; the module contains four exercises that can be used for discussion or for written assignments. A module on teaching about racism in the United States, also contributed by Lynne Healy, demonstrates the use of United Nations materials to address racism at home. Diane Drachman's module on the migration experience is a three-session segment that can be used in courses on HBSE or on Practice. As taught at the University of Connecticut, it is part of an elective MSW course on Services to Immigrants and Refugees and Cross-Cultural Helping.

The module, War and Peace in Bosnia—developed by Judy Anne Dwyer, Karl Bahm, and Haji Dokhanchi (University of Wisconsin-Superior)—demonstrates the use of a well planned travel-study option to address international learning. We hope that this will be useful as a model to educators planning travel-study courses to other countries. The final contribution is a well-developed set of Web site resources by Héctor Díaz of the University of Texas at

Arlington that can be used to enhance any course or module on international topics and can assist faculty members in furthering their own knowledge of international issues.

Criteria for Selection of Course Outlines for the Collection

Criteria for selection were carefully deliberated. Together with our nine reviewers we (the coeditors) have been encouraged by the range of effective curriculum content in existence. More than 50 outlines were submitted in response to the CSWE call for examples. It has been our emphasis to select courses and modules that could potentially be most useful as resource materials for colleagues in other social work programs. Despite some excellent submissions of country-specific courses, these have been less of a priority due to limited generalizability to other programs. The example of a course in Bosnia is included as it offers a template for use with exchanges in other countries.

All submissions were evaluated using an 11-item CSWE Publications and Media Commission instrument covering such areas as comprehensiveness of content, clarity, relevance of course content to CSWE standards, currency, creativity and innovation in assignments, instructions in delivering international content, organization, clarity of student assessment procedures, and usefulness to other programs. An additional set of criteria was used to assess courses and modules demonstrating infusion of international content to ensure sufficiency and relevance of the international components. These criteria included infusion of international perspectives in course outcomes/objectives, a global reach in readings and resources, inclusion of assignments that address international learning, and inclusion of international learning in criteria for evaluating student performance.

The call for submissions yielded a higher proportion of international social welfare courses than any other category. To ensure a range of courses and topics, we are unable to include them all here, but have invited supplemental modules to reflect the array of sources available. It is also noteworthy that we received a good number of outlines demonstrating infusion of international content in foundation courses. In *Global Perspectives in Social Work Education*, the first collection of international social work course outlines published by CSWE in 1997, only one outline demonstrating infusion in the foundation was judged adequate for publication. That we received a large number and were able to publish five examples augurs well for the implementation of EPAS. It should be cautioned, however, that the submissions were concentrated in the social policy area, with a much smaller number in HBSE. Missing were examples of solid infusion of international content in practice, research, and diversity courses.

Readers should be aware that the syllabi in this collection are out of context of their program flow. It is our hope that in publishing these courses, authors are willing to be available as mentors to faculty expanding their own international content. Also, where replication is planned, faculty members are encouraged to discuss with their colleagues and students the horizontal (connections to parallel courses in the curriculum flow) and vertical (courses with prerequisites or in a hierarchy toward graduation) context.

ACKNOWLEDGMENTS

Publication of this volume has been made possible by the interest and efforts of many. We would like to thank CSWE, especially the publications office under the direction of Michael Monti, Vicki Fanney, and Noemi C. Arthur for their interest in publishing a second collection of international outlines and for ongoing assistance in preparing the publication. The ongoing support of the International Commission, chaired by Doreen Elliott, has been invaluable. Nine members of the commission served as reviewers for the publication: M. C. "Terry" Hokenstad (Case Western Reserve University), Salewe Kawewe (Southern Illinois University Carbondale), Golam Mathbur (Monmouth University), Nazneen Mayadas (University of Texas at Arlington), Arline Prigoff (California State University, Sacramento), Irene Queiro-Tajalli (Indiana University), Uma Segal (University of Missouri–St. Louis), Sharon Templeman (Stephen F. Austin University), and Sally vander Straeten (University of Georgia).

The publication would have been particularly difficult to complete without the invaluable help of Pamela Harrison of the University of Connecticut School of Social Work. She assisted with tracking and contacting authors and reviewers, made the editing changes in the manuscript, and compiled the final manuscript for transmission to CSWE. University of Connecticut graduate students Cari Carter and Autumn Fiske also assisted in organizing the submissions.

REFERENCES

Asamoah, Y. A. (2003). International collaboration in social work education: Overview. In L. M. Healy, Y. A. Asamoah, M. C. Hokenstad (Eds.), *Models of International Collaboration in Social Work Education*. (pp. 1–14) Alexandria, VA: Council on Social Work Education.

Blevins, J. (2002, July 12). Immigrant workers are a resource the economy needs. *Minneapolis Star Tribune*, p. A6.

Clinton, W. J. (1993, January 21). Inaugural address. *The New York Times*, p. A15.

Council on Social Work Education. (2001). *Educational policy and accreditation standards*. Alexandria, VA: Author.

Elliott, D., & Mayadas, N.(1999). Infusing global perspectives into social work practice. In C. Ramanathan & R. J. Link, *All our futures: Principles and resources for social work practice in a global era* (pp. 52–68). Belmont, CA: Brooks/Cole.

Galardini, A., & Giovannini, D. (2003) *Children of Italy*. Produced by PECA International Idyl Wild Media. Distributed: Crystal Lake, Illinois: Magna Systems Inc.

Healy, L. M. (2001). *International social work: Professional action in an interdependent world*. New York: Oxford University Press.

Ife, J. (2000). Localized needs and a globalized economy: Bridging the gap with social work practice [Special issue]. *Canadian Social Work*, 2(1), 50–64.

International Federation of Social Workers (1988). *International policy papers*. Geneva: Author.

Jones, J. F., & Kumssa, A. (1999). Professional growth in a global context. In C. Ramanathan & R. J. Link, *All our futures: Principles and resources for social work practice in a global era* (pp. 206–218). Belmont, CA: Brooks/Cole.

Measuring globalization. (2001). *Foreign Policy*, 1–11, Retrieved April 3, 2001, from the InfoTrac database.

Shukovsky, P. (2003). Feds claim adopted orphans had parents, U.S. agents break up local agency dealing in Cambodia. *Seattle Post-Intelligencer*. December 17, 2003, p. A1.

State's workers suffer in a global economy. (2004, May 30). [Editorial]. *The Sunday News & Observer*, East Carolina, p. 1A.

Shiva, V. (2002). *Water Wars: Privatization, Pollution, and Profit*. Cambridge, MA: South End Press.

Trenka, J. J. (2003). *The language of blood*. Minneapolis: Minneapolis Historical Society.

United Nations Centre for Human Rights (1994). *Human rights and social work: A manual for schools of social work and the social work profession*. [Professional training series No. 1]. Geneva: Author.

UNICEF. (2002). *Building a world fit for children*. New York: UNICEF. www.unicef.org.

United Nations Development Programme. (2003). *Human development report 2003*. New York: Oxford University Press.

United States Bureau of the Census. (2003). The foreign-born population in the United States March 2002. Retrieved July 18, 2004, from www.census.gov/prod/2003pubs/p20-539.pdf

World Health Organization: www.who.int/csr/sars/en/

MINNESOTA STATE UNIVERSITY–MANKATO
DEPARTMENT OF SOCIAL WORK | MANKATO, MN
ROBIN R. WINGO

Global Perspectives on Human Need
SOWK 255

COURSE DESCRIPTION

National borders are increasingly permeable as an international economy influences an emerging global society. In a similar fashion, problems faced by people on a day-to-day basis rapidly are becoming generic; the same problems appear in every country, including the most developed ones. War, famine, epidemics, and violence continue to create unmet human needs. Historically significant cultural patterns must be reexamined as viable resources in a rapidly changing society. Immigration and mobility are increasing everywhere. The United States and other more developed countries face increasing demands for admittance and must struggle with the reality of illegal immigration. People from less developed countries are actively recruited or coerced into accepting overseas employment, often in degrading circumstances. The continuing effects of colonization add to the suffering of ordinary people in the developing world.

Governments and multinational organizations are involved in the struggle to find solutions for these and other issues. The actions of these bodies addressing human needs have had limited effect to date in improving the general lot of the poor of the world. Yet the struggle is important and must be continued. The purpose of this course is to:

- increase students' awareness of these global issues;
- allow students to understand the role of social work and other professions in developing strategies to alleviate poverty and deprivation;
- increase knowledge about the consequences of domestic and international political and economic forces on the lives of people around the globe; and
- explore the results of current strategies to alleviate poverty and deprivation.

This course meets Minnesota State University–Mankato's three-credit undergraduate general education global perspective requirement that focuses on "increasing students' awareness of the growing interdependence of nations, traditions, and peoples and develop(ing) their ability to apply a comparative perspective to cross-cultural social, economic, and political experience." This course is open to any student and therefore will offer the opportunity for a rich and thoughtful discourse representing a variety of academic programs and departments.

LEARNING OUTCOMES

Upon completion of this course, the successful student will develop the following skills, knowledge, and values:

1. Access and evaluate information on international social, health, and economic conditions;
2. Demonstrate knowledge and appreciation of cultural, social, and religious differences;
3. Analyze responses to specific social problems as they are manifested on a global scale;
4. Describe the role of governmental, multinational, and nongovernmental organizations in creating responses to human need;
5. Identify forces that oppress and exploit vulnerable populations of the world;
6. Analyze the implications of the World Bank, International Monetary Fund, United Nations Universal Declaration on Human Rights, United Nations Convention on the Rights of the Child, and other organizations and statements as they are being discussed and applied on the global scene;
7. Understand the role of the global citizen in addressing the social, economic, and health issues that face the world today; and
8. Be able to empathically understand the desire of many people to improve their countries situation AND the desire of many to emigrate (legally or otherwise) to other countries.

1

REQUIRED TEXTS

Healy, L. M. (2001). *International social work: Professional action in an interdependent world.* New York: Oxford University Press.

The Millennium Project. (2001). *Briefing papers for students: "We the people": The role of the United Nations in the twenty-first century.* New York: United Nations.

OTHER REQUIREMENTS

Online Classroom With UCompass

Internet Address for UCompass is available via the university homepage located at http://www.mnsu.edu/.

Students can check their points for each assignment as well as point totals for the semester by accessing UCompass. All scores are confidential with the use of your password.

All students must be registered on UCompass by the end of the first week. Dependent on the needs of those enrolled in this course, a lab may be scheduled to complete this registration. All students must have access to e-mail and are expected to check it for information related to this course.

UCompass will be used to provide you with additional information and resources. Any assignments, quizzes, or examinations added to UCompass after the beginning of the semester will be announced in class with ample time for completion.

COURSE EVALUATION

Students are evaluated on participation, attendance, and completion of all required learning activities. Grading guidelines will be discussed for each assignment. Grades awarded for group papers will be added to each student's total points provided that each student contributes to the group paper. In addition, students are expected to evaluate the course, the instructor, and the text. The instructor reserves the right to add a midterm exam and/or a final exam.

COURSE EXPECTATIONS

The course schedule outlines weekly topics and due dates for UCompass, reading, and writing assignments. You will be provided one copy of the syllabus and the course schedule in class. You may download additional copies from UCompass should a replacement be necessary.

- Each week the class will focus on a specific topic. This will involve lecture, large and small group discussions, guests to bring unique insights, videos, and other experiences. Students are expected to participate by asking questions, answering questions, and introducing information or ideas.
- Students will be expected to keep up with the readings, Internet assignments, and other out-of-class assignments.
- Students will break into small groups, select a country from an approved list, write papers, and produce a presentation they will share with other members of the class (outlined below).
- Each student will use this same country for the focus of his (or her) final paper.

READING ASSIGNMENTS

In fact, the instructor DOES know that you have other classes! However, the breadth of information regarding a rapidly evolving global situation far exceeds the ability of publishers to keep up. Textbook assignments are therefore augmented with suggested readings from various Web sites that are accessible via UCompass. Some current newspaper/newsmagazine articles will be made available in class. Every effort has been made to select readings carefully. You will be asked to evaluate their contribution to your learning.

WRITING ASSIGNMENTS

Group Papers

- Each member of the group should take the role of "primary author" for at least one paper. That means providing leadership for getting the information and resources organized, doing the final editing of the paper, making sure that all the assignment questions are answered, and making sure the paper is in on time.

- This does NOT mean the other group members are excused from contributing time, writing skills, references, and collaboration for clear and well-written content.
- These papers will form the foundation of the class presentation due toward the end of the semester.
- Each paper should include information as well as resource references (Web sites, journals, books, and other publications).
- Some time will be provided in class for getting organized, distributing work, and in general, moving the papers along. Students will be asked to supply an overview of tasks and decide who is responsible for each paper after the class meeting.

All writing assignments should be turned in on time (unless you have negotiated and documented an extension with the instructor), word processed, double-spaced on white paper, stapled, using a 12-point Times New Roman font, with page numbers, one-inch margins all around, and a bibliography. The bibliography does NOT count as one of the required pages. Half pages do not count as full pages.

- Any sources quoted, paraphrased, drawn on, or otherwise used should be properly cited (American Psychological Association, 5th ed. preferred) to avoid plagiarism. A minimum of two sources (beyond those supplied on UCompass) should be used for each paper.
- Papers must be submitted with a cover sheet that has the course name, each student's name (with the "primary author" first), title of the paper, and date submitted.

External links are provided on UCompass for the following papers. These are NOT the only sources of information you should access for information as you write your papers. You should use at minimum two additional sources for your papers:

- Assignment: Week 3 | Country Overview Group Paper: 50 points

  - Write a 5–7-page paper presenting a demographic, geographic, economic, and political overview of your chosen country.

- Assignment: Week 6 | WB/IMF Group Paper: 50 points

  - Visit the sites of the World Bank and the International Monetary Fund. Search for and visit the Web sites of organizations that oppose the WB/IMF programs that are active or verbal in your country. Write a 5–7-page paper answering the following questions:
  - How do the World Bank and the International Monetary Fund explain their programs of assistance to the developing world?
  - What are the concerns of the opposition groups that are active or vocal in your country? (Provide the full site address and statement of purpose of these groups.)
  - As far as you understand them, and I know that the issues are complex, do you support or oppose the way the IMF and WB are involved in your country?

- Assignment: Week 8 | Situation of Children Group Paper: 50 points

  - Using the Internet and library resources, find out the situation of children in your country. Write a short paper (5–7 pages) that describes the issues children face in your country.
  - Locate and describe at least one program that is working to help them.
  - Which articles from the Convention on the Rights of the Children are applicable to the situations you described? What information did you find about how the convention is being addressed by your country?

- Assignment: Week 10 | Human Rights Group Paper: 50 points

  - In the library or on the Internet find the Universal Declaration of Human Rights. Select two sections that especially appeal to your group and write a short paper (5–7 pages) on why those sections are important and the implications they have for the population in your country. Explain your group's interest in the particular sections that were chosen.

- Assignment: Week 12 | AIDS Pandemic Group Paper: 50 points

  - The AIDS pandemic in countries throughout the world has drawn attention to the difficulty of getting up-to-date medicines in the hands of sick, poor people; cultural attitudes toward disease; and health care services in general.

  - Describe in 5–7 pages the situation in your country, including any culturally specific perspectives or barriers that are discovered.

- Assignment: Week 15 | U.S. Role Individually Written Paper: 50 points

  - After all of the issues that we have discussed during this semester, describe in 5–7 pages what you think the appropriate role of the United States should be in responding to the issues. You may use your country as the foundation for your paper, but you should also incorporate a "global" perspective based on what you heard about in class and learned from your student colleagues or from the presentations. Support your answer.

Class Presentation | Group: 100 points

The class presentation should be based on, and roughly cover, the accumulated knowledge from the paper assignments. The primary focus should be on the people and their situation. You must also add cultural information that expands the understanding of your country beyond the statistics and issues they confront. This may take the form of a film or video clip (not to exceed 10 minutes), a short reading from a piece of literature, a display of craftwork or products, a display of artwork, a dance demonstration, and so forth. Any invitation to a guest speaker or performer MUST be cleared by the instructor IN ADVANCE.

Each group will have 30–45 minutes for its presentation. You must tell the instructor how much time you will require for scheduling purposes. Each group must provide a handout for class members. Each group member must have a speaking role in the presentation. There will be class time allotted for the groups to work on papers and/or the presentation. However, that time will be limited and you will need to spend some out-of-class time working on these projects. You may use PowerPoint, the document camera, or any other technological convenience you choose.

WEB SITES

These Web sites represent only a small sample of what is available on the Web and appear in no specific order. Please remember that sites can be hosted, founded, and maintained from any point of view by individuals, groups, and organizations. ALWAYS use good critical thinking skills as you review information regarding the host and mission of the site to help understand the information it is providing. The instructor urges you to review these and other sites that you may find thoughtfully and carefully for bias, political ideology, and truthfulness.

For example, this first listing, FAIR, doesn't sound negative, but it blames immigrants to Minnesota for the problems of urban sprawl, air pollution, poverty, and school growth! Caveat emptor!

Site: **The Federation for American Immigration Reform (FAIR)**
URL: http://www.fairus.org/
Description: FAIR is a national, nonprofit, public interest membership organization of concerned citizens united by their belief in the need for immigration reform. Founded in 1979, FAIR believes that the United States can and must have an immigration policy that is nondiscriminatory and designed to serve the environmental, economic, and social needs of our country.

Site: **Family Education Network's Information Please**
URL: http://www.infoplease.com/world.html
Description: Combining the contents of an encyclopedia, a dictionary, an atlas, and several up-to-the minute almanacs loaded with statistics, facts, and historical records, Infoplease places the resources of an entire reference information center at your fingertips.

Site: **CIA World Factbook 2001**
URL: http://www.cia.gov/cia/publications/factbook/
Description: Despite the controversy that surrounds the CIA, it does compile a tremendous amount of information about countries around the world. You will find succinct descriptions on this site.

Site: **Mother Jones**
URL: http://www.motherjones.com/
Description: Established in 1975 the Foundation for National Progress seeks to advance public understanding of, and engagement with, important issues through exemplary journalism and reporting. Its various media projects include Mother Jones magazine, MotherJones.com, and the Mother Jones International Fund for Documentary Photography. In a news world dominated by giant entertainment companies, Mother Jones provides an intelligent and provocative alternative to the homogenous and often hollow mainstream. Its work provides the base for informed and democratic change.

Site: **Newsweek Magazine**
URL: http://www.msnbc.com/news/NW-front_Front.asp
Description: Major news source. Searchable for current information regarding international issues.

Site: **Save The Children**
URL: http://www.savethechildren.org
Description: This organization works worldwide to address issues relevant to the education, safety, and development of children.

Site: **UNICEF**
URL: http://www.unicef.org/uwwide/
Description: In 1953, UNICEF became a permanent part of the United Nations system, its task being to help children living in poverty in developing countries get the care and stimulation they need in the early years of life and encourages families to educate girls as well as boys. It strives to reduce childhood death and illness and to protect children in the midst of war and natural disaster. UNICEF supports young people, wherever they are, in making informed decisions about their own lives, and strives to build a world in which all children live in dignity and security.

Site: **World Bank**
URL: http://www.worldbank.org/
Description: The World Bank Group is one of the world's largest sources of development assistance. In fiscal year 2001, the institution provided more than U.S. $17 billion in loans to its client countries. It works in more than 100 developing economies with the primary focus of helping the poorest people and the poorest countries.

Site: **International Monetary Fund Homepage**
URL: http://www.imf.org/
Description: The IMF is an international organization of 184 member countries. It was established to promote international monetary cooperation, exchange stability, and orderly exchange arrangements; to foster economic growth and high levels of employment; and to provide temporary financial assistance to countries to help ease balance of payments adjustment.

Site: **The International AIDS Trust**
URL: http://www.aidstrust.org/
Description: The International AIDS Trust was established to create strategic opportunities for galvanizing leadership, mobilizing resources, and promoting effective interventions in the global battle against AIDS. The International AIDS Trust is a single-focused nongovernmental organization.

Site: **The World Revolution**
URL: http://www.worldrevolution.org
Description: The World Revolution is an idea for a new, global grassroots social movement for progressive social change. It attempts to resolve in a definitive and comprehensive manner the major social problems of our world and our era.

Site: **The Heavily Indebted Poor Countries (HIPC) Debt Initiative**
URL: http://www.worldbank.org/hipc/
Description: The principal objective of the Debt Initiative for the heavily indebted poor countries is to bring the country's debt burden to sustainable levels, subject to satisfactory policy performance, so as to ensure that adjustment and reform efforts are not put at risk by continued high debt and debt service burdens. The HIPC Debt Initiative was proposed by the World Bank and IMF and agreed to by governments around the world in the fall of 1996. It was the first comprehensive approach to reduce the external debt of the world's poorest, most heavily indebted countries, and represented an important step forward in placing debt relief within an overall framework of poverty reduction.

Site: **Third World Network**
URL: http://www.twnside.org.sg
Description: The Third World Network is an independent nonprofit international network of organizations and individuals involved in issues relating to development, the Third World and North–South issues. Its objectives are to conduct research on economic, social, and environmental issues pertaining to the South; to publish books and magazines; to organize and participate in seminars; and to provide a platform representing broadly southern interests and perspectives at international fora such as the UN conferences and processes.

Site: **National Immigration Information Forum**
URL: http://www.immigrationforum.org/
Description: The purpose of the National Immigration Forum is to embrace and uphold America's tradition as a nation of immigrants. The forum advocates and builds public support for public policies that welcome immigrants and refugees and that are fair and supportive to newcomers in our country.

Site: **AIDS Education Global Information System (AEGiS)**
URL: http://www.aegis.org
Description: AEGiS began in the mid-1980s and has continued to be the definitive Web-based reference for HIV/AIDS-related information. The collaborative effort of many organizations and individuals has enabled the creation of this vast database of facts regarding the history, prevention and treatment of HIV/AIDS, to date, over one million files.

Site: **The WWW Virtual Library on Migration and Ethnic Relations**
URL: http://www.ercomer.org/wwwvl/select.php?selecttype = HostType&selector = NGO
Description: The WWW Virtual Library on Migration and Ethnic Relations' objective is to create a superlative and easy-to-use guide that thoroughly catalogs in an organized and meaningful way, quality Web resources on ethnic relations and migration topics. The WWW VL on Migration and Ethnic Relations is part of the much larger World Wide Web Virtual Library project.

Site: **The United Nations**
URL: http://www.un.org/english/
Description: The United Nations was established on 24 October 1945 by 51 countries committed to preserving peace through international cooperation and collective security. Today, nearly every nation in the world belongs to the UN: membership now totals 189 countries.

Site: **UNICEF Convention on the Rights of the Child**
URL: http://www.unicef.org/crc/crc.htm
Description: None

Site: **United Nations Universal Declaration of Human Rights**
URL: http://www.un.org/Overview/rights.html
Description: None

Site: **American Immigration Center**
URL: http://www.us-immigration.com/
Description (commercial site): The American Immigration Center houses one of the largest available selections of self-help immigration and citizenship products. It offers products through direct mail order from the Web site. It specializes in distributing and stocking products that are directly related to immigration, citizenship, and learning the English language.

Site: **African History Powered by the History Net**
URL: http://africanhistory.about.com/cs/eracolonialism/
Description: This site is related specifically to the issue of colonialism. There are photographs that "tell a story."

Site: **Organisation for Economic Co-operation and Development**
URL: http://www.oecd.org
Description: An international organization helping governments tackle the economic, social, and governance challenges of a globalized economy.

Site: **International Labour Organization (ILO)**
URL: http://www.ilo.org
Description: The ILO formulates international labor standards in the form of conventions and recommendations setting minimum standards of basic labor rights: freedom of association, the right to organize, collective bargaining, abolition of forced labor, equality of opportunity and treatment, and other standards regulating conditions across the entire spectrum of work-related issues.

Site: **Globalize This**
URL: http://www.globalizethis.org
Description: Site is focused on global activism.

Site: **World Vision**
URL: http://worldvision.org
Description: Founded in 1950, World Vision is a Christian humanitarian organization serving the world's poorest children and families in nearly 100 countries. World Vision, driven by faith, is a partner in enabling the world's children to realize their God-given potential by tackling the root causes of poverty.

Site: **50 Years is Enough, US Network for Global Economic Justice**
URL: http://50years.org
Description: Calls for the immediate suspension of the policies and practices of the International Monetary Fund and World Bank Group, which have caused widespread poverty, inequality, and suffering among the world's peoples and damage to the world's environment.

Site: **Statistical Profiles for Least Developed Countries**
URL: http://r0.unctad.org/conference
Description: The criteria for being on the list and getting off the list are provided. Each country is also profiled with standard and more unusual data (such as the number of telephones per 1,000 inhabitants).

Site: **Global Policy Forum (GPF)**
URL: http://www.globalpolicy.org/visitctr/about.htm
Description: Global Policy Forum monitors policy making at the United Nations, promotes accountability of global decisions, educates and mobilizes for global citizen participation, and advocates on vital issues of international peace and justice. GPF is a nonprofit, tax-exempt organization, with consultative status at the United Nations. Founded in 1993 by an international group of concerned citizens, GPF works with partners around the world to strengthen international law and create a more equitable and sustainable global society. GPF uses a holistic approach, linking peace and security with economic justice and human development, and places a heavy emphasis on networking to build broad coalitions for research, action, and advocacy. It puts its energy into well-focused and unique programs in which GPF has a special analytical and organizational edge. The GPF office is strategically located across the street from UN headquarters in New York.

Site: **Women's Human Rights Network (WHRnet)**
URL: http://www.whrnet.org
Description: Founded in 1997, WHRnet aims to provide reliable, comprehensive, and timely information and analyses on women's human rights in English, Spanish, and French. WHRnet updates readers on women's human rights issues and policy developments globally and provides information and analyses that support advocacy actions. A team of regionally based content specialists provides regular news, interviews, perspectives, alerts and campaign information, and Web highlights. The site provides an introduction to women's human rights issues worldwide, an overview of UN/regional human rights systems, a research tool that serves as gateway to the best available online resources relevant to women's human rights advocacy, and a comprehensive collection of related links.

Site: **Amnesty International (AI)**
URL: http://www.amnesty.org
Description: AI is a worldwide movement of people who campaign for internationally recognized human rights. In pursuit of this, AI's mission is to undertake research and action focused on preventing and ending grave abuses of the rights to physical and mental integrity, freedom of conscience and expression, and freedom from discrimination within the context of its work to promote all human rights. AI is free of any government, political, economic interest or religion.

Site: **United Nations High Commission on Human Rights**
URL: http://www.unhchr.ch/women/
Description: The Office of the High Commissioner for Human Rights attaches importance to practical and creative measures to realize the human rights of women: civil, cultural, economic, political, and social rights. The starting point is the recognition that there can be no human rights without women's rights, and this office is committed to ensuring that the United Nations remains the uncompromising guardian of women's human rights.

TENTATIVE CLASS SCHEDULE

Week 1

Topics/video for class discussion: Introduction, discussion of projects, overview of social work philosophy and methodology

Access and Read Compass, External Links: Course Materials/Course Folders/*SOWK Philosophy and Methodology*

Week 2

Topics/video for class discussion: Framework for understanding international social conditions; colonialism and imperialism in history and contemporary perspectives

Readings

- Healy: chapter 1, International Social Work: Why Is It Important and What Is It?; chapter 2, The History of the Development of Social Work.
- Midgley, J. (1997). The global world system. In *Social welfare in global context* (2nd ed.). Thousand Oaks, CA: Sage.

Week 3

Topics/video for class discussion: Nongovernmental organizations as factors in developments; structure of the UN that assists development

Access and Read Compass, External Links: Site: The United Nations, URL: http://www.un.org/english/. Site: The WWW Virtual Library on Migration and Ethnic Relations; URL: http://www.ercomer.org/wwwvl/select.php?select type = HostType&selector = NGO.

Reading

- Healy: chapter 6, International Relief and Development Practice.

Week 4

Topics/video for class discussion: Overview of world poverty

Access and Read Compass, External Links: Site: Statistical Profiles for Least Developed Countries; URL: http:// http://r0.unctad.org/conference/

Readings

- Healy: chapter 4, Social Work Around the World Today.
- Wang She. (2001). *Efforts to eliminate poverty*. Beijing Review, 44(7), 7.

Week 5

Topics/video for class discussion: Struggle for economic justice; the World Bank, the International Monetary Fund.

Video: Richter, R. (Producer). (1995). *Banking on life and debt* [Videorecording]. (Available from Maryknoll World Media Center, P.O. Box 408, Maryknoll, NY 10545-0308)

Access and Read Compass, External Links: Site: World Bank; URL: http://www.worldbank.org/. Site: International Monetary Fund Homepage; URL: http://www.imf.org/. Site: 50 Years Is Enough, U.S. Network for Global Economic Justice; URL:http://50years.org

Readings

- Healy: chapter 5, Global Interdependence and Social Work; The Millennium Report 11, *Globalization*; The Millennium Report 12, *Governance;* Video Viewer Guide.
- Prigoff, A. (1999). Global social and economic justice issues. In C. S. Ramanathan & R. J. Link (Eds.), *All our futures: Principles and resources for social work practice in a global era* (pp.156–173). Belmont, CA: Wadsworth.
- Hoff, M. D. (1997). Social work, the environment and sustainable growth. In M. C. Hokenstad & J. Midgley, *Issues in international social work* (pp. 27–44). Washington, DC: NASW Press.

Week 6

Topics/video for class discussion: Issues of employment; justice in the global workplace, sweatshops; employment exploitation; micro-enterprise alternative

Video: Sandys, A. (Ed.). (1987). *From sun up* [Videorecording]. (Available from Maryknoll World Media Center, P.O. Box 408, Maryknoll, NY 10545-0308)

Powerpoint: 2002 Trip to Community Development Projects in South Africa

Access and Read Compass, External Links: Site: International Labour Organization; URL: http://www.ilo.org

Readings

- Video Viewer Guide.
- Mayur, R., & Daviss, B. (1998). How not to develop an emerging nation. *The Futurist, 32*(1), 27–32.

Week 7

Topics/video for class discussion: Children in need

Video: Maryknoll Productions. (1997). *The world through kids' eyes* (Videorecording). (Available from Maryknoll World Media Center, P.O. Box 408, Maryknoll, NY 10545-0308)

Access and Read Compass, External Links: Site: UNICEF_Convention on the Rights of the Child; URL: http://www.unicef.org/crc/crc.htm

Readings

- The Millennium Report 5, *Children's Rights*; The Millennium Report 9, *Education for All*; Video Viewer Guide.
- Smallwood, G. (1995). Child abuse and neglect from an indigenous Australian's perspective. *Child Abuse and Neglect, 19*(3), 281–289.
- Mameli, P. A. (2002). Stopping the illegal trafficking of human beings: How transnational police work can stem the flow of forced prostitution. *Crime, Law and Social Change, 38*(1), 12–13.
- Kaminsky, D. C. (2000). Street children's drawings: windows into their life circumstances and aspirations. *International Social Work, 43*(1), 107–120.

Week 8

Topics/video for class discussion: Women in the developing world; eye-to-eye women

Video: Miller, N. (Producer). (1994). *Faces of change: Afghan women* [Videorecording]. (Available American Universities Field Staff, Documentary Educational Resources)

Video: Beitel, G. (Producer). (1992). *In Danku the soup is sweeter* [Videorecording]. (Available from Imageries P. B. Ltd.)

Access and Read Compass, External Links: Site: United Nations_Universal Declaration of Human Rights; URL: http://www.un.org/Overview/rights.html. Site: Women's Human Rights Network; URL: http://www.whrnet.org/index.html

Readings

- The Millennium Report 10, *Girl Child;* Video Viewer Guides.
- Nthunya, M. M. (1996). *Singing away the hunger.* Petermaritzburg, South Africa: University of Natal Press.
- Van Hook, M. P. (1994). The impact of economic and social changes on the roles of women in Botswana and Zimbabwe. *Affilia, 9*(3), 288–307.

Week 9

Topics/video for class discussion: War, refugees, immigration policy

Video: Minnesota Advocates for Human Rights. (1998). *The energy of a nation: Immigrants in America* [Videorecording]. (Available from Minnesota Advocates for Human Rights, 650 3rd Ave. South, Minneapolis, MN 55402)

Access and Read Compass, External Links: Site: American Immigration Center; URL: http://www.us-immigration.com/. Site: National Immigration Information Forum; URL: http://www.immigrationforum.org/

Readings

- The Millennium Report 4, *Child Soldiers*; The Millennium Report 7, *Disarmament*; The Millennium Report 18, *Refugees*; Video Viewer Guide.
- Asegdom, M. (2001). *Of beetles and angels: A boy's remarkable journey from a refugee camp to Harvard.* Boston: Megan Tingley Books.
- Neier, A. (2002). Bringing war criminals to justice: A brief history. *Social Research, 69*(4), 1085–1091.

Week 10

Topics/video for class discussion: AIDS and issues of accessible health care; population policy; illness and disability

Video: Basmajian, S. (Producer). (1991). *Don't take my sunshine away* [Videorecording]. (Available from the National Film Board of Canada)

Access and Read Compass, External Links: Site: The International AIDS Trust; URL: http://www.aidstrust.org/. Site: AIDS Education Global Information System; URL: http://www.aegis.org

Readings

- The Millennium Report 1, *AIDS/HIV*; The Millennium Report 8, *Drug Abuse*; Video Viewer Guide.
- Wintersteen, et al. (1997). Families and mental illness: Observations from two developing countries. *International Social Work, 40*(2), 191–207.
- Takyi, B. K. (2002). Religion and women's health in Ghana: Insights into HIV/AIDS preventive and protective behavior. *Social Science and Medicine, 56*(6), 1221–1234.

Week 11

Topics/video for class discussion: Treatment of Indigenous Populations

Video: Robinson, M. Loeterman, B. (Producers). (1999). *The triumph of evil* [Videorecording]. (Available from WGBH Educational Foundation).

Week 12

Topics/video for class discussion: Values and ethics; international and domestic practice interface

Video: Marinez, P., Sills, S. (Producers). *In service to America* [Videorecording]. (Available from PBS Video)

Readings

- Healy: chapter 7, Values and Ethics for International Professional Action; Video Viewer Guide.
- Link, R. J. (1999). Infusing global perspectives into social work values and ethics. In C. S. Ramanathan & R. J. Link (1999), *All our futures: Principles and resources for social work practice in a global era* (pp. 52–68). Belmont, CA: Wadsworth.

Week 13

Topics/video for class discussion: Concepts of social development; social work as a development function

Readings

- Healy: chapter 8, International Relief and Development Practice; chapter 9, International/Domestic Practice Interface; chapter 12, Social Work as a Force for Humane Global Change and Development
- Midgley, J. (1997). International social development. In *Social welfare in global context* (pp. 180–202). Thousand Oaks, CA: Sage.

Week 14

Topics/video for class discussion: Opportunities for international work; Peace Corp; churches

Guest Speaker

Access and Read Compass, External Links: Site: The World Revolution; URL: http://www.worldrevolution.org. Site: Amnesty International; URL: http://www.amnesty.org

Reading

- Healy: chapter 10, Understanding and Influencing Global Policy; chapter 11, Education for International Professional Action: Current Realities, Future Challenges.

Week 15

Topics/video for class discussion: Wrap-up; find the linkages and signs of hope and optimism

Social Welfare: A Worldview
Course # 450:041

I. COURSE DESCRIPTION

This course provides a basic understanding of how societies meet personal and social risks and provide for the welfare of their members. Basic concepts of social welfare, social choice, social support, and related value issues are examined. The development of social welfare ideas and systems in Western society and in societies at different stages of development in diverse cultures are analyzed. Global perspectives and comparative national welfare systems are surveyed.

This course is a part of the liberal arts/general education curriculum at the undergraduate level. It is a required course for all social work majors.

II. LEARNING OBJECTIVES

During this course it is expected that students will:

A. Identify the broad range of basic needs and social and personal "risks" (e.g., gender, old age, death, disability, illness, accidents, violence, and war) that people share throughout the world.

B. Describe the purposes, function, and structure of activities of the social welfare institutions and understand their functions in relation to other social institutions (family, education, corrections, religion, political, economic).

C. Compare philosophical stances or ideas reflected in different countries. Understand cross-cultural differences in values pertaining to treatment of women, minorities, and other vulnerable populations. Appreciate the relationship between social welfare provisions and the treatment of vulnerable populations.

D. Describe the development of social welfare in the United States, including current social welfare programs and specific provisions of the Social Security Act as amended.

E. Examine the variety of social welfare approaches that nations have developed to minimize the negative effects of social and personal risks for their populations.

F. Understand the forms and mechanisms of oppression and discrimination and the strategies of change that advance social and economic justice.

III. INSTRUCTIONAL MATERIALS AND METHODS

Required Reading

A course pack has been put together for this course and is available from Copy Central in the Rod Library. The course pack consists of readings mentioned in the Schedule of Class Topics and Reading Assignments (see pp. 6–11 of this syllabus). Readings in the course pack are arranged in the order mentioned in this schedule.

IV. CRITERIA FOR STUDENT EVALUATION

Grading Scale

Exams, group presentation, homework assignments, logs, and class participation will count toward the final grade. Maximum points—100.

A. Midterm Paper (15 points); Final Paper (20 points)

The midterm paper and final paper will cover material found in the readings, the supplemental readings, the lectures, and class exercises and presentations. Questions may be drawn from all material assigned for the units before the midterm. You will be expected to provide a reference list if you cite any sources.

B. Homework Assignments (20 points)

During the course of the semester, the instructor will make out-of-class assignments. Each assignment will focus on the content of the unit being studied and will have a specified due date. There will be four (4) assignments during the semester. The assignments will be reaction papers (2–3 pages typed, double-spaced, 12-point font) based on videos, guest lectures, class discussion topics (homework assignments are mentioned in the addendum).

C. Group Presentations (15 points)

There will be a student group presentation to the class on the social welfare system of one country. This presentation will be approximately 20 minutes for each group, followed by 10 minutes of class discussion. It will roughly follow the outline for presentations below. The class will be divided into research presentation groups for this assignment. Reports will be graded based on preparation and use of notecards, overheads or posters, maps, pictures, and so forth from the country. Do not read your report but tell us what you learned.

In addition to the verbal presentation, each student in each group will be required to submit a report that details the social welfare system of the country, as well as the time spent and activities conducted by the individual student in terms of library readings, talking to people, Web surfing, attending meetings, collecting materials, and so on. In your report, you need to tell me what you did to contribute to the presentation that the group came up with as well as what you personally learned about the social welfare system of that country. Please provide a bibliography indicating the source of your materials.

Outline for Group Presentation

You will choose a country or indigenous population. The following format pertains to countries:

I. Provide an Overview of the Country

  A. Location: Which area of the world?

    1. Asia
    2. Africa
    3. Europe
    4. South and Central America
    5. North America (including United States and Canada)

  B. Choose a particular theme (such as health, housing, family welfare, rights of immigrants, rights of prisoners, racism) or population (such as children, women, elderly, people with disabilities, minorities, indigenous populations). Describe the issues as well as welfare systems pertaining to the theme or population that you have chosen.

  C. Compare your chosen country to the United States on the theme/populations that you have selected. Why are there differences between the country you have chosen and the United States? Can some of the differences be attributed to differences in history, cultural values? If so, summarize the cultural values or history that has led to the social welfare system of the country that you have chosen.

  D. What can your country of choice and the United States learn from each other in terms of social welfare systems?

Sources: In addition to the sources suggested on your bibliography, embassies are a very good source for information about a country and its system. Also make use of the library. Hint: Sample maps and charts make presentations more interesting, especially for comparisons. Use UniStar and look under subject. Type in the country in question. The Internet is, of course, good for up-to-date information. Don't simply read an Internet report, however. See www.amnesty.org for human rights violations of your country. You are encouraged to schedule a time to meet with the instructor as a group to discuss your presentation.

D. "What in the World Is Going On?" Logs (20 points)

Each student is required to maintain logs of newspaper and magazine stories on national and international social welfare issues or problems. You are required to submit 10 logs in all. Each log is worth two points. Students may be asked to share information from the articles with the class. You are encouraged to do the first five logs from mainstream media sources such as the *New York Times, Washington Post, U.S. News and World Report, The Wall Street Journal, The Economist*, MSNBC news, local news channels, local newspapers, and so forth. You are then required to do the remaining five logs from alternative media sources, such as newsinsider. org, truthout.org, BBC, news sources of other countries, *The Nation, Yes! A Journal of Positive Futures*, and so forth. A list of recommended alternative media sources is included in Addendum II for your perusal. You are encouraged to watch *Now with Bill Moyers* on PBS on Fridays at 9 p.m. (check local timings). You may write some (not all) of your logs based on the *Now* program. Please see the reference librarian or the instructor if you are looking for more sources.

Your log entry should include (1) a complete reference in American Psychological Association (5th ed.) style, (2) a brief summary of the article, (3) a brief note on why the story is relevant to social welfare, and (4) your personal reaction to the story. Try to limit yourself to two pages (double spaced) per log.

Your log will be graded on conscientiousness, clarity, analysis, insights, and originality of source material. International social welfare issues must be addressed. All selections should be current, that is, not more than two months old.

If the log meets the criteria in the preceding paragraph and is turned in on time, the student will receive full credit of two points per log. Logs that meet the criteria in the preceding paragraph and are turned in within one week of the due date will receive one point.

One entry may describe your family/ethnic background, why your ancestors came to Iowa or the United States, if they did, and what you know about them from the early days.

E. Class Participation (10 points)

You are encouraged to participate in classroom discussions. Your participation is essential for your own as well as your classmates' learning. Please feel free to ask questions and voice your opinions.

V. SCHEDULE OF CLASS TOPICS AND READING ASSIGNMENTS

This course will be organized around four units: poverty, inequality and social welfare in the United States and abroad, democracy and human rights, globalization and its effect, and sustainable development and responsible consumerism. The pace and scope of the readings are set forth below. The instructor reserves the right to make changes in the readings with a minimum advance notice of one week.

Unit 1: Poverty, Inequality, and Social Welfare in the United States and Abroad (4 weeks)

Week 1

* DiNitto, D. (2000). Defining poverty: where to begin. In *Social welfare: Politics and policy* (pp. 66–86). Boston: Allyn & Bacon.

Week 2

* Log No. 1 due
* van Wormer. (1997). Feminization of poverty. In *Social welfare: A worldview* (pp.256–257). Chicago: Nelson-Hall.
* Shah, A. (2002). *Causes of poverty*. Available online at www.globalissues.org/TradeRelated/Poverty.asp
* Video for homework assignment No. 1: CBS *60 Minutes*. (1996, August 8). *Who's getting rich and why aren't you?* [Television broadcast]. New York: CBS Broadcasting, Inc.

Week 3

* Log No. 2 due
* DiNitto, Political ideology and social welfare, pp. 22–26.

- Midgley, J. (1997). Social welfare around the world. In *Social welfare in global context* (pp. 68–75). Thousand Oaks, CA: Sage.
- DiNitto, Government and social welfare, pp. 32–36.
- van Wormer, The great depression and the new deal, pp. 144–154.

Week 4

- Log No. 3 due
- DiNitto, Doesn't welfare cause poverty? pp. 9398.
- Midgley, Social welfare around the world, pp. 7988.
- van Wormer, A society without poverty: The Norwegian experience, pp. 279–285.
- Guest speaker/video on daily living from the perspective of a welfare recipient.

Unit 2: Democracy and Human Rights (4 weeks)

Week 5

- Homework assignment No. 1 due
- UN Center for Human Rights (1994). What rights are human rights. In *Human Rights and Social Work* (p. 4). New York: United Nations.
- UN Center for Human Rights, Basic instruments concerning human rights, pp. 15–22.
- UN Center for Human Rights, Universal Declaration of Human Rights, pp. 55–56.
- Video for homework assignment No. 2: Moyers, B. (1999). *Free speech for sale: A Bill Moyers special* [Television Broadcast]. Available from Films for the Humanities and the Sciences, PO Box 2053, Princeton, NJ, 08543-2053.

Week 6

- Smith-Ferri, D. (2002, December 20). Waiting for war. *Yes! Magazine*. Available online: http://www.yesmagazine.org/iraq/smithferri.htm
- Gordon, J. (2002, November). Cool war: Economic sanctions as a weapon of mass destruction. *Harper's Magazine*. Available online: http://globalpolicy.org/security/sanction/iraq1/2002/1100weap.htm
- Yes! Magazine (2003, Spring). The war against ourselves. An interview with Major Doug Rokke. Available online: http://www.yesmagazine.org/25environmentandhealth/rokke.htm

Week 7

- Homework assignment No. 2 due
- Rehn, E., & Sirleaf, E. J. (2002). *Women, war, and peace: The independent experts' assessment on the impact of armed conflict on women and women's role in peace-building*. New York: United Nations Development Fund for Women. Available online at: www.unifem.undp.org
- Brzezinski, M. (2002, October 27). Hady Hassan Omar's detention. *New York Times Magazine*, pp. 50–55.
- American Civil Liberties Union (2003, April 18). The rights of immigrants: ACLU position paper. Available online at: http://www.aclu.org/ImmigrantsRights/ImmigrantsRights.cfm?ID = 12413&c = 22

Week 8

- Log No. 5 due; midterm paper due
- Bergman, J., & Reynolds, J. (2002, December 2). The guns of Opa-locka: How U.S. dealers arm the world. *The Nation*, pp. 19–22.
- Stohl, R. (2001). A risky business: U.S. arms exports to countries where terror thrives. Center for Defense Information. Available online: http://cdi.org/friendlyversion/printversion.cfm
- Human Rights Watch (2003). *International criminal court*. Available online: http://www.hrw.org/campaigns/icc

- Human Rights Watch (2003). *The United States and the international criminal court.* Available online: http://www.hrw.org/campaigns/icc/
- Video: Center for Defense Information (1998). *The human cost of America's arms sales.* Available from CDI, 1779 Mass. Ave. NW, Washington DC, 20036.

Unit 3: Globalization and Its Impact

Week 9

- Log No. 6 due
- Stiglitz, J. (2001). *Globalization and its discontents.* New York: W.W. Norton. (chapter 1)
- Su, Evelyn (2000). The winners and losers: The agreement on trade-related aspects of intellectual property rights and its effects on developing countries. *Journal of International Law and Business, 23,* 169.

Week 10: Spring Break

Week 11

- Log No. 7 due
- Shand, H. (1994). Patenting the planet. *Multinational monitor, 15*(6), 9–14.
- Prigoff, A. (2000). The function of International Monetary Fund Structural Adjustment Programs. In *Economics for social workers* (pp. 121–123). Belmont, CA: Wadsworth.

Week 12

- Log No. 8 due
- Hofrichter, R. (Ed). (1993). Corporate plundering of third-world resources. In *Toxic struggles* (pp. 186–196). Philadelphia, PA: New Society.
- Landau, S. (2002). The end of the maquila era. *The Progressive, 66*(9), 24–26.
- The National Labor Committee (2002). Wal-Mart sweatshops in Honduras. Available online at: http://www.nlcnet.org
- Discuss homework assignment No. 3 on sweatshops.

Week 13

- Log No. 9 due
- Group presentations—no new readings

Week 14

- Homework assignment No. 3 due
- Group presentations—no new readings
- Handout and discuss homework assignment No. 4

Unit 4: Sustainable Development and Responsible Consumerism

Week 15

- Log No. 10 due
- Prigoff, A. The money culture: Marketing the image of wealth, pp. 97–103.
- Video: Graf, J. D., Boe, V. (1997). *Affluenza.* Available from Bullfrog Films, P.O. Box 149, Oley, PA 19547.
- Griscom, A. (2002, November 28). Beyond oil. *Rolling Stone,* pp. 73–76.
- Tokar, B. (2001). Biotechnology: Enlarging the debate. *Z Magazine.* Available online at: http://www.zmag.org/zmag/articles/june01tokar.htm

Week 16

- Homework assignment No. 4 due
- Korten, D. (1999). The new storytellers. In *The post-corporate world* (pp. 225–242). West Hartford, CT: Kumarian.
- Shah, A. (2002). Sustainable development: Introduction. Available online at: http://www.globalissues.org/TradeRelated/Development/Intro.asp
- Chief Seattle (1854, revised 2002). We may be brothers after all. Available online at: http://www.13moons.org/bos/chief_seattle.htm
- Korten, Epilogue: Planetary consciousness, pp. 277–281.

Week 17

- Finals week
- Course wrap-up
- Final paper due

BIBLIOGRAPHY

(You are encouraged to read the additional resources and consult them for your homework assignments, logs, group presentations, and midterm and final papers.)

Peace, human rights, democracy, and U.S. foreign policy

American Civil Liberties Union. (2003). *Immigrant rights*. ACLU position paper. Retrieved May 2, 2003 from www.aclu.org/ImmigrantsRights/ImmigrantsRights.cfm?ID-12413&c-22

Amnesty International. (2002). *Report 2002: United States of America*. Retrieved May 2, 2003, from http://web.amnesty.org/web/ar2002.nsf/amr/usa!Open

Arnove, A., & Abunimah, A. (2003). *Iraq under siege: The deadly impact of sanctions and war*. Cambridge, MA: South End Press.

Brzezinski, M. (2002, October 27). Hady Hassan Omar's detention. *New York Times Magazine*, pp. 50–55.

Caldicott, H. (2002). *The new nuclear danger: George W. Bush's military-industrial complex*. New York: New Press.

Caldicott, H., Kaku, M., Gould, J., & Clark, R. (1997). *Metal of dishonor: How depleted uranium penetrates steel, radiates people and contaminates the environment*. New York: International Action Center.

Chomsky, N (1992). *Deterring democracy*. New York: Hill & Wangs.

Chomsky, N. (2000). *Rogue states: The rule of force in world affairs*. Cambridge, MA: South End Press.

Chomsky, N. (2001). *9-11*. New York: Seven Stories Press.

Cruikshank, B. (1999). *The will to empower: Democratic citizens and other subjects*. Ithaca, NY: Cornell University Press.

Forsythe, D. P. (2000). *Human rights in international relations*. Cambridge, England: Cambridge University Press.

Haner, P. (2001). *Unspeakable truths: Confronting state terror and atrocity*. New York: Routledge.

James, S. (1998). Shades of othering: Reflections on female circumcision/genital mutilation. *Signs, 23*(4), 1031–1048.

Johnson, C. (2000). *Blowback: Costs and consequences of the American empire*. New York: Owl Books.

Levy, J. S. (1998). The causes of war and the conditions of peace. *Annual Review of Political Science, 1*, 139–165.

Lobell, S. (2003). *The challenge of hegemony: Grand strategy, trade and domestic politics*. Ann Arbor: University of Michigan Press.

McCormick, J. (1998). *American foreign policy and process*. Itasca, IL; Peacock.

McCormick, J. M., & Mitchell, N. J. (1989). Human rights and foreign assistance: An update. *Social Science Quarterly, 70*(4), 969–979.

Minnow, M. (1998). *Between vengeance and forgiveness.* Boston: Beacon Press.

Otero, C. P. (2003). *Chomsky on democracy and education.* New York: Routledge.

Power, S. (2003). *A problem from hell: America and the age of genocide.* Harper Perennial.

Rehn, E., & Sirleaf, E. J. (2002). *Women, war and peace: The independent experts' assessment of the impact of armed conflict on women and women's role in peace-building.* New York: United Nations Development Fund for Women. Available online at: www.unifem.undp.org

Risse, T., Ropp, S. C., & Simmkink, K. (Eds.). (1999). *The power of human rights: international norms and domestic exchange.* Cambridge, England: Cambridge University Press.

Roy, A. (2003). *War Talk.* Cambridge, MA: South End Press.

Schoeffel, J., & Mitchell, P. R. (Eds.). (2002). *Understanding power: The indispensable Chomsky.* New York: New Press.

Smith, J. W. (2002). *Why? The deeper history behind the September 11, 2002 terrorist attacks on America.* Sun City, AZ: The Institute for Economic Democracy. Available online at: www.ied.info/books/why/contents/html

Thomas, D. C. (2001). *The Helsinki effect: International norms, human rights and the demise of communism.* Princeton, NJ: Princeton University Press.

Young, I. M. (1990). *Justice and the politics of difference.* Princeton, NJ: Princeton University Press.

Young, I. M. (2000). *Inclusion and democracy.* Oxford, England: Oxford University Press.

Zakaria, F. (2003). *The future of freedom: Illiberal democracies at home and abroad.* New York: W.W. Norton.

Zinn, H. (2003). *A people's history of the United States: 1492–present.* Harper Perennial.

Impact of global economy

Chossudovsky, M. (1997). *The globalization of poverty, impact of IMF and World Bank reforms.* London: Zed Books.

Chossudovsky, M. (2002). *War and globalization: The truth behind September 11.* Ontario, Canada: Global Outlook and the Center for Research on Globalization.

Chossudovsky, M. (2003). *The globalization of poverty and the New World Order* (2nd ed.). Ontario, Canada: Global Outlook.

Chua, A. (2003). *World on fire: How exporting free market democracy breeds ethnic hatred and global instability.* New York: Doubleday.

Danaher, K. (1994). 50 years is enough: *The case against World Bank and International Monetary Fund.* Boston, MA: South End Press.

Friedmann, H. (1991). *The political economy of food: The origins of Third World food dependence.* London: Verso/ New Left Books.

George, S. (1986). *How the other half dies: The real reasons for world hunger.* New York: Penguin.

Klien, N. (2000). *No space, no choice, no logo: Taking aim at the brand bullies.* New York: Picador.

Klein, N. (2002). *Fences and windows: Dispatches from the front lines of the globalization debate.* New York: Picador.

Korten, D. C. (2000). *The post-corporate world: Life after capitalism.* San Francisco, CA: Berrett-Koehler.

Korten, D. C. (2001). *When corporations rule the world.* West Hartford, CT: Kumarian Press.

MacArthur, J. R. (2001). *The selling of free trade: NAFTA, Washington, and the subversion of American democracy.* Berkeley, CA: University of California Press.

Palast, G. (2003). *The best democracy money can buy: The truth about corporate cons, globalization and high-finance fraudsters.* New York: Plume.

Paley, J. (2001). *Marketing democracy: Power and social movements in post-dictatorship Chile.* Berkeley, CA: University of California Press.

Prigoff, A. (2000). *Economics for social workers: Social outcomes of economic globalization with strategies for community action.* Belmont, CA: Wadsworth.

Roy, A. (2002). *Power politics.* Cambridge, MA: South End Press.

Shiva, V. (2000). *Stolen harvest.* Cambridge, MA: South End Press.

Simon, A. (1984). *Bread of the world.* New York: Paulist Press.

Smith, J. W. (1994). *The world's wasted wealth: Save our wealth, save your environment.* Cambria. CA: Institute for Economic Democracy.

Smith, J. W. (2002). *Economic democracy: The political struggle of the 21st century.* Sun City, AZ: Institute for Economic Democracy. Available online at: www.ied.info/books/ed/contents.html

Stiglitz, J. E. (2002). *Globalization and its discontents.* New York: W.W. Norton.

Media, corporate ownership, and social consciousness

Barsamina, D., & Chomsky, N. (2001). *Propaganda and the public mind.* Cambridge, MA: South End Press.

Chomsky, N. (1989). *Necessary illusions: Thought control in democratic societies.* Cambridge, MA: South End Press.

Chomsky, N. (2000). *Propaganda and control of the public mind.* Cambridge, MA: AK Press.

Chomsky, N. (2002). *Media control: The spectacular achievements of propaganda* (2nd ed.). New York: Seven Stories Press.

MacArthur, J. R. (1993). *The second front: Censorship and propaganda in the Gulf War.* Berkeley, CA: University of California Press.

Said, E. S., & Chomsky, N. (2002). *Manufacturing consent: The political economy of the mass media.* New York: Pantheon Books.

General

Abramovitz, M. (1991). *Regulating the lives of women.* Monroe, ME: South End Press.

Baker, M. (1995). *Canadian family policies: Cross-national comparison.* Toronto, Canada: University of Toronto Press.

Barajas, et al. (Eds.). (1996). *Community justice: Striving for safe, secure and just communities.* Washington, DC: U.S. Dept of Justice, National Institute of Corrections.

Dominelli, L. (1989). *Feminist social work.* Basingstoke, New Hampshire: Macmillan.

Dooley, Brian. (1998). *Black and green: The fight for civil rights in Northern Ireland and Black America.* Chicago: Pluto Press.

Ehrenreich, B. (2001). *Nickel and dimed: On (not) getting by in America.* New York: Metropolitan Books.

Galaway, B., & Herdson, J. (Eds.) (1996). *Restorative justice: International perspectives.* Monsey, NY: Criminal Justice Press.

Hoff, M., & McNutt, J. (1994). *The global environmental crisis: Implications for social welfare and social work.* Aldershot, England: Avebury.

Hooks, Bell. (1995). *Killing rage: Ending racism.* New York: Henry Holt.

Marger, M. (1997). *Race and ethnic relations: American and global perspectives.* Belmont, CA: Wadsworth.

Menninger, K. (1968). *The crime of punishment.* New York: Viking Press.

Munday, Brian. (1993). *European social services.* Canterbury, England: University of Kent.

Navarro, V. (Ed.). (1994). *Why the United States does not have a national health program.* Amityville, NY: Baywood.

Navarro, V. (Ed.). (2002a). *Dangerous to your health: Capitalism in health care.* New York: Monthly Review Press.

Navarro, V. (Ed.). (2002b). *The political economy of social inequalities: Consequences for health and quality of life.* Amityville, NY: Baywood.

Oster, P. (1989). *The Mexicans: A personal portrait.* New York: Harper and Row.

Piven, F., & Cloward, R. (1993). *Regulating the poor.* New York: Vintage Books.

Salmon, J. W. (1990). *The corporate transformation of health care.* Amityville, NY: Baywood.

Sasson, J. (1992). *Princess: A true story of life behind the veil . . . in Saudi Arabia.* New York: Avon Books.

Sidel, R. (1996). *Keeping women and children last: America's war on the poor.* New York: Penguin Books.

Slater, J., Fain, S., & Rossatto, C. (Eds.). (2002). *The Freirean legacy: Educating for social justice.* New York: Peter Lang.

Tropman, J. (1989). *American values and social welfare.* Englewood Cliffs, NJ: Prentice Hall.

Van Soest, D. (1997). *The global crisis of violence: Common problems, universal causes, shared solutions.* Washington, DC: NASW Press.

Vaz, K. M. (1997). *Oral narrative research with black women.* Thousand Oaks, CA: Sage.

Weldon, M. (1999). *I closed my eyes: Revelations of a battered woman.* Center City, MN: Hazelden.

Wing, A. (Ed.). (1997). *Critical race feminism: A reader.* New York: New York University Press.

Wronka, J. (1998). *Human rights and social policy in the 21st century: A history of the idea of human rights.* New York: University Press of America.

Journals

- *British Journal of Social Work*
- *Canadian Social Work Review*
- *The Economist*
- *International Journal of Health Services*
- *International Social Work*
- *Public Culture*
- *Social Development Issues*

Videos

- Graf, J. D., Boe, V. (1997). *Affluenza.* (Available from Bullfrog Films, P.O. Box 149, Oley, PA 19547.) (on materialism and responsible consumerism)
- Moore, M., Glynn, K., Czarnecki, J., Bishop, C., Donovan, M. (Producers) & Moore, M. (Writer/Director). (2002). *Bowling for Columbine.* USA: Dog Eat Dog Films.
- Jhally, S. (Producer), & Ericsson, S. (Director). (2001). *Constructing public opinion: How politicians and the media misrepresent the public.* USA: Media Education Foundation.
- Moyers, B. (1999). *Free speech for sale: A Bill Moyers special.* (Available from Films for the Humanities and the Sciences, PO Box 2053, Princeton, NJ, 08543-2053.) (on propaganda and corporate ownership of media and implications for democracy)
- Meissonnier, M. (Producer/Director). (2000). *Invisible war, depleted uranium and the politics of radiation. France: Canal Plus.* (Available from Capa Presse TV, 80 rue de la Croix Nivert 75015 Paris. http://www.capatv.com)

- Brohy, A. & Ungerman, G. (Producers/Directors). (2000). *Hidden wars of Desert Storm*. New York: Free Will Productions.
- Black, S. (Producer/Director). (2001). *Life and debt*. New York: Tuff Gong Pictures Production. (Documentary Web site www.lifeanddebt.org on impact of International Monetary Fund and World Bank policies [structural adjustment programs] on the economy and social welfare of Jamaica)
- Siegel, A. (Producer/Director). (1991). *Lifting the fog*. USA: Maljack productions (on U.S. foreign policy and Middle East conflict)
- Achbar, M., & Wintonick, P. (Producers/Directors). (1992). *Manufacturing consent: Noam Chomsky and the media*. Canada: National Film Board of Canada; Zeitgeist Films.
- WGBH Boston, Science Unit. (1990). *Race to save the planet* [Television series]. S. Burlington, VT: Annenberg/ CPB Multimedia Collection.
- Center for Defense Information (1998). *The human cost of America's arms sales*. (Available from CDI, 1779 Mass. Ave. NW, Washington DC, 20036.)
- CBS *60 Minutes*. (1996, August 8). *Who's getting rich and why aren't you?* [Television broadcast]. New York: CBS Broadcasting Inc.
- National Labor Committee (1995). *Zoned for slavery: Child behind the label*. New York: Crowing Rooster Arts (on sweatshops).

Other Resources

- www.nyu.edu/socialwork/wwwrsw
- South End Press: www.southendpress.org
- Langendoen, R., & O'Brien, D. (2003). Resources for democracy. *Yes! Magazine*, Winter, pp. 47–48. Available online http://www.yesmagazine.org
- http://globalresearch.ca

ADDENDUM

1. Homework assignments

Homework assignment 1: 2–3-page reaction paper to the video *Who's getting rich and why aren't you?* (CBS *60 Minutes*), or any other video related to globalization and U.S. economy.

Homework assignment 2: 2–3-page reaction paper to the video *Free speech for sale, a Bill Moyers special*.

Homework assignment 3: Sweatshop assignment as below

Write a 2–3-page paper answering questions on any one topic below (Nike, Gap, Coca-Cola, or any other). You may refer to the list of resourceful Web sites on sweatshops that follow.

1. Nike
   a. Where are Nike shoes made?
   b. Look for any description of the workers: Are the workers primarily men, women, children? Age range? Socioeconomic status?
   c. Compare cost of a pair of Nike shoes in the United States at retail versus per day/per piece wages paid to workers.
   d. What are the typical conditions of workers who work for Nike contractors?
   e. Describe some of the initiatives being undertaken to stop/question sweatshops or improve working conditions.
   f. What can you as a consumer do to promote fair trade?

2. GAP

    a. Where is GAP clothing made?

    b. Look for any description of the workers: Are the workers primarily men, women, children? Age range? Socioeconomic status?

    c. Compare cost of a pair of GAP blue jeans in the United States at retail versus per day/per piece wages paid to workers.

    d. What are the typical conditions of workers who work for GAP contractors?

    e. Describe some of the initiatives being undertaken to stop/question sweatshops or improve working conditions

    f. What can you as a consumer do to promote fair trade?

3. Coca-Cola

    a. Where are Coca-Cola products made?

    b. Look for any description of the workers: Are the workers primarily men, women, children? Age range? Socioeconomic status?

    c. Look for typical earnings of Coca-Cola workers.

    d. What are the typical conditions of workers who work for Coca-Cola contractors?

    e. Describe some of the initiatives being undertaken to stop/question sweatshops or improve working conditions.

    f. What can you as a consumer do to promote fair trade?

4. Any other product of your choice: try to find information along above lines

Useful Web sites for homework assignment 4 on sweatshops:

The following organizations and Web sites represent a variety of perspectives about sweatshops. You may also use these Web sites to learn more about particular issues.

*   United Students against Sweatshops (http://www.studentsagainstsweatshops.org)
*   Sweatshop Watch (http://www.sweatshopwatch.org/)
*   Behind the Label (http://www.behindthelabel.org/)
*   Corporate Watch (http://www.corpwatch.org/)
*   Fair trade: Co-op America (http://www.coopamerica.org/sweatshops/index.html)
*   National Labor Committee (http://www.nlcnet.org/)
*   Global Exchange (http://www.globalexchange.org/)
*   Human Rights Watch (http://www.hrw.org/)
*   UNITE—Union of Needletrades, Industrial and Textile Employees (http://uniteunion.org/sweatshops/sweatshop.html)
*   Triangle Fire Web site (http://www.ilr.cornell.edu/trianglefire)
*   Campaign for Labor Rights (http://www.campaignforlaborrights.org)
*   Lawyers Committee for Human Rights (http://www.lchr.org)
*   National Interfaith Committee for Worker Justice (http://www.igc.org)
*   Los Angeles Jewish Commission on Sweatshops (http://www.isber.ucsb.edu)
*   Feminists Against Sweatshops (http://www.feminist.org)
*   Maquila Solidarity Network (http://www.maquilasolidarity.org)
*   National Retail Federation (http://www.nrf.com)
*   Clean Clothes Campaign (http://www.cleanclothes.org)

- Oxfam Community Aid Abroad (http://www.oxfam.org.au)
- U.S. Department of Labor, Office of Wage and Hour (http://www.dol.gov)

Homework assignment 4: 2–3-page reaction paper to a chapter/journal article from one of the books/journals selected by the instructor from the general bibliography on U.S. foreign policy and international relations.

2. Alternative media sources

- Bill Moyers *Now* (TV program—for timings see www.pbs.org/now)
- *Boston Globe*: www.boston.com/globe/
- British Broadcasting Corporation: www.bbc.co.uk
- Center for Global Research http://globalresearch.ca
- Democracy Now!: www.democracynow.org
- Global Issues: www.globalissues.org
- Newsinsider: www.newsinsider.org
- *The Guardian*: www.guardian.co.uk/
- *The Nation*: www.thenation.com
- *The Progressive*: www.progressive.org
- Truth Out: www.truthout.org
- World news: www.worldnews.com
- *Yes! Magazine*: www.yesmagazine.org
- *Z Magazine*: www.zmag.org

ACKNOWLEDGMENT

Katherine van Wormer contributed to the development of an earlier version of this course.

Social Welfare Policy and Services II

SSW 702

PURPOSE

Social Welfare Policy and Services II: Special Topics in Social Welfare Policy and Services focuses on a selected social welfare issue or special population. It is a required MSW course. This specialization extends the foundations of social welfare policy by applying knowledge obtained in Social Welfare Policy and Services I to a particular social welfare issue or population and by refining the analytic skills needed to synthesize and interpret critically the complexities of social welfare policy. This course explores policy dynamics, patterns, and changes through a closer look at selected history, theories, frameworks, ethical issues, forces of oppression, and various paths to social, economic, and political justice relevant to a special population. The focus on a special issue/population includes recognition of some of the needs of diverse groups within that special population or those affected by the special issue. While developing expertise about particular clients and communities, as well as social agencies and government programs, students also learn the social welfare principles applicable to one group may be generalized to other policies and populations. More specific objectives for students follow.

OBJECTIVES

1. Deepen foundations of social welfare policy and services by applying principles of social welfare policy learned in Social Welfare Policy and Services I to particular social welfare issues/populations.

2. Apply historical knowledge, theoretical frameworks, and social science findings to the development and assessment of social welfare policy with particular populations or social issues as its targets.

3. Understand diverse needs, beliefs, interests, and experiences of a particular population or those affected by particular social issues as well as internal group differences based on race, gender, class, sexual orientation, age, ethnicity, culture, religion, or mental and physical abilities.

4. Examine developments and effects of structure and operation of social welfare programs and current trends in social welfare policy on special populations or issues at which they are aimed.

5. Explore how complex dynamics of discrimination, economic deprivation, and institutionalized oppression create social problems and place particular populations and subgroups within them at risk; how prejudice based on race, gender, class, sexual orientation, and other factors limit the well-being of populations and groups, and how institutionalized oppression may influence the capacity of social welfare policy and service programs to mediate, address, and redress social issues and otherwise ensure social, economic, and political justice.

6. Recognize and address situations in which the operation of social welfare policy and the delivery of social services to selected populations may violate social work values and ethics, including personal dignity, self-determination, respect for differences, adequacy of resources, and responsiveness of social programs.

7. Learn how social welfare policy aimed at special issues/populations can help or hinder efforts to meet client needs, modify existing programs, change social conditions, and otherwise promote social, economic, and political justice.

8. Learn how social welfare policy knowledge and skills developed for work with one issue or population may be applied to others.

OUTCOMES

Upon successful completion of Social Welfare Policies and Services II: Special Topics in Social Welfare Policy and Services, students will be able to demonstrate a range of competencies related to stated course objectives. In class projects, written assignments, and class discussions, students will be required to demonstrate their ability to:

1. Apply foundations of social welfare policy to specific issues, populations, or problems.

2. Synthesize and use historical knowledge, theoretical frameworks, and social welfare principles in ways that reflect advanced understanding of how social welfare policy influences particular social conditions and the needs of special populations.

3. Discuss a range of needs, beliefs, interests, and experiences found among members of special populations, as well as a diversity of needs, beliefs, interests, and experiences of subgroups within those populations; discuss importance of creating social welfare policies and social welfare programs that take diversity at many levels into account.

4. Describe the structure and operation of social welfare programs aimed at special populations or issues, and effects of current trends in social welfare policy on capacities of agencies and programs to meet the needs of populations.

5. Understand roles of social welfare policy in addressing discrimination, economic deprivation, and oppression faced by members of various populations because of injustice based on race, class, gender, sexual orientation, age, ethnicity, culture, religion, or mental and physical ability.

6. Assess social policies and services for compatibility with social work values, including personal dignity, self-determination, respect for differences, adequacy of resources, and responsiveness of social programs, as well as the need for the profession to address resulting conflicts.

LEARNING EXPERIENCES

In addition to readings that represent an array of perspectives on international social welfare, students will learn from lectures and class discussions, as well as presentations by experts in the field; study international agencies; take relevant field trips (e.g., to the UN); and examine selected case studies to deepen their understanding of special issues facing populations in industrialized and developing countries, as well as transitional societies. Extensive use will be made of social and economic indicators issued by national and international agencies and advocacy organizations.

ASSIGNMENTS

In addition to presentation and analysis of readings students will select a country to research collectively in depth. Using the grid provided, students will select three channels in order of preference (the grid outlines political, economic, sociocultural, social protection, and environment categories, with subheadings or "channels" within each category), of which one will be assigned. The instructor will ensure that all channels are covered across the class. students will prepare a formal research paper on the "channel" selected, which intersects with all the others. For example, a student who selects "nutrition" follows the nutrition channel across the grid, examining nutrition in the chosen country as it relates to each of the "inherent characteristics": race, gender, age, and so on. All studies must be in the context of social welfare in the chosen country, and all students will examine the same country. After grading, students have the opportunity to revise their papers and make a copy for each class member. This collective study provides extensive research and a template and example that can be applied to the study of any other country.

OUTLINE OF CLASS SECTIONS

Readings and other materials for the course are drawn from a wide range of international sources. To provide broad diversity of perspectives on issues and proposed social work interventions to address them, they are presented by scholars from many countries on every inhabited continent as well as persons employed in international social and social welfare organizations.

I. Introduction: Review and Overview

Reviews key definitions of terms and themes from Social Welfare Policy and Services I; discusses application to international social welfare of principles of social welfare policy developed in Social Welfare Policy and Services I; provides overview of Social Welfare Policy and Services II.

A. *Course overview.* Brief class discussion of particular interests and experiences of students enrolled in the course.

B. *Current context.* Reviews key definitions of social policy; current international economic issues; social welfare systems in selected countries in comparison with U.S. models.

- Atherton, C., & Bolland, K. (2002). Postmodernism: A dangerous illusion for social work. *International Social Work, 45*(4), 421–433.
- Estes, R. (1995). Education for social development. *Social Development Issues, 16*(3), 68–90.
- Lusk, M., & Stoesz, D. (1994). International social work in a global economy. *Journal of Multicultural Social Work, 3*(2), 101–113.
- Midgley, J. (1995). International and comparative social welfare. In R. Edwards (Ed.), *Encyclopedia of Social Work* (19th ed.)(pp. 1490–1499). Washington, DC: NASW Press.
- Nagy, G., & Falk, D. (2000). Dilemmas in international and cross-cultural social work education. *International Social Work, 43*(1), 49–60.

II. Theories, frameworks, models

Examines theories, frameworks, and ideologies that inform analysis of key social issues, experiences of diverse populations, and the social provision, adequacy, and delivery of social welfare services in selected venues, with specific attention to health, poverty, crime, and human security.

- Dixon, J. (2001). A global perspective on social security programs for the unemployed. *International Social Work, 44*(4), 405–422.
- Dixon, J., & Scheurell, R. (Eds.) (1995). *Social security programs*. London: Greenwood.
- Dolgoff, R. (1999). What does social welfare produce? *International Social Work, 42*(3), 295–307.
- Drover, G. (2000). Redefining social citizenship in a global era. *Canadian Social Work, 2*(1), 29–48.
- Ferge, Z. (1997, July). *And what if the state fades away?* Paper delivered at the European Sociological Association 3rd Annual Conference, Essex University, Essex, UK.
- Rondeau, G. (2000). Empowerment and social practice, or the issue of power in social work. *Canadian Social Work, 2*(1), 216–222.

III. Needs, rights, and services in an international context.

Explores, assesses, and analyses social welfare policies and services in the context of different cultures, economies, and traditions. Examines the development of social welfare policies and services in relation to social, political, and cultural contexts. Explores the effect of social, political, and economic changes on the definitions, provisions, and adequacy of social welfare policies and services, with particular attention to children, including child laborers and soldiers, women, refugees, unskilled workers, and victims of ethnic conflicts.

A. Social welfare as an international issue and problems.

- Caragata, L., & Sanchez, M. (2002). Globalization and global need. *International Social Work, 45*(2), 217–238.
- *Human Development Report.* (Annual). New York: Oxford University Press (for the United Nations). (Selected issues; selected readings)
- Johanneson, T. (1997). Social work as an international profession. In M.C. Hokenstad & J. Midgley (Eds.), *Issues in International Social Work* (pp. 146–155). Washington, DC: NASW Press.
- *State of the World's Children.* (Annual). New York: Oxford University Press (for UNICEF). (Selected issues; selected readings)
- *World Development Report.* New York: Oxford University Press (for the World Bank). (Updated periodically; selected issues; selected readings)

B. Social problems and social services in relation to special populations.

- Allén, T. (1996). The Nordic model of gender equality: The welfare state, patriarchy, and unfinished emancipation. In V. Moghadam (Ed.), *Patriarchy and Social Development* (pp. 303–326). Oxford, England: Clarenden Press.
- Mupedziswa, R. (1997). Social work with refugees. In M.C. Hokenstad & J. Midgley (Eds.), *Issues in International Social Work* (pp. 110–124). Washington, DC: NASW Press.

- Ogwu-oju, D. (2000, December 4). Should my tribal past shape Delia's future? *Newsweek*, p. 14.
- Sadisivam, B. (1997). The impact of structural adjustment on women: A governance and human rights agenda. *Human Rights Quarterly, 19*(3), 636–665.
- Seipel, M. (1994). Disability: An emerging global challenge. *International Social Work, 37*(2), 165–178.
- Tsui, M. (2000). The harm reduction approach revisited. *International Social Work, 43*(2), 243–251.

C. International initiatives in social policy and social welfare provisions.

- Cox, D. (1989). *Welfare practice in a multicultural society*. Sydney, Australia: Prentice-Hall.
- Flanagan, C., Bowes, J., Jonsson, B., Csopo, B., & Sheblanova, E. (1998). Ties that bind: Correlates of adolescents' civic commitments in seven countries. *Journal of Social Issues, 54*(3), 457–475.
- Mok, B., & Liu, J. (1999). In the service of market socialism: The quest for a welfare model in China. *Journal of Sociology & Social Welfare, 26*(3), 137–150.
- Mupedziswa, R. (1996). The challenge of economic development in an African developing country: Social work in Zimbabwe. *International Social Work, 39*(1), 41–54.

IV. Professional issues: international social welfare and the social work profession

Examines social work as an international profession. Reviews various roles of social workers in international agencies and policy-making bodies with specific attention to contrasts among industrialized, developing, and transitional societies. Examines status, practices, and influence of social workers worldwide and within various venues. Explores possibilities for employment internationally.

A. Review of international social work organizations and their activities.

- Fernando, J., & Heston, A. (1997). NGOs between states, markets, and civil society. *Annals of the American Academy of Political and Social Science, 554*(November), 8–21.
- Healy, L. (1995). International social welfare: Organizations and activities. In R. Edwards (Ed.), *Encyclopedia of Social Work* (19th ed.) (pp. 1499–1510). Washington, DC: NSAW Press.
- Torczner, J. (2000). Globalization, inequality and peace building. *Canadian Social Work, 2*(1), 123–145.

B. Examination of selected case examples of issues and special populations served by international social work organizations.

- Al-krenawi, A., & Graham, J. (2000). Islamic theology and prayer. *International Social Work, 43*(3), 289–304.
- Gamble, D., & Varma, S. (1999). International women doing development work define needed skills for sustainable development. *Social Development Issues, 21*(1), 47–56.
- Landim, L., & Thompson, A. (1997). *Voluntas*, 8(4), (December), 337–350.
- Wagner, A. (1995). Reassessing welfare capitalism: Community-based approaches to social policy in Switzerland and the United States. *Journal of Community Practice, 2*(3), 45–63.

C. Analysis of trends in international social work with particular attention to the emergence of not-for-profit, non-governmental organizations in world social welfare policy and service.

- Campfens, H. (1997a). International review of community development: Theory and practice. In H. Campfens (Ed.), *Community development around the world: Practice, theory, research, training* (pp. 11–46). Toronto, Canada: University of Toronto Press.
- Campfens, H. (1997b). Comparisons and conclusions: An international framework for practice in the twenty-first century. In H. Campfens (Ed.), *Community development around the world: Practice, theory, research, training* (pp. 437–470). Toronto, Canada: University of Toronto Press.
- Fukuyama, F. (1995). Social capital and the global economy. *Foreign Affairs, 74*(5), 89–103.
- Ife, J. (2000), Localized needs and a globalized economy. *Canadian Social Work, 2*(1), 50–64.

NOTE

In addition to the readings listed, students are expected to read and refer to the following:

- *Convention on the Rights of the Child.* (1996). New York: United Nations.
- *International Code of Ethics for Professional Social Workers.* (1994). http://www.ifsw.org
- *Universal Declaration of Human Rights.* (1948). New York: United Nations.

References will be made to special editions of and articles from:

- *Human Development Report.* New York: Oxford University Press (for the United Nations). Updated annually.
- *State of the World's Children.* New York: Oxford University Press (for UNICEF). Updated annually.

SSW702 – INTERNATIONAL SOCIAL WELFARE COUNTRY RESEARCH GRID

Inherent Characteristics						
	Race	Gender	Age	Ethnicity	Disability	Sexual
Political						
voting rights						
participation						
Economic						
income security						
work opportunity						
job security						
income adequacy						
unemployment aid						
old-age security						
Social Cultural						
nutritition						
education						
health						
shelter						
religion						
travel						
Social Protection						
public police						
public firemen						
equal justice						
privacy						
Environment						

Human Behavior in the Social Environment
MSW 500

COURSE DESCRIPTION

This course provides the knowledge basic to an understanding of human growth through the life cycle and the interplay of sociocultural, biological, spiritual, and psychological factors that influence the growth of individuals and families in contemporary world society. The role of the "nurturing environment" in relation to human development, the effect of the "sustaining environment," and ecological issues relevant to growth are emphasized. The course stresses the link between social issues and individual problems and considers the cultural inclination in some countries to explain behavior in individual terms and in other countries to consider the common human condition.

The theme of our course is to approach life and development in a holistic way. The experiences of people from diverse cultures will expand our understanding of sustainable human growth in a global context.

TEACHING METHODS

We will build in this course on the philosophy of Paulo Freire and Barbara Bryant Solomon that empowerment is at the heart of learning. Our class will be a community of learners, including faculty, students, and guests. All of us will share our knowledge and experience with each other. We will make an effort to identify our own cultural biases in the learning process and will constructively and respectfully challenge and support each other. We are co-learners; we will share objectives, ideas, concerns, and questions and be interdependent, expanding the boundaries of our learning to include international resources and experience.

COURSE OBJECTIVES

(Students are invited to develop their own objectives in consultation with their classmates.)

a. Identify and describe human growth within a historical, cultural, and global context.

b. Identify and describe the various phases and stages of the life cycle of individuals and families.

c. Identify theory and practice that demonstrates how to maintain a dual focus on both the person and his (or her) environmental conditions.

d. Gain an understanding of the family as a social system and how the family as a social system can nurture or impede human growth and development.

e. Identify the effect of family systems and relationships on child and adult lives (with special reference to multiple stressors, abusive relationships, drug addiction, divorce, and single parenting). Begin to identify how social workers work with families in many countries.

f. Gain an understanding of how individuals and families are affected by the societal application of prejudice and discrimination and the resulting effect on human development.

g. Complete a research experience that implements theories in the students' own practice through individual research and exposure to other colleagues' work.

h. Facilitate an understanding of special populations (i.e., women, elderly, and other so-called minorities).

i. Facilitate the identification of the effect of social systems and social organizations on individuals and groups. Begin to identify how social workers affect social systems in a global context.

j. Facilitate the understanding of U.S. cultural bias toward explaining problems individualistically and strengthen the link between human development and larger social, political, and global systems. Begin to identify how social workers can intervene with social systems and demand social justice for the benefit of human growth and development worldwide.

COURSE OUTCOMES

a. Demonstrate knowledge of and ability to critique prevalent theories of human growth and development so that these can be applied in practice in a global context.

b. Use human development theory to assess various family, individual, and community issues.

c. Identify the concepts of social systems theory and apply these concepts to a variety of systems advocacy and social work situations.

d. Be able to identify and describe the various phases and transformations of individuals and families as they develop over the life cycle; incorporate a broad-based perspective on the range of "normal" and "delayed" phases of development.

e. Identify and describe development within a historical and global cultural context. Recognize one's own cultural norms and compare these with diverse communities locally, nationally, and internationally.

f. Specify biological, cultural ethnic, psychological, spiritual, and sociological factors that influence the behaviors of individuals, families, communities, and cultures at various phases of life.

g. Identify and describe developmental tasks/circumstances specific to women, people with disabilities, gays and lesbians, elderly potentially "at-risk" groups, and a range of cultures.

h. Identify how society assigns worth to individuals and how oppression hinders development worldwide.

TEXTS

Required

Ashford, J. B., LeCroy, C. W., & Lortie, K. L. (2001). *Human behavior in the social environment: A multidimensional perspective*. Pacific Grove: Wadsworth.

UNICEF. (2003). *The state of the world's children*. New York: UNICEF.

Pinderhughes, E. (1989). *Understanding race, ethnicity and power*. New York: The Free Press.

Kotlowitz, A. (1991). *There are no children here*. Doubleday: New York.

Recommended

Ramanathan, C., & Link, R. (1999). *All our futures: Principles & resources for social work practice in a global era*. Pacific Grove, CA: Wadsworth.

UNICEF. (1997) The progress of nations 1997. Available online at: pubdoc@unicef.org

The New Internationalist, (2004), NI: The People, the ideas, the action in the fight for world development. Lewiston, New York: New Internationalist publications. Online at: www.newint.org

COURSE ASSIGNMENTS

All assignments must include references from a variety of cultures and global resources.

Begin a journal from the first class onward to generate material for assignment 2.

1. Due Session 2: points 10

    The practice of systems theory. Describe the major characteristics and concepts of systems theory as it relates to social work. Apply your description to practice with reference to any system you are familiar with (agency, community group, client family, etc). Briefly analyze the contribution of systems theory to social work (e.g., in comparison to the pre-1970s emphasis in the United States, for example, on individual clients), and comment on how far you see this perspective articulated and applied in the workplace. Choose whether to use a diagram or illustration. Change any names to protect confidentiality. Approximately 1,000 words (4 pages).

2. Due Session 3: points 10

    Journal information about yourself and your family. Incorporate class discussion, readings, and topics in your journal. Include how the family expresses emotion, what roles individuals play, family norms, rules, overt and covert forms of communication, and so forth. Compare your experience with one of the global families portrayed in the film (Haines-Stieles, G. [1991] *Childhood Series, Part 1, Great Expectations*, PBS, New York: Ambrose.) or from other global resources, such as our discussion of articles on discipline in Sweden and Norway. Type a summary of not more than 1,000 words.

3. Presentations due Session 5: points 15—student and faculty evaluation

    Group Research Project. Discuss and agree together ways to present group's chosen theories to class in a 20-minute presentation. Connecting theory to practice is a key element in this assignment. Groups must include in their presentation a component addressing how the theory influences and informs practice and the global resources they have used. A bibliography or reference list must be typed and submitted to class members on day of presentation. If audiovisual aids are needed, please contact the Augsburg Library for videos available and the audiovisual department for equipment (our classroom will have a monitor).

    Choose groups:

    a. Gender roles and cultural transmission theorists, for example, Carol Gilligan, Wilson Schaeff, Leon Chestang, Devore and Schlesinger, Lum, Balgopal, Tripodi; explore global resources and include a practice illustration.

    b. European-American psychosocial, determinist (stage) theorists, for example, Erikson, David Elkind; psychosocial humanist (nonstage) theorists, for example, Carl Rogers, Virginia Satir; explore differences in approach to psychosocial theory internationally; include a practice illustration.

    c. Psychoanalytic/personality (determinist) theorists, for example, Sigmund Freud, Carl Jung, Myers-Briggs; contrast with alternative culturally based approaches to personality; include a practice illustration.

    d. Learning and behavior—environment theorists, developmental tasks, for example, Robert Havinghurst; draw on global resources (for example, case studies from the *New Internationalist* or *Progress of Nations*); include practice illustration.

    e. Cognitive theorists and cognitive behavioral approaches, for example, Jean Piaget, Michael Fraser, Katherine van Wormer (connects to models of restorative justice), David Elkind, (Elkind often combines psychosocial and cognitive theory in his analysis of development); draw on global resources and include a practice illustration.

    f. Empowerment, advocacy, and social exclusion theorists, for example, Solomon, Gaudier, Wolfe (in Ramanathan and Link), Saleeby, Rees, Gutierrez.

    We will discuss organizational theorists in class.

4. Due Session 6: points 15

    Interview a social work practitioner to ascertain her approach to human behavior and development; discuss the opportunities he or she has had to encounter theories and ask how her or his theoretical orientation influences and informs practice. Include questions relating to the social worker's international experience or encounters with service users from countries outside the United States. Ask what global issues have an effect on services. Hand in a short (one page) summary of your reflections and learning from the dialogue (see handout attached).

5. Due Session 7: points 15

    Critical assessment: Choose a community, organization, or individual with whom you are not familiar. Visit and assess the historical implications and the nurturing and sustaining factors in the lives/life of the person(s)/organization chosen. Read Norton's "Dual Perspective Revisited" as you prepare for this. In the past, students have visited various culturally specific community centers, synagogues, temples, and churches and places of spiritual celebration and alternative healing; we can brainstorm in class to extend this list.

    Re: Assignment No. 5: This is not a paper, it is an activity. To receive your grade of 15 points you will (a) describe the experience in a small class group; (b) hand in a sheet that gives date, description of event, and brief summary on one page.

- Due: Session 7.

This assignment is an attachment for assignment No. 6. It will provide experience and background for your discussion of dual perspectives; the culture or faith identified need not be the same as your case study, but there will be a parallel process in relation to nurturing and sustaining factors. Turn it in with assignment No. 6.

6. Due on or before session 8: points: 25

Self-analysis and cultural competence: Refer to pages 240–241 of Pinderhughes and her assignment on the significance of cultural interface in social work assessment and practice.

Complete a case analysis on yourself and your wider environment, utilizing both micro and macro concepts and public and private issues. How have you been affected by your class, ethnicity, location in the world, and age? What effect do your values have upon your behavior and practice? How has the community influenced you? Assess what barriers or limitations you might experience in an agency setting. Incorporate your journal in this paper (2,500–3,000 words). An outline for this assignment will be distributed in class.

EVALUATION

Self-evaluation; due Session 8 (assess grade and identify objectives covered).

In human development, we flourish when we are self-aware concerning our accomplishments and open concerning areas for development. Self-evaluation is therefore considered to be an important aspect of growth. Students will share responsibility for evaluation with faculty and the class as a whole. Each student will complete a self-assessment based on personal reflection, faculty, and group feedback. Forms of grade and weight for different assignments will be discussed when we meet.

The final grade is therefore based on a combination of:

1. Points for assignments assigned by faculty and one student group exercise.
2. Participation in class (10 points available—includes reading presentation).
3. Self-evaluation: a guide will be distributed in class.

CALENDAR

Session I

Welcome, introductions, syllabus review

- *Topics*: An ecological perspective: Human development, survival, or self-actualization; exploring the nature/nurture debate.

  - Review syllabus
  - Plan assignments
  - Introduction to systems theory
  - Nature or nurture in a global context.

- *Required Readings:*

  - Our Text: Ashford, Le Croy, Lortie, chapters 1–4; Pinderhuges: chapters 1–2
  - Van der Veer, G. (2000). Empowerment of traumatized refugees: a developmental approach to prevention and treatment. *Torture*, *10*(1), pp. 2–4.

- *Video:* Haines-Stieles, G. (1991). *Childhood Series, Part 1, Great Expectations* (in Japan, Russia, USA, Brazil), PBS, New York: Ambrose.

Theme throughout the trimester: exploring ethnicity, difference, power, ethnocentrism, and geocentrism in an interdependent world.

Criteria in grading assignments to be reviewed in class.

Session 2

Assignment No. 1 Due

- *Topics:* The Community: Micro/macro concepts and systems theory; connecting theory to practice; family transformation; infancy and childhood

  - Defining micro perspectives through personal childbirth experience and access to health care.
  - Macro concepts, common human condition, and social exclusion.
  - Mezzo concepts of community support across cultures.
  - The effect of violence on young children: the handgun debate and family safety and well-being.
  - Tracing connections between micro experience and macro realities.

- *Speaker:* Approaches to childbirth; a healthy or medical process? Comparisons with birthing, midwife services, and nurturing patterns in different countries

- *Required Readings:*

  - Ashford, LeCroy and Lortie, chapters 5–6
  - Bausch, R. S., & Serpe, R. T. (1997) Negative outcomes of interethnic adoption of Mexican American children. *Social Work, 42,*136–143.

- *Recommended Readings:*

  - Kalil, A., & Kunz, J. (1999). First births among unmarried adolescent girls: Risk and protective factors. *Social Work Research, 23*(3), 197–209.
  - Bachman, D., & Lind, R. (1997) Perinatal social work and the high risk obstetrics patient. *Social Work in Health Care, 24*(33/4), 3–19.

Session 3

Assignment No. 2 Due

- *Topics:* The family as a social institution: Definition of family; diversity in families due to history, social conditions, and cultural traditions; place of families within a community context; functions and organization of families as they respond to their social environment; "sustaining" social institutions and their organizational effect on families; becoming a couple and the parenting option.

  Diversity in families: history, social conditions, cultural traditions; special populations in the Midwest; functions and organization of families as they respond to the social environment and human conditions; sustaining social institutions and their organizational effect on families.

- *Speaker:* to facilitate—Alpha Beta—playing a culture game.

- *Required Readings:*

  - Ashford, LeCroy, Lortie, chapters 7–8

- *Recommended Readings:*

  - Mendez-Negrete, J. (2000). "Dime con quien andas": Notions of Chicano and Mexican American families. *Families in Society, 81*(1), 42–48.
  - Berg, I., & Jaya, A. (1993). Different and same: Family therapy with Asian-American families. *Journal of Marital and Family Therapy, 19*(1), 31–38.
  - Defining Social Exclusion: in Ramanathan & Link, All our Futures.

Session 4

- *Topics:* Building healthy families with adolescents; family patterns and the lives of children around the world; family resilience; special stressors in adolescent and daily development; including families in planning services.

- *Required Readings:*

  - Ashford, LeCroy, Lortie, chapter 9. UNICEF. (2003). The state of the world's children. New York: UNICEF.
  - Weston, K. (1991). *Families we choose: Lesbians, gays, kinship.* New York: Columbia University Press. (reserve)

- *Recommended Readings:*

  - DuBray, W., & Sanders, A. (1999). Interactions between American Indian ethnicity and health care. *Journal of Health and Social Policy, 10*(4), 67–84.
  - Carbonell, D., Reinherz, H., & Giaconia, R. (1998). Risk and resilience in late adolescence. *Child and Adolescent Social Work Journal, 15*(4), 251–272.
  - Beeler, J., & DiProva, V. (1999). Family adjustment following disclosure of homosexuality by a member: Themes discerned in narrative accounts. *Journal of Marital and Family Therapy, 25*(4), 443–459.
  - Rosemary to present: Link, R. (1995). British family centres and family participation. *Community Alternatives, 7*(1), 81–105.

Session 5

- *Topics:* The family stressors: macro change such as migration; mezzo change such as school, peers, workplace; micro change such as separation, health; family stressors; special populations and migration; adolescent development.

- *Readings:*

  - Kotlowitz, A. *There are no children here* (*choose a chapter*).
  - Garbarino, J. (1999). *Lost boys.* New York: Free Press. (*choose a chapter*).
  - Pipher, M. (1994). *Reviving Ophelia.* New York: Ballantine.
  - *Colorin Colorado: The art of Indian children.* (1994). Mexico City: Trust for the Health of the Indian Children of Mexico. (Link to distribute)
  - Williams, C. (1995). Adolescent pregnancy. In *Encyclopedia of social work* (19th ed.) (pp. 34–40. Washington, DC: NASW Press.
  - Guterman, N. B., & Cameron, M. (1997). Assessing the impact of community violence on children and youths. *Social Work, 42,* 495–505.
  - Smith, J., O'Connor, I., & Berthelsen, D. (1996). The effects of witnessing domestic violence on young children's psycho-social adjustment. *Australian Social Work, 49,* 3–10.

Session 6

- *Topics:* Issues of cultural oppression and institutional "isms"; mental health and assessment; family well-being; physical and psychological well-being; DSM-V.
- *Speaker:* Mental health assessment
- *Video:* King, D. (1992). Peace of mind: Exeter health authority, England, de-institutionalization project during the 1980–1990s. Exeter, UK: Exeter Health Authority. Patient contribution to the evaluation "Tell Them Thank You."
- *Required Readings:*

  - Ashford, LeCroy & Lortie, chapter 2
  - Pinderhughes, chapter 7

- *Recommended Readings:*

  - Hackl, K. L., Somlai, A. M., Kelly, J. A., & Kalishman, S. C. (1997). Women living with HIV/AIDS: The dual challenge of being a patient and caregiver. *Health and Social Work, 22,* 53–62.

- Cook, J. A., Cohler, B. J., Pickett, S. A., & Beeler, J. A. (1997). Life-course and severe mental illness: Implications for caregiving within the family of later life. *Family Relations*, 46(4), 427–436.

Session 7

Assignment No. 4 due

- *Topic:* Group presentations; comparing theories; group presentations concerning psychosocial, psychoanalytic, cultural transmission, social exclusion, cognitive theorists; constructing a "theory wheel" expanding global references; presentations; family transitions, losses and growth: death and dying, theory, frameworks, and indicators for practice.
- *Required Readings:*

    - Kubler-Ross, E, (1969). *On death and dying.* New York: Macmillan.
    - Irish, D., Lundquist, K, & Nelsen, V. (1993). *Ethnic variations in dying, death and grief: Diversity in universality.* Washington, DC: Taylor & Francis.

- *Recommended Reading:*

    - Barnes, G. (1999). Divorce transitions: Identifying risk and promoting resilience for children and their parental relationships. *Journal of Marital and Family Therapy*, 25(4), 425–441.

Session 8

Assignment No. 5 and 6 due and self-evaluation.

- *Topics:* Endings and social approaches to transition and renewal: the elderly family; nurturing living places, workplaces, and human awareness; summary and review; endings; the elderly family; nurturing across the life span.
- *Required Readings:*

    - Ashford, LeCroy, and Lortie, chapter 12
    - Weisbord, M. (1987). *Productive workplaces: Organizing and managing for dignity, meaning and community.* San Francisco: Jossey-Bass. (class handout)
    - Pinderhughes, chapter 8.

- *Recommended Readings:*

    - Sheehy, G. (2002, September). September widows. *Vanity Fair*, pp. 263–282.
    - Browne, C., & Broderick, A. (1994). Asian and Pacific Island elders: Issues for social work practice and education. *Social Work*, 39, 252–259.
    - Crow Dog, M., & Erdoes, R. (1991). *Lakota Women.* New York: Harper Perennial.

- *Video:* Gurievitch, G. (1985). *Kicking high in the golden years.* Hohokus, New Jersey: New Day Films.

Congratulations: your first trimester accomplished . . .

"Gracias a la vida que me ha dado tanto"
(Thanks to life that has given me plenty)
—Gabriela Mistral, 1889–1957, Chile

GUIDELINES TO ASSIGNMENT NO. 2. DUE SESSION 3

Points 10 | Length: 1,000 words (4 pages, font 12)

Journal information about yourself and your family. This means regularly writing notes about experiences that help you reflect on human behavior. These notes are your private reflection and you do not hand them in. You will summarize and quote from them for your assignment:

Incorporate class discussion, readings, and topics in your journal and then in your assignment. It is very important to integrate class dialog, reading, and observation in your reflections. For example, you may have observed how the Japanese family live out the saying "In Japan, children live with the gods until they are seven." Children are treated as though they are precious and close to "gods"; they are a particular focus for families, family legislation, and community support—is this our experience in the United States and in our own communities and families?

In your assignment include:

- how the family expresses emotion;
- what roles individuals play (are they openly assigned or covertly ascribed?);
- family norms (are these explicitly discussed or part of tradition?);
- rules (who makes them, breaks them, ignores them);
- overt and covert forms of communication;
- rituals and celebrations.

Compare your experience with one of the global families portrayed in the film (*Childhood*, PBS) or from other global resources (reserve).

Global Community Practice
SW 518 01

COURSE DESCRIPTION

This course, required of all graduate social work majors, focuses on the community as the unit of intervention. Students will be introduced to the spectrum of macro social work practice from a global perspective. Students will learn the skills necessary for conceptualizing and facilitating social change, whether at the agency, neighborhood, state, federal, or international level. Direct action (grassroots) organizing will be the framework for learning about social change. The course will also examine international organizing movements and how these compare to organizing efforts in the United States.

COURSE RATIONALE

Social workers need to have an understanding of the role of the community in their clients' lives. Central to this thesis is the assumption that direct practice cannot be divorced from community practice. Social change (reform) is needed to overcome dysfunctional systems, which regenerate psychosocial problems requiring direct practice intervention. Reform can only take place when social work practitioners, working directly with clients, initiate change at the macro level. This course will teach students the skills necessary to make this happen, whether working on the local, national, or international level.

COURSE OBJECTIVES AND EDUCATIONAL OUTCOMES

Overarching:

1. Students will be able to apply critical thinking skills to social work practice knowledge, values, and skills within the generalist model and at the macro level;
2. Students will be able to demonstrate the professional use of self in interactions with clients, agencies, and communities;
3. Students will understand the values and ethics of the social work profession and apply them at the macro level;
4. Students will be able to demonstrate greater awareness of diversity of one's self and others and how these diversities influence clients, ethical practice, and communities;
5. Students will be able to demonstrate the ability to incorporate cultural competencies in the assessment, intervention, and evaluation of work at the macro level;
6. Students will explore and understand the implications and consequences of inequality, injustice, and oppression in society and the effect of these social phenomena on communities;
7. Students will be able to demonstrate the ability to promote the empowerment of and strengthen the capacities of vulnerable individuals, families, groups, and communities;
8. Students will understand the interdependence of nations and the global nature of social problems and how these are enacted at the community level.

Foundation Objectives:

1. Students will be able to demonstrate written and verbal skills appropriate for social work practice at the macro level;
2. Students will be able to become familiar with the technology appropriate for social work practice;
3. Students will be able to demonstrate an ability to contract with groups and communities, problem solve situations, and implement and evaluate interventions using culturally competent practice;
4. Students will learn macro change efforts through the direct action organizing model;
5. Students will understand the local connections to social problems at the global level and familiarize themselves with solutions that are global in nature.

Course Objectives:

1. To understand the spectrum of macro social work practice;
2. To demonstrate a beginning familiarity with the United Nations and the organizations involved in working at an international level;
3. To develop specific macro skills in writing press releases, designing workshops, and designing brochures and other literature needed for organizing campaigns;
4. To understand how to work with a board of directors;
5. To understand and examine international community-organizing efforts.

REQUIRED READING

Brueggemann, W. (2002). *The practice of macro social work*. Belmont, CA: Brooks/Cole.

McKnight, J. L., & Kretzman, J. P. (1997). Mapping community capacity. In M. Minkler (Ed.), Community organizing and community building for health (pp. 157–172). New Brunswick, NJ: Rutgers University Press.

Rivera, F., & Erlich, J. (1998). *Community organizing in a diverse society* (3rd ed.). Boston: Allyn & Bacon.

Specht, H., & Courtney, M. E. (1994). *Unfaithful angels: How social work has abandoned its mission*. New York: The Free Press.

United Nations. (1996). *Platform for action and the Beijing declaration*. Fourth World Conference on Women, Beijing, China, September 1995.

Wahid, A., & Hus, M. (2000). The Grameen Bank of Bangladesh: History, procedures, effects & challenges. *Asian Affairs, 31*(2), 160–170.

Warren, R. B., & Warren, D. I. (1977). How to diagnose a neighborhood. In R. B. Warren & D. I. Warren (Eds.), *The neighborhood organizing handbook* (pp. 167, 173–195). Notre Dame, IN: University of Notre Dame Press.

RECOMMENDED READINGS

Bobo, K. (1996). *Organizing for social change: A manual for activists in the '90s*. Santa Anna, CA: Seven Locks Press.

Ramanathan, C., & Link, R. (1999). *All our futures: Principles and resources for social work in a global era*. Belmont, CA: Wadsworth.

WEB SITES UTILIZED FOR THE COURSE

* http://www.ssw.upenn.edu/ ~ restes/praxis.html: PRAXIS Web page
* http://bubl.ac.uk./link/d/developmentstudies.htm: Social Development Resources Web page

DESCRIPTION OF ASSIGNMENTS

PRAXIS Web page

An excellent Internet resource on social development is located at the University of Pennsylvania School of Social Work. Students will be required to explore this Web page in depth, and every three weeks submit a 2–3 page paper on a different aspect or link of this Web page. The location of the page is: www.ssw.upenn.edu/ ~ restes/praxis. html. A total of four papers will be collected based on this Web resource. Take the opportunity to explore four different international or global issues with these papers.

Ethno-Racial-Cultural Identity and Community Practice Assignment

The purpose of this assignment is to have the student learn more about ethnic, racial, and cultural backgrounds to begin to understand their effect on community practice. Students will submit a 2–3-page paper answering the following questions:

1. Choose an ethno-racial-cultural background different from your own. Describe significant historical, religious, and/or cultural factors that have shaped the values of this group.

2. What values do you associate with this ethno-racial-cultural identity? Give examples of what might be considered both positive and negative values.

3. Most important, what historical and contemporary aspects of your group's ethno-racial-cultural background are forces for and/or against community development (macro) practice?

Use both journal articles and appropriate Internet Web sites to complete the paper. Make sure you include how the Web sites and articles stimulated your thinking and values about the group you have chosen.

Oral Recitation

Each student will (in random order) present a reaction to the premise of *Unfaithful Angels: How social work has abandoned its mission*. The orator will present their reaction/position and build on, add to, or challenge previous positions/presentations. Each presentation should be approximately five minutes in duration.

Community Assessment and Intervention Project

Class members will be divided into groups to complete projects based on community-organizing components. For the neighborhood diagnosis paper, each group must choose a neighborhood unfamiliar to the group. Using the Warren and Warren article on "Diagnosing a Neighborhood," diagnose or assess this neighborhood as much as possible. Each group will submit one paper for the group, and members will receive their grade based on the grade for the paper (with presentation and self-analysis of your role in the group accounting for 35% of individual grade). In the paper (6–8 pages), discuss your methods and what you discovered about the neighborhood. Also include a community asset map using the McKnight and Kretzman article identifying the resources and networks available to the community.

Using the community chosen above, decide what issue the neighborhood needs to organize around, using a multicultural perspective. Using the examples given in class, describe what your organizing effort would look like. Each project must include at least five of the following:

1. public service announcements
2. press releases
3. advisory board
4. press conference
5. a workshop
6. a public hearing
7. literature
9. brochures
10. campaign posters
11. flyers

The final paper should describe the organizing effort to the fullest extent as well as include the above information as content or appendices. Each paper will also reflect how the efforts described can be applied to international community development. Use the appropriate articles in the bibliography of the syllabus to help you compare international community development to the efforts outlined in your paper. Each group will give a 30-minute presentation to the class on its project.

All papers must be typed, double-spaced, and run between 6–8 pages in length (without appendices). Late papers will not be accepted. Considerations for grading will include resources used, writing style, quality and depth of analytical thought.

Groups will present progress reports in class on an ongoing basis (as part of class discussion), reflecting on lessons learned about the process, experience, and strategies used in their respective CD projects. A final report on the project will be presented in class (15% of overall grade for project).

Based on self-analysis and feedback from class discussion following the presentations, each student will submit via e-mail a maximum three-page summary and analysis of his/her role in the CD process (20% of overall grade for project). Formative (process) and summative (outcomes) evaluations of the project will make up the basis of this report. Individuals should keep journals and minutes of meetings to assist them with preparation of their final report.

To be included in the report (one-page addition to the appendix) is a description of the assignments/contributions of individual members working within the group. Students working with groups are expected to share the load evenly. If members of the group are concerned that one or more of their members is not doing his or her fair share, it is in the first instance up to them to negotiate to rectify the situation. However, should that prove to be ineffective, it behooves the affected members of the group to approach the course instructor expeditiously to seek a solution. Groups who do not include the workload distribution in their final report or do not ensure that the workload is evenly spread among their members may have their group grade lowered.

Outcomes Assessment Evaluation

A requirement in the Department of Social Work is the administration of an outcomes assessment test. This testing is done on both the undergraduate and graduate levels and is one of several tools that the department uses to assess whether students are performing and learning the objectives of the social work program. The evaluation will be administered during Week 13.

COURSE OUTLINE

Week 1: Introduction to the Course

Course Requirements: Overview of PRAXIS Web page

Week 2: Defining Macro Skills

Readings: Brueggemann, chapter 1: Overview of the Practice of Macro Social Work; chapter 15: Social Work at the Global Level; Review of the U.S. Bill of Rights; Review of the Declaration of Human Rights

Week 3: Social Change Making

Readings: Brueggemann, chapter 2: Social Problems and Social Change; Rivera, chapter 1: A Time of Fear, A Time of Hope; Community Asset Mapping; McKnight & Kretzman, Neighborhood Diagnosis; Warren & Warren

- PRAXIS paper No. 1 due
- Ethno-racial-cultural assignments due

Week 4: Understanding Communities

Readings: Brueggemann, chapter 5: Communities; Ramanathan & Link, chapter 3: Understanding the Human Condition in a Global Era; Rivera, chapter 2: Native American Community Development; Rivera, chapter 3: Chicanos, Community & Change

Week 5: Understanding Organizations

Readings: Brueggemann, chapter 9: The Social Sector and the Rise of the Social Organization; chapter 12: Becoming an Organizational Developer; Ramanathan & Link, chapter 4: Infusing Global Perspectives into SW Practice; Ethics in Organizational Development

Week 6: Global Approaches to Social Welfare

Readings: Ramanathan & Link, chapter 6: Global Approaches to Social Welfare Policy; Beijing Conference Proceedings, UN, pp. 1–30; Needs Assessment in Community practice

- PRAXIS Paper No. 2 due

Week 7: Organizing with People of Color

Readings: Rivera, chapter 4: The House on Midland; chapter 5: Practice with Puerto Ricans; chapter 6: Organizing with Women of Color; Beijing Conference Proceedings: Women and Poverty, pp. 37–46

Week 8: The Fundamentals of Direct Action Organizing

Readings: Bobo, chapter 1: Introduction; chapter 2: The Fundamentals of Direct Action Organizing

Week 9: Becoming a Community Organizer

Readings: Brueggemann, chapter 8: Becoming a Community Organizer; Bobo, chapter 3: Choosing an Issue; chapter 4: Developing a Strategy chapter 5: A Guide to Tactics; chapter 7: Designing Actions; Beijing Conference

Proceedings: Women's Issues in Beijing, pp. 46–109; The Grameen Bank of Bangladesh: History, Procedures, Effects and Challenges

- PRAXIS Paper No. 3 due

Week 10: Oral Recitation on *Unfaithful Angels*

Week 11: Organizing Skills Part I and II

Readings: Bobo, chapter 8: Holding Accountability Sessions; chapter 12: Planning and Facilitating Meetings; chapter 13: Being a Great Public Speaker; chapter 14: Using the Media; chapter 15: Designing and Leading a Workshop; Rivera, chapter 7: Organizing in the Chinese-American Community; chapter 8: The Japanese American Community and Community; Organizing; chapter 9: The Philippino American Community ; chapter 12: Community Development and Restoration

Week 12:

Readings: Ramanathan & Link, chapter 9: Global Social and Economic Justice Issues; chapter 11: Social Development in Social Work; chapter 13: Future Visions for Global Studies in SW

- PRAXIS Paper No. 4 due

Week 13: Outcomes Assessment Test

Week 14: Managing Resources

Readings: Bobo, chapter 20: Grassroots Fundraising; chapter 21: Controlling your work: Administrative Systems; chapter 22: Using Computers for Organizing; chapter 23: Supervision; chapter 24: Financial & Legal Matters

- Project Presentations
- Community Assessment and Intervention Project due

Week 15: Project Presentations

BIBLIOGRAPHY

Community Development

Adato, M., & Haddad, L. (2002). Targeting poverty through community-based public works programmes: Experience from South Africa. *Journal of Development Studies*, *38*(3), 1–36.

Addams, J. (1910). *Twenty years at Hull House.* New York: Macmillian.

Addams, J. (1930). *The second twenty years at Hull House.* New York: Macmillan.

Bender, T. (1978). *Community and social change in America.* Baltimore, MD: Johns Hopkins University Press.

Biddle, W., & Biddle, L. (1965). *The community development process: The recovery of local initiative.* New York: Holt, Rinehart & Winston.

Carlton-LaNey, I., & Burwell, N. Y. (Eds). (1996). *African American community practice models: Historical and contemporary responses.* New York: Haworth Press.

Du Plessis, R. (2002). The narrative approach and community development: A practical illustration. *Africanus*, *32*(2), 76–92.

Eversole, R. (2003). Managing the pitfalls of participatory development: Some insight from Australia. *World Development*, *31*(5), 781–95.

Fellin, P. (1987). *The community and the social worker.* Itasca, IL: Peacock Publishers.

Halpern, R. (1995). *Rebuilding the inner city: A history of neighborhood initiatives to address poverty in the U.S.* New York: Columbia University Press.

Hussein, M. K. (2003). The role of Malawian local government in community development. *Development South Africa*, *20*(2), 271–82.

Jones, J. F., & Xu, Q. (2002). Grass-roots organization and community development: Evaluating the Chinese urban neighborhood committee. *Regional Development Studies, 8,* 99–117.

McHombu, K. (2002). Sharing knowledge for community development and transformation: A handbook. London: Oxfam.

Midgley, J. (1995). *Social development: The developmental perspective in social welfare.* London: Sage.

Otzen, U. (2003). Community development: the key to reducing poverty in Africa's rural regions. *Agriculture and Rural Development, 10*(1), 3–6.

Sakai, M. (2002). Enabling self-help activities through loan services in Thailand: The Urban Community Development Office's strategies for low-income community development. *Regional Development Dialogue, 23*(1), 136–51.

Shanmugaratnam, N., Mamer, D., & Kenyi, M. R. (2002). From emergency relief to local development and civil society building: A review of Norwegian People's Aid's interventions in Southern Sudan. Narobi, Kenya: Drylands Corporation Group.

Suttles, Gerald. (1972). *The social construction of communities.* Chicago: University of Chicago Press.

Tropman, E., & Rothman, J. (Eds.) (1995). *Tactics and techniques of community intervention* (3rd ed.). Itasca, IL: Peacock Publishers.

Wald, L. (1934). *Windows on Henry Street.* Boston: Little, Brown.

Wang, S. (2002). On the politics and participation in the development of urban communities in China. *Social Sciences in China, 23*(2), 3–13.

World Bank. (2003). Fostering community-driven development: What role for the state? *Policy Research Working Papers* (No. 2969). Geneva, Switzerland.

Community Organizing

Betten, N., & Austin, M. (1990). *The roots of community organizing: 1917 to 1939.* Philadelphia, PA: Temple University Press.

Cookingham, F., & Linthicum, R. (1994). Community organizing in Madras: evaluating an innovative urban advance project. *World Vision International, 19,* 1–40.

Freire, P. (1992). *Pedagogy of the oppressed.* New York: Continuum.

Kahn, S. (1970). *How people get power: Organizing oppressed communities for action.* New York: McGraw-Hill.

Mondros, J. B., & Wilson, S. M. (1994). *Organizing for power and empowerment.* New York: Columbia University Press.

Perlman, R., & Gurin, A. (1972). *Community organization and social planning.* New York: Wiley.

Wong, C. K. (1993). State-funded social work projects for social reform: Reflections from community organizing in Hong Kong. *International Social Work, 36*(3), 249–60.

Leadership

Bethel, S. (1990). *Making a difference: Twelve qualities that make you a leader.* New York: Putnam.

Greenleaf, R. K. (1977). *Servant leadership: A journey into the nature of legitimate power and greatness.* New York: Paulist Press.

Hersey, P. (1985). *The situational leader: The other 59 minutes.* New York: Warner Books.

Kouzes, J., & Posner, B. (1987). *The leadership challenge: How to get extraordinary things done in organizations.* San Francisco, CA: Jossey-Bass.

Kouzes, J., & Posner, B. (1993). *Credibility: How leaders gain it and why people demand it.* San Francisco, CA: Jossey-Bass.

Oakley, E., & Krug, D. (1993). *Enlightened leadership: Getting to the heart of change.* New York: Simon & Schuster.

Perlmutter, F., & Slavin, S. (Eds.). (1980). *Leadership in social administration: Perspectives for the 1980s.* Philadelphia, PA: Temple University Press.

Tropman, J. E. (1997). *Successful community leadership: A skills guide for volunteers and professionals.* Washington, DC: NASW Press.

Oppression and Injustice

Axford, B. (1995). *The global system: Economics, politics and culture.* Cambridge, England: Polity Press.

Barnet, R. J., & Cavanagh, J. (1994). *Global dreams: Imperial corporations and the new world order.* New York: Touchstone.

Barry, T. (1995). *Zapata's revenge: Free trade and the farm crisis in Mexico.* Boston: South End Press.

Bussey, G., & Tims, M. (1980). *Pioneers for peace: Women's International League for Peace and Freedom, 1915–1965.* London: George Allen & Unwin.

Cherniack, M. (1986). *The Hawk's Nest incident: America's worst industrial disaster.* New Haven, CT: Yale University Press.

Elling, R. H. (1986). *The struggle for workers' health: A study of six industrialized countries.* New York: Baywood Publishing.

Foster, C. (1989). *Women for all seasons: The story of the Women's International League for Peace and Freedom.* Athens: University of Georgia Press.

Green, J. (Ed.). (1983). *Workers' struggles, past and present: A "radical America" reader.* Philadelphia, PA: Temple University Press.

Lofgren, D. (1989). *Dangerous premises: An insider's view of OSHA enforcement.* Ithaca, NY: Cornell University Press.

McWilliams, C. (1971). *Factories in the field: The story of migratory farm labor in California.* Santa Barbara, CA: Penguin.

Riis, J. (1903). *Children of the tenements.* New York: Macmillan.

Rossi, P. H. (1989). *Down and out in America: The origins of homelessness.* Chicago: University of Chicago Press.

Simon, B. Levy. (1994). *The empowerment tradition in social work practice: A history.* New York: Columbia University Press.

Steinbeck, J. (1939). The *grapes of wrath.* New York: Viking Press.

Steinbeck, J. (1945). *Cannery Row.* New York: Viking press.

Organizations

Etzioni, A. (1964). *Modern organizations.* Englewood Cliffs, NJ: Prentice-Hall.

Hummel, R. (1977). *The bureaucratic experience.* New York: St. Martin's Press.

Kamat, S. (2003). The NGO phenomenon and political culture in the Third World. *Development, 46*(1), 88–93.

Lipsky, M. (1980). *Street-level bureaucracy: Dilemmas of the individual in public services.* New York: Russell Sage Foundation.

Mintzberg, H. (1983). *Power in and around organizations.* Englewood Cliffs, NJ: Prentice-Hall.

Perrow, C. (1979). *Complex organizations: A critical essay* (2nd ed.). Glenview, IL: Scott, Foresman.

Simon, H. (1976). *Administrative behavior.* New York: Free Press.

Taylor, F. W. (1947). *The principles of scientific management.* New York: Norton.

Social Action and Social Justice

Alinsky, S. (1969). *Reveille for radicals*. New York: Vintage Books.

Alinsky, S. (1971). *Rules for radicals*. New York: Random House.

Allen, R. (1983). *Reluctant reformers: Racism and social reform movement in the United States*. Washington, DC: Howard University Press.

Anderson, W. (1989). *The age of protest*. Pacific Palisades, CA: Goodyear.

Carson, M. (1990). *Settlement folk: Social thought and the American settlement movement, 1885–1930*. Chicago: University of Chicago Press.

Davis, A. (1967). *Spearheads for reform: The social settlements and the Progressive Movement, 1890–1914*. New York: Oxford University Press.

Dayaratne, R., & Smarawickrama, R. (2003). Empowering communities in peri-urban areas of Colombo. *Environment & Urbanization, 15*(1), 101–110.

Halkatti, M., Purushothaman, S., & Brook, R. (2003). Participatory action planning in the peri-urban interface: The twin city experience, Hubi-Dharwad, India. *Environment and Urbanization, 15*(1), 149–158.

Reeser, L. & Epstein, I. (1990). *Professionalization and activism in social work: The sixties, the eighties, and the future*. New York: Columbia University Press.

Sinclair, U. E., Sagaren & A. Teichner (Eds.) (1963). *Cry for justice: An anthology of the literature of social protest* (Rev. ed.) New York: Lyle Stuart.

Walters, R. G. (1978). *American reformers: 1815–1860*. New York: Hill and Wang.

Social Leaders

Costin, L. B. (1983). *Two sisters for social justice: A biography of Grace and Edith Abbott*. Urbana: University of Illinois Press.

Finks, P. D. (1984). *The radical vision of Saul Alinsky*. New York: Paulist Press.

Wilson, D. C. (1975). *Stranger and traveler: The story of Dorothea Dix, American reformer*. Boston: Little, Brown.

Brinkley, A. (1983). *Voices of protest: Huey Long, Father Coughlin & the Great Depression*. New York: Random House.

Social Development

Boutros-Ghali, B. (1995). *An agenda for development, 1995*. New York: United Nations Public Information Office.

Brown, L., et. al. (1997). *State of the world: A Worldwatch Institute report: Progress towards a sustainable society*. New York: W. W. Norton.

Caufield, C. (1996). Masters of illusion: The World Bank and the poverty of nations. New York: Henry Holt.

Craig, G. (2003). Globalization, migration and social development. *Journal of Social Development in Africa, 18*(2), 49–76.

Igoe, J. (2003). NGOs, wheat, and civil society: The story of Tanzania's Hanang community development project (paper No. 243). Boston, MA: Boston University, African Studies Center.

Hickey, S. (2002). Transnational NGDOs and participatory forms of rights-based development: converging with the local politics of citizenship in Cameroon. *Journal of International Development, 14*(6), 841–57.

Momsen, J. H. (2002). NGOs, gender and indigenous grassroots development. *Journal of International Development, 14*(6), 859–67.

Van Reisen, M. (2002). *Directing EU policy towards poverty reduction: From commitments to targets to results*. Brussels, The Netherlands: European Centre for Development Policy Management.

International Social Work and Social Welfare
Social Work 780

International Social Work and Social Welfare is a graduate-level elective available to all second-year MSW students at San Diego State University (SDSU). SDSU has two concentrations: direct practice and administration; and three fields of service: mental health; children, youth, and families; and health and aging. Material in this course complements all fields of service and all concentrations, though its emphasis is on macro practice. Social Work 780 complements SDSU's efforts to focus on border issues and international social work.

PURPOSE AND DESCRIPTION

The purpose of this course is to expose students to salient global issues and to relate how the institution of social welfare has developed in different regions of the world. The course examines globalization and its effect on social welfare and human need. The fields of comparative social welfare analysis and social development are surveyed briefly. Special attention is given to the linkage of human rights and social work. As a way of understanding how different regions and countries have responded to human need, the course explores the specific problem areas of women in developing countries, street children and child labor, HIV in the developing world, and the plight of refugees. The course explores the international practice of social work as one of the primary professions associated with social welfare. Finally, the course delves into the role of international organizations, such as the World Bank, the International Monetary Fund (IMF), and the agencies of the United Nations (UN), and nongovernmental organizations (NGOs) such as Catholic Relief Services and Save the Children, in shaping international welfare policy and services.

COURSE OBJECTIVES

Knowledge

1. Understand how different countries approach and configure their social welfare systems and social services.
2. Identify the role of globalization in shaping social problems and country-specific responses to social problems.
3. Demonstrate a working knowledge of key international social welfare organizations and their social welfare orientation.
4. Understand the functions and contributions of social work in countries around the world.

Skills

1. Articulate different approaches to structuring social welfare programs and services.
2. Identify major resources for research in international social welfare.
3. Assess the prevalence of social problems, such as poverty, AIDS, and human rights violations, in specific countries.
4. Identify how social work is practiced in a specific country.

Values

1. Identify the need to strengthen and enhance social welfare systems in the face of globalization.
2. Recognize social work as a global profession.
3. Associate human rights with social welfare and social work practice.
4. Recognize value conflicts that influence global and international social interventions.

Outcomes

1. Become familiar with key concepts and issues in international social welfare.
2. Recognize the effect of globalization on social work and social welfare.
3. Identify organizational actors involved in international social work and social welfare.
4. Identify resources and data used in analyzing global social conditions and international social welfare.

REQUIRED TEXT

Midgley, J. (1997). *Social welfare in global context*. Thousand Oaks, CA: Sage.

OPTIONAL TEXTS

Healy, L. (2001). *International social work*. New York: Oxford University Press.

Ife, J. (2001). *Human rights and social work*. New York: Cambridge University Press.

REQUIRED READINGS

Copies of all the nontextbook readings will be placed on reserve at Love Library. A course reader is available for purchase at Cal Copy.

SOURCE MATERIALS

The United Nations Development Programme's *Human Development Report* (2002, New York: Oxford University Press) will be held on reserve at Government Documents. The latest *World Development Report* from the World Bank (2002, New York: Oxford University Press) is in the reference room.

The following books have been placed on reserve at the Reserve Room at Love Library:

- Hokenstad, M. C., Khinduka, S. K., & Midgley, J. (Eds.). (1992). *Profiles in international social work*. Washington, DC: NASW Press. (chapters on social work practice in countries throughout the world)
- Hokenstad, M. C., & Midgley, J. (Eds.). (1997). *Issues in international social work*. Washington, DC: NASW Press. (chapters on international issues)
- Mayadas, N. S., Watts, T. D., & Elliot, D. (Eds.). (1997). *International handbook on social work theory and practice*. Westport, CT: Greenwood Press. (chapters on social work practice throughout the regions and countries of the world)
- Ramanathan, S. C., & Link, R. (1999). *All our futures: Principles and resources for social work practice in a global era*. Pacific Grove, CA: Brooks/Cole.

ASSIGNMENTS

1. **Discussion Questions**: For four classes, you are to develop a minimum of two discussion questions per reading and send the set of discussion questions to the instructor at least one day before the class (late questions will be docked two points). Two sets of discussion questions should relate to the conceptual portion of the course (Weeks 1 to 7), one set to vulnerable populations (Weeks 8 to 11), and one set to professional or organizational interventions (Weeks 12 to 15). The discussion questions should demonstrate that you have read and thought about the materials. Questions should link the readings and explore common themes. To receive the maximum points per set of questions, you should bring copies of the questions to class and share them with your colleagues to help shape class discussion. **40 points**

2. **International Social Work and Social Welfare Portfolio**: Select a developing country and provide the following:

   1. a brief history of the country;
   2. an outline specifying its major ethnic/racial groups;
   3. a demographic profile (e.g., total population, population growth rate, age structure, percent of urban population, life expectancy, infant mortality rates, maternal mortality rates, fertility rates, HIV rates);

4. a poverty profile (e.g., income inequality, poverty levels, access to clean water, per capita health expenditures, adult literacy rate, global poverty ranking, ranking on the human development index);

5. an economic profile (e.g., GDP, GDP growth rate, major industries, major agricultural products, military expenditures, level of high-technology exports, level of foreign investment);

6. a social welfare profile (what types of social assistance and social insurance programs the country offers);

7. information on the country's human rights issues or track record;

8. two scholarly articles that discuss a social problem(s) that affects a vulnerable population;

9. two journalistic articles that discuss a social problem(s) that affects a vulnerable population;

10. a description of social work (whether the country has a school of social work, what type of social work is practiced);

11. a description of World Bank, World Health Organization, UNICEF, or International Labour Organization programs;

12. a description of NGO activity;

13. a description of social work, human services, public health, and/or Peace Corps voluntary opportunities.

All the materials in the preceding list are to be submitted in the form of a portfolio:

• **Items 1–5:** These items serve as an assessment of the country. What do the data tell you about the country and its level of human development? It may help to examine how the country compares to others in the region. You may also find it helpful to organize the information into tables. The assessment should be no more than five pages long. **10 points**

• **Item 6:** Given your country assessment, how does the formal social welfare system correspond to and deal with the country's social conditions? No more than two pages; include reference material. **5 points**

• **Item 7:** Using the information gathered, identify and describe the state of human rights in the country. No more than two pages; include reference material. **5 points**

• **Items 8–9:** Include in portfolio and develop a brief summary of the articles, including why you chose them. No more than three pages. **10 points**

• **Item 10:** Include information on topic in portfolio.

• **Item 11:** Provide information on topic in portfolio and develop a brief assessment of the appropriateness of the projects given the country's socio/political/economic conditions. No more than two pages.

• **Item 12:** Include information on topic in portfolio and assess the importance of the work being done. No more than two pages.

• **Item 13:** Include information on topic in portfolio.

The final portfolio should include all materials and previous written work. It should include a statement that synthesizes your grasp of the material and what you have found most interesting, troubling, or exciting about the process of exploring social welfare and social work in the country you chose. No more than 10 pages. **60 points** (including the 30 points from Items 1–9)

CLASS SCHEDULE

Week 1: Introduction

Overview of the course and introductory comments

Required Reading

• Midgley, Social welfare in global context, Introduction and chapter 1: The field of international social welfare.

Suggested Reading

• To keep up with international developments, you will need to read regularly one of the major newspapers. Almost all have Web versions:

- www.nytimes.com
- www.washingtonpost.com
- www.latimes.com
- www.iht.com (*The International Herald Tribune*)
- Additionally, Dr. Richard Estes has an excellent Web page with international hyperlinks: http://caster.ssw. upenn.edu/ ~ restes/praxis.html

Week 2: Globalization

These two sections review competing theories of globalization and examine how global economic and social change influence the provision of social welfare in developing countries. Data sources for documenting socioeconomic conditions are reviewed.

Required Reading

- Deacon, B. (1997). *Global social policy.* Thousand Oaks, CA: Sage. (pp. 11–27)
- Foek, A. (1997). Sweat-shop Barbie: Exploitation of third world labor. *Humanist, 57*(1), 9–13.
- Micklethwait, J., & Woolridge, A. (2001). The globalization backlash. *Foreign Policy, 126,* 16–26.
- Midgley, chapter 2: The global world system.

Suggested Reading

- Friedman, T. (2000). *The Lexus and the olive tree.* New York: Anchor Books.

Week 3: Globalization

Required Reading

- Midgley, chapter 3: Social conditions in global context.
- Drager, N., Woodward, D., Beaglehold, R., & Lipson, D. (2001). Globalization and the health of the poor. *Development, 44*(1), 73–76.
- www.cia.gov/cia/publications/factbook (This Web page provides summary data and analysis on the social, economic, and political conditions of virtually every country.)
- State Department: http://www.state.gov/

Suggested Reading

- Estes, R. J. (1997). The world social situation: Social work's contribution to international development. In R. Edwards (Ed.), *Encyclopedia of social work* (supplement to the 19th ed.) (pp. 21–36). Washington, DC: NASW Press. (available in reference room, Love Library)
- Midgley, chapter 4: Description of social welfare around the world.
- For the latest data on global trends in social welfare, see the World Bank, *World Development Report,* and the United Nations Development Programme, *Human Development Report,* which are annual publications.

Week 4: Comparative Social Welfare

This section examines different approaches to comparative social welfare and assesses the relevance of formal social welfare programs to developing countries.

Required Reading

- Midgley, chapter 5: Theories of state welfare.
- Midgley, chapter 6: The impact of state welfare.

Suggested Reading

- Dixon, J. (1999). *Social security in global perspective.* Westport, CT: Praeger.
- Esping-Andersen, G. (Ed.). *Welfare states in transition: National adaptation in global economies.* Thousand Oaks, CA: Sage. (This volume has contributed chapters on social welfare in all regions of the world except Africa.)
- Richard Estes, R. (1995). International social welfare: Comparative systems. In R. Edwards (Ed.), *Encyclopedia of social work* (pp. 957–969). Washington, DC: NASW Press.
- Social Security Administration. (1999). *Social Security programs throughout the world—1999.* Washington, DC: U.S. Government Printing Office. (This annual publication describes the provision of social welfare for more than 172 countries.)
- Ward, P. M. (1993). Social welfare policy and political opening in Mexico. *Journal of Latin American Studies, 25*(3), 613–628.

Week 5: Social Development

This section examines the concept of social development and provides examples of social development activities in India and Bangladesh.

Required Reading

- Dominelli, L. (1997). International social development and social work. In M. C. Hokenstad & J. Midgley (Eds.), *Issues in international social work* (pp. 74–91). Washington, DC: NASW Press.
- Midgley, chapter 9: International social development.

Suggested Reading

- Berstein, J. (1995). Redefining social work's emphasis on the "social": The path to development. *International Social Work, 38,* 53–67.
- Estes, R. J. (1993). Toward sustainable development: From theory to praxis. *Social Development, 15*(3), 1–29.
- Khinduka, S. K. (1997). Development and peace: The complex nexus. *Social Development Issues, 10*(3), 19–30.
- Midgley, J. (1998). *Social development: The developmental perspective in social welfare.* Thousand Oaks, CA: Sage.

Week 6: Social Exclusion and Human Rights

The concept of social exclusion is examined and its utility for understanding poverty is assessed, especially in regard to the developing world. Human rights are reviewed as a component of social work practice.

Required Reading

- Grant, E., Blue, I., & Harpham, T. (2000). Social exclusion: A review and assessment of its relevance to developing countries. *Journal of Developing Societies, 16*(2), 201–222.
- Ife, J. (2001). *Human rights and social work.* New York: Cambridge University Press. (chapter 2: The three generations of human rights)

Suggested Reading

- Jones, A., & Smyth, P. (1999, September). *Social exclusion: A new framework for social policy analysis?* Paper presented at the 26th AASW National Conference, Brisbane, Australia.
- Amnesty International: www.amnesty.org
- Human Rights Watch: www.hrw.org
- United Nations Office of High Commissioner for Human Rights: http://www.unhchr.org/
- U.S. State Department, Human Rights: http://www.state.gov/g/drl/hr/
- U.S. State Department, Human Rights Country Report: www.state.gov

Week 7: Human Rights

This section focuses on the debate and conflict over human rights. Efforts to ban child labor serve to illustrate the tension between competing human rights agendas.

Required Reading

- Bissell, S. (2001). Young garment workers in Bangladesh: Raising the rights question. *Development*, *44*(2), 75–80.
- Ife, J. (2001). *Human rights and social work*. New York: Cambridge University Press. (chapter 10: Achieving human rights through social work practice)
- Myers, W. (2000). The right rights? Child labor in a globalized world. *Annals*, *575*, 38–55.

Suggested Reading

- George, J. (1999). Conceptual muddle, practical dilemma: Human rights, social development and social work education. *International Social Work*, *43*(1), 15–26.
- United Nations Universal Declaration of Human Rights: www.unhchr.ch/udhr/lang/eng.htm

Week 8: Women in the Developing World

This section examines the status of women in the developing world through two problem areas: sexual trafficking and poverty. A human rights perspective is reviewed to address both problems.

Required Reading

- Bertone, A. M. (2000). Sexual trafficking in women: International political economy and the politics of sex. *Gender Issues*, *18*(1), 4–22.
- Buvinic, M. (1997). Women in poverty: A new global underclass. *Foreign Policy*, *108*, 38–52.
- Reichert, E. (1998). Women's rights are human rights: Platform for action. *International Social Work*, *41*, 371–384.
- U.S. Department of State, Office of the Senior Coordinator for International Women's Issues. (2001, October 30). *Fact sheet: Women and girls in Afghanistan*. Washington, DC: Author.

Suggested Reading

- Harcourt, W. (2001). Women's health, poverty and globalization. *Development*, *44*(1), 85–90.
- United Nations Convention on the Elimination of Discrimination against Women: www.un.org/womenwatch/daw/cedaw/
- U.S. Department of State, Agency for International Development. (n.d.). *Trafficking in persons: USAID's response*. Washington, DC: Author.

Week 9: Children

This section examines street children, child slavery, and child soldiers as problems experienced by children in many countries of the world. Efforts to assist street children are reviewed. The UN Declaration of the Rights of the Child is examined.

Required Reading

- Robinson, S., & Palus, N. (2001, April 30). An awful human trade. *Time*, pp. 40–41.
- Scheper-Hughes, N., & Hoffman, D. (1998). Brazilian apartheid: Street kids and the struggle for urban space. In N. Scheper-Hughes & C. Sargent (Eds.), *Small wars* (pp. 352–358). Berkeley, CA: University of California Press.
- Trussell, R. P. (1999). The children's streets: An ethnographic study of street children in Cuidad Juarez, Mexico. *International Social Work*, *42*(2), 189–199.

Suggested Reading

- Estes, R., & Weiner, N. A. (2001). *The commercial sexual exploitation of children in the U.S., Canada, and Mexico*. Philadelphia, PA: Center for the Study of Youth Policy, University of Pennsylvania. (There is a chapter on children in Tijuana in this report.)

- le Roux, J. (1996). The worldwide phenomenon of street children: Conceptual analysis. *Adolescence, 31*(124), 965–970.
- Mufane, P. (2000). Street youth in Southern Africa. *International Social Science Journal, 52*(164), 233–244.
- United Nations Children's Fund (UNICEF): www.unicef.org
- United Nations Convention on the Rights of the Child: www.unicef.org/crc/crc.htm

Week 10: HIV/AIDS

The epidemic of HIV/AIDS has affected many developing countries in Africa and Asia. The social and economic costs of the epidemic are reviewed. Efforts to provide antiretroviral medications are examined, as are community-based projects to assist persons with HIV/AIDS (such as AIDS *wats* in Thailand).

Required Reading

- Dixon, S., McDonald, S., & Roberts, J. (2001). HIV/AIDS and development in Africa. *Journal of International Development, 13*, 381–389.
- Mancoske, R. J. (1997). The international AIDS crisis. In M. C. Hokenstad & J. Midgley (Eds.), *Issues in international social work* (pp. 125–145). Washington, DC: NASW Press.
- Rosenberg, T. (2001, April 18). Look at Brazil. *The New York Times Magazine*, pp. 26–36.
- Cohen, J. (2003). Thailand and Cambodia: Two hard-hit countries offer rare success stories. *Science, 301*, 1658–1662.

Suggested Reading

- Kawewe, S. (2000, July 29). *Globalizing HIV/AIDS treatments: A holistic service delivery approach for social justice in Sub-Saharan Africa.* Paper presented at the 29th Joint World Conference of the International Schools of Social Work and International Federation of Social Workers, Montreal, Canada.
- McGeary, J. (2001, February 12). Death stalks a continent. *Time*, pp. 36–45.
- McGeary, J. (2001, February 12). Paying for AIDS cocktails. *Time*, p. 54.
- UNAIDS: www.unaids.org

Week 11: Refugees

This section reviews refugees and internally displaced persons as vulnerable populations. The refugee experience prior to resettlement is examined and programs to deal with trauma are explored. Human rights documents providing protection to refugees are covered.

Required Reading

- de Jong, K., Ford, N., & Kleber, R. (1999). Mental health care for refugees from Kosovo: The experience of Médécins San Frontières. *The Lancet, 353*, 1616–1617.
- East Timor as violence descended: Testimonies from East Timorese refugees. (2000). *Bulletin of Concerned Asian Scholars, 32*(1/2), 125–129.
- Mupedziswa, R. (1997). Social work with refugees. In M. C. Hokenstad & J. Midgley (Eds.), *Issues in international social work* (pp. 110–124). Washington, DC: NASW Press.

Suggested Reading

- Crisp, J. (2000). A state of insecurity: The political economy of violence in Kenya's refugee camps. *African Affairs, 99*, 601–632.
- Lobo, M., & Mayadas, N. S. (1997). International social work practice: A refugee perspective. In N. S. Mayadas, T. D. Watts, & D. Elliot (Eds.), *International handbook on social work theory and practice* (pp. 411–428). Westport, CT: Greenwood Press.
- State Department—Office of International Migration: http://usinfo.state.gov/regional/ar/
- UNHCR: www.unhcr.ch
- United Nations Convention Relating to the Status of Refugees: www.unhchr.ch/html/menu3/b/o_c_ref.htm

Week 12: International Social Work

These two sections examine the global profession of social work with special attention to social work in developing countries. The role of the International Federation of Social Workers and the International Association of Schools of Social Work in promoting social work is discussed. Social work in Armenia, Mexico, and Colombia is highlighted.

Required Reading

- Johannesen, T. (1997). Social work as an international profession. In M. C. Hokenstad & J. Midgley (Eds.), *Issues in international social work* (pp. 146–148). Washington, DC: NASW Press.
- Midgley, chapter 8: Social work in international context.
- Turner, G. (2001, Winter). The puzzling world of international social work careers. *The New Social Worker*, 4–7.
- International Federation of Social Workers (IFSW): http://www.ifsw.org/
- International Association of Schools of Social Work (IASSW): http://www.iassw.soton.ac.uk/

Suggested Reading

- Healy, L. (2001). *International social work.* New York: Oxford University Press.
- Hokenstad, M. C., & Kendall, K. A. (1995). International social work education. In R. Edwards (Ed.), *Encyclopedia of social work* (pp. 1511–1520). Washington, DC: NASW Press.
- Hokenstad, M. C., Khinduka, S. K., & Midgley, J. (Eds.). (1992). *Profiles in international social work.* Washington, DC: NASW Press. (chapters on social work practice in countries throughout the world)
- Hokenstad, M. C., & Midgley, J. (Eds.). (1997). *Issues in international social work.* Washington, DC: NASW Press. (chapters on international issues)
- Mayadas, N. S., Watts, T. D., & Elliot, D. (Eds.). (1997). *International handbook on social work theory and practice.* Westport, CT: Greenwood Press. (chapters on social work practice throughout the regions and countries of the world)

Week 13: International Social Work

Required Reading

- From either the *International handbook on social work theory and practice* or *Profiles in international social work*, pick one chapter on social work practice in Asia and one on Africa.
- Queiro-Tajalli, I. (1997). Latin America. In N. S. Mayadas, T. D. Watts, & D. Elliot (Eds.), *International handbook on social work theory and practice* (pp. 51–59). Westport, CT: Greenwood Press.
- Marian Angela Aguilar, Mexico, in *International handbook on social work theory and practice.*

Week 14: Global Organizational Actors

This section reviews the role of global organizations, such as the World Bank, IMF, and assorted UN agencies, in supporting social welfare in the developing world. Competing visions of social welfare are assessed.

Required Reading

- Deacon, B. (1997). *Global social policy.* Thousand Oaks, CA: Sage. (chapter 3: The social policy of global agencies)
- Fox, J., & Gershman, J. (2001). The World Bank and social capital: Lessons from ten rural development projects in the Philippines and Mexico. *Policy Sciences, 33*, 399–419.
- Healy, *International social work*, chapter 6: International social welfare organizations and their functions.

Suggested Reading

- International Committee of the Red Cross (ICRC): www.icrc.org
- International Labour Organization (ILO): www.ilo.org

- International Monetary Fund (IMF): www.imf.org
- United Nations (UN): www.un.org
- United Nations Development Programs (UNDP): http://www.undp.org/
- United Nations Economic and Social Development: http://www.un.org/esa/
- World Bank: www.worldbank.org
- World Health Organization (WHO): www.who.int
- World Trade Organization (WTO): http://www.wto.org/

Week 15: International NGOs

This section investigates the role of smaller international and national NGOs in the developing world. Focus is on NGO efforts to promote human rights and to develop antipoverty programs.

Required Reading

- Chowdhry, G., & Beeman, M. (2001, May). Challenging child labor: Transnational activism and India's carpet industry. *Annals, 575,* 158–175.
- Salinas-Ardaya, N., & Schachinger, C. (2001). Strengthening the rights of children and women in Bolivia. *Development, 44*(2), 99–103.

Suggested Reading

- Padilla, Y. C., & Daigle, L. E. (1998). Inter-agency collaboration in an international setting. *Administration in Social Work, 22*(1), 65–81.
- CARE: www.care.org
- Catholic Relief Services: www.catholicrelief.org
- Oxfam International: http://www.oxfam.org/
- Peace Corps: www.peacecorps.gov
- Save the Children: www.savethechildren.org

Issues in International Social Development
SSS 886

I. COURSE PURPOSE

This course, an elective course in the National Catholic School of Social Service Doctoral Program, which is also open to students in the Master's Program, builds upon and expands on the knowledge, values, and skills of social policy, development, and evaluation. The intention of this course is to broaden a student's perspective of the world, its problems, and needs and to examine the role of the professional in addressing these issues. As the world grows smaller given the revolutions in communication and technology, there is increasing pressure to form regional, international, and indeed global agreements and structures for economic, political, and environmental cooperation. As these changes take place, a number of social consequences have become apparent that are of concern to professionals.

The goal of this offering is the review of three interrelated themes: (1) globalization and its social, economic, political, and cultural consequences; (2) comparative social policies; and, (3) social and economic development as strategies of change and progress. An understanding of sociocultural differences is crucial to practicing overseas or in our own internationalized communities. Specifically, the course will address the following topics:

- Unit One: Globalization and social problems

    A. AIDS/HIV

    B. Economic displacement; migration and refugees

    C. Poverty, inequality, and inequity

- Unit Two: International work in a globalized world

    A. Framework for analysis of social policies and services

    B. Analyses of fields of practice

        1. Child welfare

        2. Mental health

        3. Family services

        4. The elderly and social security

- Unit Three: Social Development

    A. Models of social and economic development

    B. Case examples

        1. Africa

        2. Asia

        3. South and Central America

- Unit Four: Multicultural understandings

    A. Sociocultural issues in international work

    B. International work at home and abroad

    C. Opportunities in international work

II. EDUCATIONAL OBJECTIVES

A. Knowledge Objectives

1. To understand the concept of globalization, with its economic, political, environmental, and technological dimensions.
2. To become familiar with the benefits and disadvantages of globalization in the lives of individuals, families, and communities.
3. To comprehend the consequences of globalization for professionals.
4. To discern a model for the analysis of social polices of other nations.
5. To acquire a familiarity with the strategies of service delivery for children, families, the mentally ill, and the elderly.
6. To understand the social and economic approaches to development.
7. To interpret the development activities in selected countries in Africa, Asia, and South and Central America.
8. To see the relevance for international practice at home.
9. To understand where the opportunities for international practice exist.

B. Affective Objectives

1. To be cognizant of the nature of problems resulting from globalization.
2. To be aware of the importance of culture, social structure, values, and norms in defining social problems and their solutions.
3. To be conscious of the problems and needs of children, families, and the elderly in Third World countries.
4. To perceive the needs and problems of immigrants, aliens, and refugees in this country.

C. Skill Development

1. To acquire the tools necessary to understand the positive and negative trends and effects of globalization.
2. To become comfortable with various roles in assisting populations in need.
3. To develop an ability to analyze social policies and services in other countries.
4. To understand the necessary expertise in social development, especially its application to multicultural groups in this country.
5. To be able to adapt one's interventions to meet the needs of these populations.
6. To demonstrate a proficiency in understanding and adapting the findings in the international literature to one's own professional practice.
7. To demonstrate beginning competence in formulating research questions, methodological approaches, and findings relevant to one's practice.

III. COURSE REQUIREMENTS

A. Required Texts

The following texts are required for this course:

*   Hokenstad, M.C., & Midgley, J. (1997). *Issues in international social work*. Washington, DC: NASW Press.
*   Midgley, J. (1997). *Social welfare in global context*. Thousand Oaks, CA: Sage.
*   Stoesz, D., Guzzetta, C., & Lusk, M. (1999). *International development*. Needham Heights, MA: Allyn & Bacon.

A suggested text is:

*   Midgley, J. (1995). *Social development*. Thousand Oaks, CA: Sage.

These texts are available at the CUA Bookstore.

B. Course Assignments

Participants in this course will be required to do the following assignments:

- Make a 30-minute class presentation on a topic related to social policy, programs, or service delivery. The student will provide a bibliography and appropriate handouts for class participants, who will have an opportunity for questions and comments after the formal presentation. This activity will commence the seventh week of the semester. It will be graded and account for 25% of a student's grade. The date of the presentation will be agreed upon between instructor and student.

- Write a scholarly paper on the above topic due the last class. This project will account for 60% of a student's grade.

- Class participation will be graded and add 15% to the final grade.

IV. CLASS SCHEDULE

Unit One: Globalization and Social Problems

Lecture One. Globalization: Overview

Required Reading

- Cetingok, M., & Rogge, M. (2001). Turkey's Southeast Anatolia Project (GAP): Environmental justice and the role of social work. *Social Development Issues*, *23*(3),13–17.
- Hirst, P., & Thompson, G. (1999). *Globalization in question*. Cambridge, England: Polity Press. (pp. 1–18)
- Hokenstad, M.C., & Midgeley, J. (1997). Realities of global interdependence. In M.C. Hokenstad & J. Midgley, J. (Eds.), *Issues in international social work* (pp. 1–10). Washington, DC: NASW Press
- Hoff, M. D. (1997). Social work, the environment, and sustainable growth. In M.C. Hokenstad & J. Midgley (Eds.), *Issues in international social work* (pp. 27–44). Washington, DC: NASW Press.
- Khan, P., & Dominelli, L. (2000). The impact of globalization on social work in the UK. *European Journal of Social Work*, *32*, 95–108.
- Midgley, J. (1997). *Social welfare in global context*. Thousand Oaks, CA: Sage. (chapter 2: The global world system, pp. 21–40)
- Wagner, A. (1997). Social work and the global economy. In M. C. Hokenstad & J. Midgley (Eds.), *Issues in international social work* (pp. 45–56). Washington, DC: NASW Press.

Suggested Reading

- Starke, L. (2002). *State of the world, 2002: A Worldwatch report on progress toward a sustainable world*. New York: W.W. Norton.

Lecture Two. Global Social Issues: Poverty, inequality, insecurity, unemployment, and economic dislocation

Required Reading

- Atherton, C. R. (1994). Minimizing inequality in a market economy: Implications for Eastern Europe in transition. *International Social Work*, *37*(2), 127–136.
- Estes, R. (1999). The poverties: Competing definitions and alternative approaches to measurement. *Social Development Issues*, *21*(2), 11–21.
- Kentor, J. (2001). The long-term effects of globalization on income inequality, population growth, and economic development. *Social Problems*, *48*(4), 435–455.
- Midgley, J. (1997). *Social welfare in global context*. Thousand Oaks, CA: Sage. (chapter 3: Social conditions in a global context, pp. 43–67; chapter 6: The impact of state welfare: An international assessment, pp. 111–133)
- Silva, K. T., & Athukorala, K. (1996). South Asia: An overview. In E. Oyen & S. M. Miller (Eds.), *Poverty: A global view* (pp. 65–85). Oslo, Norway: Scandinavia University Press.

Lecture Three. Global Social Issues: Human Rights | The Treatment of Children | The Plight of Women

Required Reading

- Cagan, E., & Julia, M. (2000). Women, democracy and global transformation: Toward a reconceptualization. *Social Development Issues, 22*(2/3), 24–31.
- Lusk, M. (1992). Street children in Rio de Janeiro. *International Social Work, 35*(3), 293–305.
- Nichols-Casebolt, A., Krysik, J., & Hermann-Currie, R. (1994). The povertization of women: A global phenomenon. *Affilia, 9*(3), 288–307.
- Osirim, M. J. (1992). The state of women in the Third World: The informal sector and development in Africa and the Caribbean. *Social Development Issues, 14*(2/3), 74–87.
- UNIHCHR (1990).*Convention on the rights of the child.* New York: United Nations. See: http://www.unhchr.ch/html/menu3/b/k2crc.htm
- van Wormer, K. (1997). *Social welfare: A worldview.* Chicago: Nelson-Hall Publishers. (Worldwide abuse of women, pp. 512–521)
- Wetzel, J. W. (1992). Profiles on women: A global perspective. *Social Work and Health Care, 16*(3),13–27.

Lecture Four. Global Social Issues: The International Aids Epidemic

Required Reading

- Bassett, M., & Mholyi, M. (1991). Women and AIDS in Zimbabwe: The making of an epidemic. *International Journal of Health Services, 21*(1), 143–156.
- Mancoske, R. J. (1997). The international aids crisis. In M. C. Hokenstad & J. Midgley (Eds.), *Issues in international social work* (pp. 125–145). Washington, DC: NASW Press.
- United Nations. (2004). *UN report on global HIV/AIDS epidemic.* Retrieved on October 5, 2004. See: http://www.unaids.org/bangkok2004/report.html

Lecture Five. Global Social Issues: Migration, Immigration, and Refugees

Required Reading

- Ahearn, F. L. (1995). Displaced people. In R. L. Edwards (Ed.), *Encyclopedia of social work* (19th ed.) (pp. 771–780). Washington, DC: NASW Press.
- Mupedziswa, R. (1997). Social work with refugees. In M. C. Hokenstad & J. Midgley (Eds.), *Issues in international social work* (pp. 110–124). Washington, DC: NASW Press.
- United Nations High Commissioner for Refugees. (2003). *2003 global refugee trends.* See: http://www.unhcr.org/
- United States Committee for Refugees. (2002). *World refugee survey 2002.* Washington, DC: Immigration and Refugee Services of America. See www.uscr.org/WRS2002.cfm#

Suggested Reading

- Vella, D. (Ed.). (2000). *Everybody's challenge: Essential documents of Jesuit refugee service 1980–2000.* Rome: Jesuit Refugee Service.

Unit Two: International Social Work in a Globalized World

Lecture Six. Social Policy and Social Services in a Global Context: Frameworks for social policy analysis and factors influencing these policy decisions

Required Reading

- Hokenstad, M.C., Khinduka, S.K., & Midgley, J. (1992). The worlds of international social work. In M. C. Hokensatd, S. K. Khinduka, & J. Midgley (Eds.), *Profiles in international social work* (pp. 1–11). Washington, DC: NASW Press.

- Langmore, J. (2001). Globalization and social policy. *Social Work in Health Care, 34*(1/2),11–29.
- Lusk, M. W., & Stoesz, D. (1994). International social work in a global economy. *Journal of Multicultural Social Work, 3*(2), 101–113.
- Midgley, J. (1997). *Social welfare in global context*. Thousand Oaks, CA: Sage. (chapter 1: The field of international social welfare, pp. 3–20; chapter 4: Social welfare around the world, pp. 68–88; chapter 5: Theories of state welfare, pp. 89–110)
- Midgley, J. (1992). The challenge of international social work. In M. C. Hokensatd, S. K. Khinduka, & J. Midgley (Eds.), *Profiles in international social work* (pp. 13–27). Washington, DC: NASW Press.

Lecture Seven. Comparison of Social Policies and Services in a Global Context: Child Welfare Services

Required Reading

- Ahmed, M. A. (1991). Child labor in Pakistan: A study of the Lahore area. *Child Welfare, 70*(2), 261–267.
- Johnson, A. K., et al. (1993). Foster care and adoption policy in Romania: Suggestions for international intervention. *Child Welfare, 72*(5), 489–506.
- Khan, M. B. A. (1991). The foster care system in India. *Child Welfare, 70*(2), 243–259.
- Lusk, M. W. (1989). Street children programs in Latin America. *Journal of Sociology and Social Welfare, 16*(1), 55–77.
- Midgley, J. (1997). *Social welfare in global context*. Thousand Oaks, CA: Sage. (chapter 6: The impact of state welfare: An international assessment, pp. 111–133).
- UNICEF. (2005). *The state of the world's children 2005*. See: http://www.unicef.org/sowc04/index_sowc05.htm

Lecture Eight. Comparisons of Social Policies and Services in a Global Context: Family Services

Required Reading

- Haynes, A. W., & Singh, R. N. (1993). Helping families in developing countries: A model based on family empowerment and social justice. *Social Development Issues, 15*(1), 27–37.
- Kammerman, S., & Kahn, A. (1995). Innovations in toddler day care and family support services: An international overview. *Child Welfare, 74*(6), 1281–1300.
- Pierce, L., & September, R. (2000). Reconceptualizing child maltreatment: Providing better services for children and families in South Africa. *Social Development Issues, 22*(1), 30–34.
- Rao, M. (1995). International year of the family: Key issues in global policy evolution and implementation. *Social Development Issues, 17*(1), 68–73.
- Spakes, P. (1996). Equality and family policy in international perspective: Toward a feminist theory of the state. *Journal of Sociology and Social Work, 23*(2), 113–130.
- Textor, M. R. (1995). Youth and family welfare services in Germany. *International Social Work, 38*(4), 379–386.

Suggested Reading

- Kamerman, S. B., & Kahn, A. J. (1978). *Family policy: Governments and families in fourteen countries*. New York: Columbia University Press. (Families and the idea of family policy, pp. 1–16; Family policy as field and perspective, pp. 476–503).
- Kahn, A. J., & Kamerman, S. B. (1977). *Social services in international perspective*. Washington, D.C.: U.S. Department of Health, Education, and Welfare. (chapter 1: Personal social services emerge, pp. 1–19; chapter 9: Social services in eight countries, pp. 313–360).

Lecture Nine. Comparisons of Social Policies and Services in a Global Context: The Elderly and Social Security

Required Reading

- Cox, C. (2001). Who is responsible for the care of the elderly? A comparison of policies in the United States, the United Kingdom, and Israel. In F. L. Ahearn (Ed.), *Issues in global aging* (pp. 33–46). New York: Haworth Press.

- Hokenstad, M. C., & Johanssen, L. (2001). Retirement patterns and pension policy: An international perspective. In F. L. Ahearn (Ed.), *Issues in global aging* (pp. 25–32). New York: Haworth Press.
- George, J. (1997). Global graying. In M. C. Hokenstad & J. Midgley (Eds.), *Issues in international social work* (pp. 57–73). Washington, DC: NASW Press.
- Korpi, W. (1995). The position of the elderly in the welfare state: Comparative perspectives on old age care in Sweden. *Social Services Review, 69*(2), 242–273.
- Kurata, Y., & Oya, K. (2000). A consideration on changes of welfare institutions for the aged though the history of Japan. *Japanese Journal of Social Services, 2*(May), 7–15.
- Leung, J., & Wong, Y. C. (2002). Community-based services for the frail elderly in China. *International Social Work, 45*(2), 205–216.
- Midgley, J. (1997). *Social welfare in global context.* Thousand Oaks, CA: Sage. (chapter 7: Social change and the future of state welfare, pp. 134–156)
- Takamura, J. (2001). The future is aging. In F. L. Ahearn (Ed.), *Issues in global aging* (pp. 3–16). New York: Haworth Press.

Suggested Reading

- Diamond, P. A., Lindeman, D. C., & Young, H. (Eds.). (1996). *Social security: What role for the future?* Washington, DC: National Academy of Social Insurance. (chapter 5: Social security around the world, pp. 181–208)
- Dixon, J. E. (1999). Global overview of social security practices: Patterns and recent developments. In J. E., Dixon (Ed.), *Social security in global perspective* (pp. 81–110). Westport, CT: Praeger Publishers.
- Mesa-Lago, C. (1994). *Changing social security in Latin America: Toward alleviating the social costs of economic reform.* Boulder, CO: Lynne Rienner.
- Midgley, J., & Tracy, M. B. (1996). *Challenge to social security: An international exploration.* Westport, CT: Auburn House.
- Thursz, D., Nusburg, C., & Prather, J. (Eds.). (1995). *Empowering older people: An international approach.* Westport, CT: Auburn.

Unit Three: Social Development

Lecture Ten. Models of Social Development

Required Reading

- Dominelli, L. (1997). International social development and social work: A feminist perspective. In M. C. Hokenstad & J. Midgley (Eds.), *Issues in international social work* (pp. 74–91). Washington, DC: NASW Press.
- Estes, R. J. (1993). Toward sustainable development: From theory to praxis. *Social Development Issues, 15*(3), 1–29.
- Kramer, J. M., & Johnson, C. D. (1996). Sustainable development and social development: Necessary partners for the future. *Journal of Sociology and Social Welfare, 23*(2), 75–91.
- Midgley, J. (1993). Ideological roots of social development strategies. *Social Development Issues, 5*(1), 1–13.
- Midgley, J. (1995). *Social development.* Thousand Oaks, CA: Sage. (chapter 1: A definition of development, pp. 12–36; chapter 2: The historical context, pp. 37–66; chapter 3: Theoretical debates, pp. 67–101; chapter 4: Strategies for social development, pp. 102–138; chapter 5: Achieving social development: The institutional perspective, pp. 139–176)
- Stoez, D., Guzzetta, C., & Lusk, M. (1999). *International development.* Boston: Allyn & Bacon. (chapters 7, 8, and 14, pp. 128–168, 242–264)

Suggested Reading

- David, G. (1987). Peace and development: Toward a more just and global society. *Social Development Issues, 11*(1), 21–37.

- Midgley, J. (1981). *Professional imperialism: Social work in the Third World.* London: Heinemann.
- Moser, C. O. N. (1993). *Gender planning and development.* London: Routledge. (chapter 4: Third world policy approaches to women in development, pp. 55–79)

Lecture Eleven. Social Development Case Examples: Africa

Required Reading

- Ankrah, E. M. (1992). Social work in Uganda: Survival in the midst of turbulence. In M. C. Hokenstad, S. K. Khinduka, & J. Midgley (Eds.), *Profiles in international social work* (pp. 145–162). Washington, DC: NASW Press.
- Mampheswana, D., & Netshisiwinzhe, B. (1999). Promoting development and change through truth and reconciliation: A case of South Africa. *Social Development Issues, 21*(3), 66–74.
- Mazibuko, F., McKendrick, B., & Patel, L. (1992). Social work in South Africa: Coping with apartheid and change. In M. C. Hokenstad, S. K. Khinduka, & J. Midgley (Eds.), *Profiles in international social work* (pp. 115–127). Washington, DC: NASW Press.
- Osirim, M. J. (1992). The state of women in the Third World: The informal sector and development in Africa and the Caribbean. *Social Development Issues, 14*(2/3), 74–87.
- Stoez, D., Guzzetta, C., & Lusk, M. (1999). *International development.* Boston: Allyn & Bacon. (chapter 3, pp. 40–57)

Lecture Twelve. Social Development Case Examples: South America

Required Reading

- Estes, R. J. (1996). Social development trends in Latin America, 1970–1994: In the shadows of the 21st century. *Social Development Issues, 18*(1), 25–52.
- Jimenez, M., & Aylwin, N. (1992). Social work in Chile: Support for the struggle of justice in Latin America. In M. C. Hokenstad, S. K. Khinduka, & J. Midgley (Eds.), *Profiles in international social work* (pp. 29–41). Washington, DC: NASW Press.
- Lusk, M. (1992). Social development and the state in Latin America: A new approach. *Social Development Issues, 14*(1), 10–21.
- Prigoff, A. (1992). Women, social development, and the state in Latin America. *Social Development Issues, 14*(1), 56–69.
- Stoez, D., Guzzetta, C., & Lusk, M. (1999). *International development.* Boston: Allyn & Bacon. (chapter 2, pp. 22–39)

Lecture Thirteen. Social Development Case Examples: Asia

Required Reading

- Bose, A. B. (1992). Social work in India: Developmental roles for a helping profession. In M. C. Hokenstad, S. K. Khinduka, & J. Midgley (Eds.), *Profiles in international social work* (pp. 71–83). Washington, DC: NASW Press.
- Hong, S. (1999). Services for the homeless in Korea. *Arete, 23*(2), 9–14.
- Lee, P. C. (1992). Social work in Hong Kong, Singapore, South Korea, and Taiwan: Asia's four little dragons. In M. C. Hokenstad, S. K. Khinduka, & J. Midgley (Eds.), *Profiles in international social work* (pp. 99–114). Washington, DC: NASW Press.
- Matsubara, Y. (1992). Social work in Japan: Responding to demographic dilemmas. In M. C. Hokenstad, S. K. Khinduka, & J. Midgley (Eds.), *Profiles in international social work* (pp. 85–97). Washington, DC: NASW Press.
- Stoez, D., Guzzetta, C., & Lusk, M. (1999). *International development.* Boston: Allyn & Bacon. (chapter 1, pp. 1–21)

Unit Four: Multicultural Issues

Lecture Fourteen. Multicultural Understanding and Social Work Practice: Opportunities for Practice at Home and Abroad

Required Reading

- Healy, L. M. (2001). International social work: Why is it so important and what is it? In L. M. Healy, International Social Work (pp. 1–18). New York: Oxford University Press.

- Hokenstad, M. C., Khinduka, S. K., & Midgley, J. (1992). Social work today and tomorrow: An international perspective. In M. C. Hokenstad, S. K. Khinduka, & J. Midgley (Eds.), Profiles in international social work (pp. 181–193). Washington, DC: NASW Press.

- Johannesen, T. (1997). Social work as an international profession: Opportunities and challenges. In M. C. Hokenstad, & J. Midgley (Eds.), Issues in international social work (pp. 146–158). Washington, DC: NASW Press.

- Midgley, J. (1997). Social welfare in a global context. Thousand Oaks, CA: Sage. (chapter 8: Social work in an international context, pp. 159–179; chapter 10: International cooperation in social welfare, pp. 203–224)

- Morgan, E., & Van Weigel, Dr. (1989). Credits and credibility: Educating professionals for cultural sensitivity. *Social Development Issues*, 12(2), 60–70.

- Rosenthal, B. S. (1991). Social workers' interest in international practice in the developing world. A multivariate analysis. *Social Work*, 36, 248–252.

Suggested Reading

- Ramanathan, C. S., & Link, R. J. (1999). *All our futures: Principles and resources for social work practice in a global era.* Belmont, CA: Wadsworth Publishing.

Comparative Social Welfare
SW750

I. COURSE DOMAIN AND BOUNDARIES

This is a required graduate-level course.

Social welfare is the major institutional vehicle through which societies assure a minimal level of living for all their citizens. Building on both the core curriculum and the foundational courses, the content of this course focuses on achieving a fuller understanding of the social, political, and economic dynamics of contemporary welfare development, and, in turn, social development in the United States and other countries. Problems of global poverty, social injustice, and inequality and issues of racial, ethnic, and cultural diversity will receive special attention. The multi-faceted contributions of social work, the social services, and social welfare in advancing national and international social development within rich and poor countries will be emphasized. Students will be expected to demonstrate at least beginning skill in the use of comparative methods in analyzing a cross-national social welfare or social development dilemma of particular interest to them.

II. COURSE OBJECTIVES

Within the context of achieving a fuller understanding of the social, political, and economic dynamics of contemporary welfare development, and, in turn, social development, this course will:

1. introduce students to the dynamics of national and international social development across societies and under differing social, political, and economic systems;

2. introduce students to the unique social development dilemmas confronting the "developing" and "least developing" countries of Asia, Africa, and Latin America;

3. introduce students to the profound national and international forces that impede progress toward more rapid patterns of social and economic development for historically disadvantaged population groups, including racially, ethnically, and culturally diverse population groups;

4. introduce students to the unique contributions made by social workers and the social services in promoting more fully integrated social and economic development in the United States and other countries;

5. introduce students to issues of social and economic justice within an international context; and

6. provide opportunities for students to deepen their understanding of the complex value and ethical dilemmas inherent in national and international social development practice.

III. EDUCATIONAL OUTCOMES

Building on the content of the core curriculum, their field practica, and the foundational courses, through this course students will:

1. provide evidence of increased understanding of the national and international dynamics of social development across societies and under differing social, political, and economic systems;

2. demonstrate increased understanding of the unique social development dilemmas confronting the "developing" and "least developing" countries of Asia, Africa, and Latin America;

3. demonstrate a deepened awareness of the profound national and international forces that impede progress toward more rapid patterns of social and economic development for historically disadvantaged population groups (including women, the aged, the poor, children and youth, disabled persons, political and economic refugees, and the mentally ill, as well as groups of persons who have been disadvantaged by virtue of race, religion, ethnicity, social class, caste, culture, sexual orientation, or national origin);

4. demonstrate a deepened appreciation for the contributions of social workers and the social services in promoting more fully integrated social and economic development in both the United States and other countries;

5. demonstrate increased understanding of the role of social work and the social services in promoting increasingly higher levels of social and economic justice both nationally and internationally; and

6. demonstrate sensitivity to the unique ethical and value dilemmas inherent in social development practice.

IV. READINGS

The majority of the course readings can be found in the following required books that have been ordered for purchase from the university bookstore. In some cases, additional readings have been placed on reserve in the Reserve Book Reading Room. Note: Readings preceded by an asterisk (*) are required for the unit shown; all other readings are recommended but not required.

Required

Estes, R. J. (1998). *Resources for social and economic development: A guide to the scholarly literature.* Philadelphia: University of Pennsylvania School of Social Work.

Healy, L. (2001). *International social work: Professional action in an interdependent world.* New York: Oxford University Press.

Midgley, J. (1997). *Social welfare in global context.* Thousand Oaks, CA: Sage.

United Nations Development Programme (UNDP). (2003). *Human development report, 2003: Millennium development goals.* New York: Oxford University Press.

World Bank (2003). World development report, 2003: *Sustainable development in a dynamic world.* New York: Oxford University Press.

Required Books Available Without Cost Via the Internet

U.S. Department of Health and Human Services. (2004). *Social security programs throughout the world: Europe, 2003.* Washington, DC: Social Security Administration. (Access without cost via Praxis)

U.S. Department of Health and Human Services. (2002). *Social security programs throughout the world: Africa, 2002.* Washington, DC: Social Security Administration. (Access without cost via Praxis)

U.S. Department of Health and Human Services. (2002). *Social security programs throughout the world: Asia and the Pacific, 2002.* Washington, DC: Social Security Administration. (Access without cost via Praxis)

U.S. Department of Health and Human Services. (2004). *Social security programs throughout the world: The Americas, 2003.* Washington, DC: Social Security Administration. (Access without cost via Praxis)

NOTE: Electronic versions of the UNDP (2003) and World Bank (2003) texts also are available via the Internet; however, many electronic versions often exclude the statistical annexes needed for this course.

V. ORGANIZATION OF COURSE

The course is divided into two parts: Part 1—*Conceptual Underpinnings of International Social Development*; and Part 2—*Dilemmas in International Development*. Each part builds on foundational content and supports the development of knowledge, skills, and values for social work practice in international social development. A detailed course outline is provided in Section VIII.

VI. ASSIGNMENTS AND GRADING CRITERIA

Two written assignments and one oral presentation have been designed to assist students in achieving the course's learning objectives:

1. For courses taught outside of Penn as an intensive institute, a proposal for the semester-end comparative research project is due to me in Philadelphia by October 20. The proposal first must have been reviewed by the course teaching assistant prior to being sent to the course instructor. Therefore, students will need to reserve

sufficient time to allow for the preparation of a draft proposal, its review by the teaching assistant, and the mailing of a polished version of the proposal so that the course instructor receives it in Philadelphia by the due date.

2. A report of your semester-end comparative research project focused on the preapproved international/comparative social welfare/social development topic. The completed paper is due no later than December 15. Before the paper is sent to the instructor, it will first be read and commented upon by the course teaching assistant; therefore, reserve sufficient time in your schedule to allow for the preparation of the report, its review by the teaching assistant, and the mailing of the report so that the instructor receives it by the due date.

3. During the second part of the course, students will be given an opportunity to summarize their research to other members of the class. Due to the size of the class, a variety of formats will be used in structuring these presentations.

All assignments must be completed fully and submitted on a timely basis. Assignments will not be accepted after the date they are due.

Assignment I. Project Proposal

Students are required to prepare a formal research proposal as part of this course. The proposal must include:

1. a working title for the project (not more than 10 words);

2. a general outline of the project including:

    a. a brief statement of the question or problem that will be studied (see the instructions for the second paper for a general approach to the selection of your research topic);

    b. a listing of and rationale leading to the selection of at least three countries for inclusion in the comparative analysis; and

    c. a summary of the general methods or approaches that will be used to locate and collect the data and information needed to complete the comparative analysis.

3. a working list of experts on the topic (at least two) with whom the student plans to consult—one must be local and the other associated with an appropriate international nongovernmental organization (NGO), the United Nations, or other international development entity;

4. a working bibliography of at least 6 to 10 annotated references of *direct relevance* to the proposed project;

5. a working timetable showing step-by-step activities to be taken leading to the completion of the project by the date due; and,

6. any supplemental material that the student judges will help the instructor better assess the quality of the proposed project.

    The 3–4-page research proposal must be typed double-spaced with 1-inch margins throughout. Please do not use a binder or other type of cover when submitting the proposal.

Assignment II. Semester-End Paper

Following approval of their research proposal, students may immediately begin to work on their approved projects. Students may select their topic from among a broad range of subjects. In general, approved topics will focus on the analysis of some combination of the following issue areas:

1. Sociopolitical factors that are affecting the changing "welfare mix" (e.g., the "expected" contribution of individuals, families, informal care systems, the voluntary sector, and government in responding to welfare needs) within selected countries during particular historical periods.

2. Sociopolitical factors that influence societal response to the welfare needs of particular *groups or populations* (e.g., racial/ethnic minorities; refugees; orphans; veterans; the disabled, sick, mentally ill; the aged; the poor, etc.);

3. Sociopolitical factors that influence the establishment of categories of welfare programs or services (e.g., income security, feeding and nutritional support services, housing, health care, social service provision, etc.);

4. The contribution of culture and cultural forces in shaping welfare development in particular locales (e.g., the effect of religion, ethnicity, language, etc., on particular approaches to welfare systems or welfare service provision);

5. Sociopolitical factors that influence welfare development in contrasting groupings of nations (e.g., patterns of welfare development in the so-called "developed," "developing," or "least developing" countries; welfare development trends in "rich" vs. "poor" countries or in "first" world vs. "third" world countries, etc.);

6. Sociopolitical and other philosophical traditions that influence welfare development in particular geopolitical regions (e.g., welfare development in Asia, Europe, Latin America, North America, etc.).

Students also may chose, and indeed are encouraged, to combine two or more of the above areas into a common paper, for example, "social, political, and economic factors influencing the development of income-support programs for single parents in post–WWII Europe," or "sociopolitical-economic factors influencing housing development for the aged poor in Asia's 'newly industrializing countries.'"

Regardless of the topic selected for study, all papers must:

1. provide evidence of considerable independent scholarship, including an extensive discussion of the relevant comparative welfare/social development literature;

2. offer useful insights into understanding the complex social, political, economic, and other national and international forces that influence(d) welfare development/social development over time and/or in specific cultural contexts;

3. achieve a balance between statistical and nonstatistical data sources, including in the use of either historical or contemporary data, or both; and,

4. report a comparative analysis of welfare development/social development patterns for a minimum of three (3) countries, at least one of which must be the student's own country of origin.

One hard copy of the completed project report and an electronic copy of the report's bibliography and charts are due at the end of the final session. The report may not exceed 15 pages (exclusive of tables, charts, and any appended materials).

Oral Presentations

Each student will have the opportunity to present an oral summary of her/his semester-end report. These presentations will take place during the second half of the course and will in all cases be based on the work in the student's written report. Oral presentations should not entail new or supplemental research on your part.

A variety of formats may be used in making these presentations: panels (i.e., groups of 3–4 students presenting on a single theme); roundtables (4–5 students discussing a topic of mutual interest under the guidance of 1–2 students who have undertaken research in that area); or poster sessions ("walk-through" sessions during which individual students summarize their work to others who visit their poster). Panel and roundtable presentations will be thematic in focus and, thus, need to be more or less integrated so as to avoid duplication of coverage.

For presentations involving three or more students, the instructor will appoint a student "convener" to work with each group in organizing the content and format of the presentation. No convener will be appointed for poster sessions, however, inasmuch as such presentations typically involve only 1–2 students.

Determination of the most appropriate format for your presentation will be decided jointly by the student, instructor, and teaching assistant following approval of the project proposal.

In all cases, sufficient time and electronic equipment (overhead projector, data projector, etc.) will be made available for student use in making presentations.

PART I: CONCEPTUAL UNDERPINNINGS OF INTERNATIONAL SOCIAL DEVELOPMENT

Session 1

*   **Unit 1** Course organization, readings, semester-end paper, and so forth.

*   **Unit 2** The Language of International Social Work, Social Welfare, and Social Development: Part I

    *   Unit Learning Objective

        This unit will introduce students to the concept of "globalization" and its implications for international social development, especially for the development of poorer countries. Emphasis will be placed on the imbalance that exists between rich and poor countries vis-à-vis access to and control over resources that are essential to broad-based social and economic development. Value and ethical dilemmas for social workers practicing at the international level also will receive attention.

- Readings (Read at least two of the following)

    - *Castex, G. M. (1993) Frames of reference: The effects of ethnocentric map projections on professional practice. *Social Work*, *38*, 685–693.

    - Editors. (2001, September 29). Globalisation and its critics: A survey of globalization. *The Economist* (special supplement), pp. 1–30.

    - *Estes, R. J. (1990). Development under different political and economic systems. *Social Development Issues*, *13*(1), 5–19.

    - *Healy, L. (2001). *International social work: Professional action in an interdependent world.* New York: Oxford University Press. (chapter 1: International social work: Why is it important and what is it?, pp. 1–18; chapter 7: Values and ethics for international professional action, pp. 151–169)

- **Unit 3** The Language of International Social Work, Social Welfare, and Social Development: Part II

    - Unit Learning Objective

    Social workers have practiced at the international level for more than a century. This unit will review aspects of that history and place international social work in the context of international social development. Tensions between micro- versus macro-level practice within an international context, as well as the ethical and value dilemmas that are intrinsic to international practice, also will be explored.

    - Readings

        - Elliott, D., & Mayadas, N. (1996). Integrating clinical practice and social development. *Journal of Applied Social Sciences*, *21*, 61–68.

        - *Estes, R. J. (1993). Toward sustainable social development: From theory to praxis. *Social Development Issues*, *15*, 1–29.

        - *Healy, *International social work: Professional action in an interdependent world.* (chapter 5: Global interdependence and social work, pp. 105–125)

        - Lowe, G. R. (1995). Social development. In R. I. Edwards (Ed.), *Encyclopedia of Social Work* (19th ed.) (pp. 343–359). Washington, DC: NASW Press.

        - *Midgley, *Social welfare in global context.* (chapter 2: The Global World Systems, pp. 21–42; chapter 8: Social Work in International Context, pp. 159–179; chapter 9: International Social Development, pp. 180–202)

        - Stoesz, D., et al. (1999). *International development.* Boston: Allyn & Bacon. (chapter 8: Sustainable Development, pp. 154–168)

- **Unit 4** Ideology in Comparative Social Development: Part I—The Contribution of the "Anti-" and "Reluctant Collectivists" to Social Welfare Development and to Social Development Theory and Practice

    - Unit Learning Objective

    Ideology functions as a lens through which policy makers view the world and, in turn, frame their policy decisions. Units 4 and 5 will identify the five major ideological traditions that have most influenced social welfare and social development conceptual development.

    - Readings

        - *George, V., & Wilding, P. (1994). *Welfare & ideology* (2nd ed.) Brighton, UK: Harvester Wheatsheaf. (chapter 1: Ideologies of Welfare; chapter 2: The New Right)

        - Midgley, *Social welfare in global context.* (chapter 5: Theories of State Welfare, pp. 89–110)

- **Unit 5** Ideology in Comparative Social Development: Part II—The Contribution of the Fabian Socialists and Marxists to Social Welfare and Social Development Theory and Practice

    - Readings

        - *George & Wilding, *Welfare & ideology*. (chapter 3: The Middle Way; chapter 4: Democratic Socialism; chapter 5: Marxism; chapter 8: Conclusions)
        - Stoesz, et al., *International development*. (chapter 6: Strategies of economic development, pp. 102–127)

Session 2

- **Unit 6** The Comparative Method in International and Comparative Social Welfare Research

    - Unit Learning Objectives

        Comparative social research is a specialized area within social science research. This unit will identify both the conceptual foundations of undertaking comparative studies and the unique methods that are required to conduct comparative social welfare/social development studies with scientific rigor.

    - Readings

        - *Dubey, S. (1980). Conceptual framework for comparative analysis of social policies. *Social Development Issues, 4*, 63–78.
        - Hoeffer, R. (1996). A conceptual model for studying social welfare policy comparatively. *Journal of Social Work Education, 32*(1), 101–113.
        - *Tracy, M. B. (1992). Cross-national social welfare policy analysis in the graduate curriculum: A comparative process model. *Journal of Social Work Education, 28*(3), 341–352.
        - U.S. Department of Health and Human Services. (2002). *Social security programs throughout the world, 2002* (special issues on Europe, Asia and the Pacific, and Africa). Washington, DC: Social Security Administration. (Review those entries for countries of particular interest to you.)

- **Unit 7** Computer lab demonstration of PRAXIS

    - Unit Learning Objectives

        A vast array of electronic resources currently exist to assist comparative researchers with their investigations. This laboratory will introduce students to the electronic sources currently available to assist them with the conduct of their own research.

    - Readings

        - *Estes, R. J. (1998). Informational tools for social workers: Research in the global age. In C. S. Ramanathan & R. J. Link (Eds.), *All our futures: Principles and resources for social work practice in a global era* (pp. 121–137). Pacific Grove CA: Brooks/Cole.

- **Unit 8** Understanding the Contemporary "Welfare Mix"

    - Unit Learning Objectives

        Many "actors" contribute to the planning and implementation of social welfare and social development, especially at the international level. This unit will identify the major private- and public-sector actors that are most responsible for development-related policy, planning, and service delivery at the local, national, regional, and international levels.

    - Readings

        - Evers, A. (1988). Shifts in the welfare mix introducing a new approach for the study of transformations in welfare and social policy. In A. Evers & H. Wintersberger (Eds.), *Shifts in the welfare mix* (pp. 7–30). Vienna, Austria: Center for Social Welfare Training and Research.

- *Healy, International social work: Professional action in an interdependent world. (chapter 6: International social welfare organizations and their functions, pp. 126–150)

- Midgley, *Social welfare in global context*. (chapter 7: Social change and the future of state welfare, pp. 134–158)

- **Unit 9** The Public/Private "Mix" Illustrated: European and Asian Experiences

  - Unit Learning Objective

    Everywhere in the world, the role of "the state" is shrinking vis-à-vis human services and social development. This unit will explore the conceptual foundations of this shift and suggest alternative actors who are likely to replace the state in the performance of certain "public sector" responsibilities.

  - Readings (Read at least two chapters from the following book)

    - *Johnson, N. (1987). *The welfare state in transition: The theory & practice of welfare pluralism*. Amherst: University of Massachusetts Press.

- **Unit 10** Development Ideologies in Action: The U.S. and Global Markets

Session 3

- **Unit 11** Social Work, Social Welfare, and Social Development: The Sociopolitical Context for International Social Work Practice

  - Unit Learning Objectives

    Social work and social work professionals are integral to social development at all levels of practice. This unit will conceptualize the multiple levels of intervention in which social workers engage internationally and will suggest the knowledge, value, and skill base associated with each of these levels of practice.

  - Readings

    - Midgley, *Social welfare in global context*. (chapter 1: The field of international social welfare, pp. 3–20; chapter 4: Social welfare around the world, pp. 68–88; chapter 6: The impact of state welfare: An international assessment, pp. 111–133; chapter 10: International collaboration in social welfare, pp. 203–224)

    - Stoesz, et al, *International development*. (chapter 7: Community development, pp. 128–153; chapter 14: An integrative model of development, pp. 242–266)

- **Unit 12** Organization of Student Projects

PART II

Session 4

- **Unit 13** Review of students' work

- **Unit 14** Trends in World Social Development: Regional Disparities

  - Unit Learning Objectives (Unit 14)

    This unit will explore the "state" of social development for the world as a whole and for each major geopolitical region. The instructor's own research will serve as the basis for this analysis.

  - Readings

    - *Estes, R. J. (1997). The world social situation: Social work's contribution to international development. In R. Edwards (Ed.), *Encyclopedia of social work* (Supplement to the 19th ed.) (pp. 21–36). Washington, DC: NASW Press.

- Midgley, *Social welfare in global context*. (chapter 3: Social conditions in global context, pp. 43–67)
- World Bank. (2003). *World development report, 2003: Sustainable development in a dynamic world—Transforming institutions, growth and quality of life*. New York: Oxford University Press. (Read chapters 1 and 2 and carefully review the volume's statistical annex.)

- **Unit 15** Threats to World Social Development

  - Unit Learning Objectives

    Contemporary trends in world development pose many challenges and opportunities for rich and poor countries alike: (1) continuing high rates of population growth; (2) increasing militarism in some regions of the world; (3) diversity-related social conflict, including ethnic divisiveness; (4) continuing assaults on the physical environment; and (5) a host of "reactive threats," that is, those that occur in response to the often impossible conditions under which people living in the poorest countries must cope (e.g., collapse of traditional family and kinship systems, internal migration, emergence of urban agglomerations and economic trading blocs, the absence of meaningful programs of public provision for the "poorest of the poor," among many others). This unit will explore the implications of these trends for social workers practicing in both the national and international context.

- **Unit 16** Women in Development: Tradition and Subjugation

  - Unit Learning Objectives (Units 16 and 17)

    Women and children make up two-thirds of the global population, but have been among the most neglected in terms of international development efforts. These units will focus on the unique situation of women in development—as persons in their own right and as members of larger social collectivities. Alternative approaches for advancing the social and economic status of women will be explored.

  - Readings For Units 16 and 17 (required, plus one additional reference)

    - Clifford, D. (2002). Resolving uncertainties? The contribution of some recent feminist ethical theory to the social professions. *European Journal of Social Work, 5*(1), 31–42.
    - *George & Wilding, *Welfare & ideology*. (chapter 6: Feminism)
    - *Julia, M. (2001). Social development and the feminist tradition. *Social Development Issues, 23*(1), 14-25.
    - Kinnear, K. L. (1997). *Women in the third world: A reference handbook*. Santa Barbara, CA: ABC-CLIO, Inc.
    - Matusi, Y. (1999). *Women in the new Asia: From pain to power*. New York: Zed Books.
    - Meintjes, S., Pillay, A., & Turshen, M. (Eds.). (2002). *The aftermath: Women in post-conflict transformation*. London: Zed Books.
    - Meyer, M., & Prugl, E. (Eds.). (1999). *Gender politics in global governance*. Lanham, MD: Rowman & Littlefield.
    - Stephen, L. (1997). *Women and social movements in Latin America: Power from below*. Austin: University of Texas Press.
    - United Nations Children's Fund. (2003). *The state of the world's mothers, 2003*. New York: Oxford University Press. (Available for download via Praxis)
    - *World Bank Group. (2003). *Genderstats: Database of gender statistics*. Available at: http://www.worldbank.org

  - Student Presentations: Women and Development

- **Unit 17** Women in Development (continued)

  - Cases Studies in Helping to Move Women From Poverty to Economic Self-Sufficiency

- World Neighbors (2001). *The quiet revolution: The power of women's groups—Nepal* (A-V). Oklahoma City: World Neighbors.

- World Neighbors (2001). *The quiet revolution: Stimulating micro enterprise—Arkansas.* (A-V). Oklahoma City: World Neighbors.

- World Neighbors (2001). *The quiet revolution: micro-credit—Bangladesh* (A-V). Oklahoma City: World Neighbors.

- Student Presentations: Economic Development and Women

Session 5

- **Unit 18** Review of the previous day's discussions and Vulnerable Populations: The Poor and Poverty

  - Unit Learning Objectives

    Despite recent progress in raising global wealth, poverty continues to increase worldwide. This unit will explore the multifaceted nature of poverty in rich and poor countries and will attempt to put a "human face" on those hundreds of millions of people worldwide who struggle to survive on a day-by-day basis.

  - Readings

    - *Estes, R. J. (1999). The "poverties": Competing definitions and alternative approaches to measurement. *Social Development Issues, 21*(2), 11–21. (May be downloaded from the "Selected Papers by RJE" subdirectory of Praxis)

    - Lee, W. K. (2002). Poverty policy in Hong Kong: Western models and cultural divergence. *Social Development Issues, 24*(1), 45–55.

    - Mathbor, G. M., & Mohammad A. K. (2002). Interpretation of poverty in a welfare state: The case of Norway. *Social Development Issues, 24*(1), 25–32.

    - Roe, K. (2001). From Dhaka to Dallas: Application of the Grameen model in an American city. *Social Development Issues, 23*(2), 18–26.

    - Sen, A. (1999). *Development as freedom.* Oxford, England: Oxford University Press.

    - Sherraden, M. (1991). *Assets and the poor: A new American welfare policy.* Armonk, NY: M.E. Sharpe.

    - Stiglitz, J. (1996). *Globalization and its discontents.* New York: W.W. Norton.

    - *UNDP, *Human development report, 1997.* (chapter 1: Poverty in the human development perspective: concept and measurement; chapter 2: Progress and setbacks; chapter 3: Resisting new forces of poverty in a changing world; chapter 4: Globalization: Poor nations, poor people; chapter 5: Politics of poverty eradication; chapter 6: Eradicating human poverty worldwide)

    - *UNDP. (2003). *Human development report, 2003: Millennium development goals—A compact among nations to end human poverty.* New York: Oxford University Press. (Read chapters 1 and 2 and carefully review the volume's statistical annex.)

  - Student Presentations: Poverty and Threats to Economic Security

- **Unit 19** Vulnerable Populations: Children

  - Unit Learning Objectives (Units 19–22)

    In addition to women and the poor, many other population groups also are not fully enfranchised members of the societies in which they live, including children, older people, people with disabilities, racial and ethnic minorities, "first peoples," and sexual minorities. This unit will focus on the social, political, and economic dynamics that lead to social marginalization and on remedies that can be used to empower people.

  - Readings (required, plus one additional reference under each subheading)

    (Note: In every case, the UN has developed a declaration, covenant, or convention related to the social protection and advancement of the following historically vulnerable population groups. Visit the UN home page and try to identify those international documents of relevance to a group in which you have a special interest or commitment.)

- Centre for Child and Society. (2002). *International perspectives on child protection.* Glasgow: University of Glasgow.
- Children's Defense Fund. (2003). *The state of America's children: Yearbook 2003.* Washington, DC: Children's Defense Fund.
- Estes, R. J., & Weiner, N. A. (2001). *The commercial sexual exploitation of children in the United States, Canada and Mexico.* Philadelphia: University of Pennsylvania School of Social Work. (http://caster. ssw.upenn.edu)
- *UNICEF. (2003). *The state of the world's children, 2003.* New York: Oxford University Press.

First Peoples

- Stoesz, et al., *International development.* (chapter 10: First Nations Development Institute, pp. 184–196)
- Also, review the content listed on at least two of the "First Peoples'" homepages contained on Praxis. Many of these Web sites are for first peoples located in various world regions (e.g., the Maori of New Zealand, the aboriginal peoples of Australia, etc.)

Persons with Disabilities

- Driedger, D. (1989). *The last civil rights movement: Disabled peoples international.* London: Hurst Publications.
- Seipel, M. O. (1994). Disability: An emerging global challenge. *International Social Work, 37*(2), 165–178.
- Shapiro, J. P. (1994). *No pity: People with disabilities forging a new civil rights movement.* New York: Random House.

Sexual Minorities

- Baird, V. (2001). *Sexual minorities and the law: A world survey.* London: Verso Books.
- For the current status of laws, legal protections, and legal reforms related to sexual minorities world-wide explore the many international resources listed on the Web site of Choike.org (2004): A portal on Southern civil societies (Uruguay) (http://www.choike.org)

- Student Presentations: Children, Youth, and Development

- **Unit 20** Vulnerable Populations: Migrants and Refugees

- Student Presentations: Migrants, Refugees, and Development

- Readings (Read at least one reference under each heading)

Migrants

- Ahearn, F. (Ed.). (2000). *Psychosocial wellness of refugees. Issues in qualitative and quantitative research.* London: Berghahn Books.
- Bommes, M., & Geddes, A. (Eds.). (2000). *Immigration and welfare: Challenging the borders of the welfare state.* New York: Routledge.
- Cohen, R., & Deng, F. (Eds.). (1998). *The forsaken people: Case studies of the internally displaced.* Washington, DC: Brookings Institution.
- Held, D., McGrew A., Goldblatt, D., & Perraton, J. (1999). *Global transformations: Politics, economics and culture.* Cambridge, England: Polity Press. (chapter 6: People on the move, pp. 283–326.)

Refugees

- Herscovitch, L. (2001). International relief and development practice. In L. Healy (Ed.), *International social work: Professional action in an interdependent world* (pp. 170–192). New York: Oxford University Press.
- Healy, *International social work: Professional action in an interdependent world.* (chapter 9: International/domestic practice interface, pp. 193–218)
- Potocky, M. (1996). Toward a new definition of refugee. *International Social Work, 39*(3), 245–56.
- United Nations High Commissioner for Refugees. (2003). *The state of the world's refugees, 2003.* London: Penguin.

- **Units 21 and 22** Vulnerable Populations: Racial, Religious, and Ethnic Minorities

Cultural and Religious Diversity

- Amnesty International. (2002). *Amnesty International report, 2003.* London: Amnesty International.
- Haught, J. (1995). *Holy hatred: Religious conflicts of the 1990s.* Amherst, MA: Prometheus Books.
- Randall, A. B. (1998). *Theologies of war and peace among Jews, Christians and Muslims.* Lewiston, PA: The Edward Mellon Press.
- Taras, R., & Ganguly, R. (1998). *Understanding ethnic conflict: The international dimension.* New York: Longman.

Session 7

- **Unit 23** Review of previous day's discussions and Regional Dilemmas in Development

  - Unit Learning Objectives
    Building on the content of Units 14 and 15, this unit will explore in greater depth the "state" of social development for major geopolitical regions of special interest to the students.

  - Readings

  Asia

  - Estes, R. J. (1996). Social development trends in Asia, 1970–1994: Reflections on 25 years of social and economic development. *Social Indicators Research, 37*(2), 119–148. (May be downloaded from the "Selected Papers by RJE" subdirectory of Praxis).
  - Stoesz, et al., *International development.* (chapter 1: Asia: Awakening giants, pp. 1–21)

  Africa

  - Estes, R. J. (1995). Social development trends in Africa: The need for a new development paradigm. *Social Development Issues, 17*(1), 18–47.
  - Stoesz, *International development.* (chapter 3: Africa: The fourth world, pp. 40–57)

  Latin America

  - Estes, R. J. (1996). Social development trends in Latin America, 1970–1994: In the shadows of the 21st Century. *Social Development Issues, 18*(1), 25–52.
  - Stoesz, et al., *International development.* (chapter 2: Latin America: Five hundred years of purgatory, pp. 22–39)

Middle East

- Estes, R. J. (1999). Social development trends in the Middle East, 1970–1997: The search for modernity. *Social Indicators Research, 50*(1), 51–81.

Europe

- *Estes, R. J. (2003). European social development trends, 1970–2000. In J. Vogel (Ed.), *Good times and bad times: Swedish social development during the 1990s* (pp. 435–468). Stockholm: Statistics Sweden.
- Stoesz, et al., *International development.* (chapter 4: Eastern Europe, pp. 58–84)

Commonwealth of Independent States (successor states to the Soviet Union)

- Estes, R. J. (1998). Social development trends in the successor states to the former Soviet Union: The search for a new paradigm. In R. H. Kempe (Ed.), *Challenges of transformation and transition from centrally planned to market economies* (UNCRD Research Report Series No. 26) (pp. 13–30). Nagoya, Japan: United Nations Centre for Regional Development

- Student Presentations: Development Challenges Facing Economies in Transition

- **Unit 24** The Changing Public-Private Partnership in Development

  - Readings

    - *Healy, *International social work: Professional action in an interdependent world.* (chapter 10: Understanding and influencing global policy, pp. 219–237; chapter 12: Social work as a force for humane global change and development, pp. 260–280)

  - Student Presentations: Shifts in the Public-Private Partnership in Development

OUTLINE FOR FINAL PAPER

Part I Introduction (1–2 pages)

Must introduce reader to the comparative welfare dilemma selected for analysis. Includes a brief review of the relevant literature and a statement of the major questions or hypothesis that are explored in the paper.

Part II Methodology (1 page)

Contains a summary of the major research methods that were used to collect and analyze the data.

Part III Findings (8–6 pages)

This section is divided into two parts: country-specific findings and cross-national findings. Begin your discussion with the findings that relate most directly to your study's central questions and then proceed to a discussion of secondary or more detailed findings.

Part IV Conclusions With Recommendations for Action (2–3 pages)

This is the so-called "so what" section, that is, the section in which you summarize the study's most important findings and suggest a range of solutions that will advance resolution of the continuing issues or problems identified through your research. Therefore, this section reflects both your empirical findings and your own views concerning how to achieve a more socially just world.

Appendix

The appendix section will vary considerably from student to student depending on the nature and scope of the particular study undertaken. In general, the appendix should include detailed descriptions of the social, political, and economic structure of each country selected for analysis. The appendix may also contain tables, charts, and graphs that are too large to contain in the main text.

GENERAL FORMAT FOR COMPARATIVE TABLES TO BE INCLUDED IN SEMESTER-END PAPERS

Note: The recommendations that follow are of a general nature only. The format used for individual papers should conform to the reporting requirements of each paper.

Table 1: Country Description

Using the *CIA World Fact Book*, provide a brief summary of the social, political, and economic conditions of each of your comparison countries. In all cases, the table should include type of polity and economy and, as possible, information concerning the geographic size, location, population pyramid, and other relevant descriptive information for each country.

Table 2: Country Profile on Your Major Dependent Variable

Identify the profile of each country on your major dependent variable using a variety of indicators appropriate to that variable, for example, for "poverty" identify the definitions used to classify poor, the number of people who are poor by this definition, and other factors related to poverty (e.g., gender, age, racial/ethnic factors).

Table 3: Country Approaches to Resolving/Responding to the Issue of Concern to You

Use this table to identify the range of social policies/programs adopted by your countries to resolve the dilemma or social problem described in Table 2. In terms of poverty, for example, this table would include major policies and programs adopted by each country. Simply list the initiatives, and, as possible, describe their intended outcomes.

Table 4: Pre-/Post-Policy or Program Effect

This table is used to show the effect of each country's approach to solving the social problem/issue identified in Tables 2 and 3. In terms of poverty alleviation, for example, show the effect of various cash- and social-transfer programs on reducing poverty for the particular age/population groups of particular interest to you.

Individual papers are likely to contain more tables than the four listed above. These are "anchoring" tables, and, as such, are offered as a way for you to communicate simply a lot of descriptive information concerning the social need/problem of interest to you.

UNIVERSITY OF ST. LOUIS
DEPARTMENT OF SOCIAL WORK | ST. LOUIS, MO
MARGARET SHERRADEN

WASHINGTON UNIVERSITY
GEORGE WARREN BROWN SCHOOL OF SOCIAL WORK | ST. LOUIS, MO
SHIRLEY PORTERFIELD

Social and Economic Development Policy
UMSL SW 6250/WU S40 5861

I. COURSE DOMAIN AND BOUNDARIES

This is a required policy course for MSW students concentrating in Community and Organizational Development (UMSL) or Social and Economic Development (WU).

Although social development and economic development are traditionally separate fields of inquiry and policy making, this course views social development and economic development as interrelated and often complementary.

The perspective of the course is that "underdevelopment" in the United States has much in common with "underdevelopment" in the rest of the world. Moreover, problems and solutions in one country can inform policy in other countries. Within this context, the course introduces social workers to social and economic development issues and policy in the United States and in developing countries.

II. COURSE OBJECTIVES

1. Students will know the history and content of social and economic development policy and programs affecting households and communities, particularly as it relates to the values and mission of the social work profession.

2. Students will know how social and economic development policy is delivered in programs and services to households and communities, particularly as it relates to social work practice and ethics.

3. Students will be able to evaluate social and economic development policies and services for households and communities, particularly regarding their effects on populations at risk, including those affected by issues of gender, race, religion, class, disability, and sexual orientation.

4. Students will be able to analyze and recommend reforms in social and economic development policy in households and communities in the United States and some developing countries.

III. EDUCATIONAL OUTCOMES

1. Students will demonstrate an ability to apply the above educational objectives in discussion, exercises, and the policy analysis project.

2. Students will further demonstrate their learning in the course by planning and taking concrete steps to apply their knowledge of social and economic development policy to an organization engaged in implementation.

IV. RELATIONSHIP TO PRACTICUM LEARNING OBJECTIVES

Students will be able to apply in the practicum setting knowledge of current public, nonprofit, and for-profit policies related to social and economic development. Specifically, knowledge gained in the course will provide a basis for meeting the following practicum learning objectives:

1. The student will integrate theoretical knowledge about social, economic, and political issues with practice issues.

2. The student will demonstrate knowledge of current policies and their effect on at-risk populations.

3. The student will demonstrate an understanding of values and ethics relevant to social work practice.

V. TEXT/REQUIRED READING

All students in the course are required to do the course readings. Each week there is a required set of readings. Students, however, are expected to read on the relevant topics from books on reserve and from their own collections of relevant journal articles and books.

Required Reading

Two textbooks are available for purchase from the university bookstore or online through the Barnes and Noble college textbook store (www.bn.com).

- Ferguson, R. F., & Dickens, W. T. (Eds.). (2001). *Urban problems and community development*. Washington, DC: Brookings University Press.
- Murphy, P. W., & Cunningham, J. V. (2003). *Organizing for community controlled development: Renewing civil society*. Thousand Oaks, CA: Sage.

Most required readings are available on reserve in the library or on the course Web site at My Gateway. A few readings are available on the Web or through the library online resources as noted in the syllabus.

Additional Reading

Students are expected to be knowledgeable about current social, economic, and public policy issues. This knowledge is essential for meaningful participation in class discussions. To stay abreast of current issues, students should read at least one daily newspaper and several weekly or monthly periodicals, preferably from diverse political viewpoints.

Recommended newspapers in St. Louis are the *St. Louis Post-Dispatch*, the *St. Louis American*, and the *Riverfront Times*. National newspapers are the *Washington Post*, *Wall Street Journal*, and the *New York Times* (especially the Sunday *Times* if you do not have time to read it every day). Pay particular attention to in-depth stories and op-ed commentaries that provide analyses of current issues, and learn to read the business section of the *New York Times* if you have been overlooking this part of the paper in the past.

Other suggested reading on current issues includes magazines and commentary journals. Moving approximately from right to left on the political spectrum, look at periodicals such as the *National Review*, *The Public Interest*, *Business Week*, *Economist*, *National Journal*, *Congressional Digest*, *The Atlantic Monthly*, *The New Republic*, *New York Review of Books*, *American Prospect*, *Nation*, and *In These Times*.

Internet connections to social and economic development topics are emerging continually. As you find valuable resources, please take time to disseminate the information to others in the class. A folder will circulate during each class session with resources and policy events in St. Louis and the region. Please post sources on My Gateway.

VI. ORGANIZATION OF THE COURSE

The course is organized as a combination of discussion and lectures, with occasional videos and guest speakers. When the class size is small, there will be an opportunity to structure the class as a seminar. This will require active participation during every session, as students assume a greater role in teaching and analysis. Social and economic policy events and presentations outside the classroom will be assigned as well.

VII. COURSE ASSIGNMENTS

Readings

Students are expected to do the assigned readings and to engage in cogent class discussions.

Attendance at Special Events

A number of special events and opportunities will occur throughout the semester that are relevant to the topics in this class. At a minimum, students are expected to attend at least two special events during the semester. Suggested events are included in the "Special Information and Events" folder available during each class, and some will be listed on My Gateway. Please add your suggestions!

Commentary on Reading Assignments

Comments (1–2 pages typed) on readings are intended to facilitate understanding and help integrate course content with students' professional interests and plans. Comments on readings are due each week and should include the following:

1. Briefly summarize the major point(s) (or ask well-thought-out questions) in each of the readings.

2. Apply at least one aspect of what you have read to something you are working on in your job, practicum, or volunteer work. You will not be able to cover every point; choose issues as appropriate.

3. Feel free to add other thoughts, ideas, or information to your comments as appropriate.

Students are also expected to complete a study and make a class presentation (see guidelines below).

The Social and Economic Development Policy Study

Each student in the class will conduct research on a program/organization that is engaged in social and economic development. These projects provide a mechanism for applying content from readings, discussions, lectures, and guest lectures to the reality of social and economic development. The instructor will provide suggestions. Alternatives are possible but must be approved by the instructor.

Our view is that graduate students are capable of meaningful work with potential for policy or program application at the local, state, national, or international level. This is expected of all projects and papers. Students will develop a plan for application of their work and take concrete steps toward this application. Some of the possibilities for application include conducting research or organizing a project for the organization; sending a proposal for policy to key policy makers; participating in legislative processes; connecting with relevant interest groups, committees, or task forces; giving speeches, workshops, or other public education appearances; publishing in academic journals, newsletters, or the general press; or organizing a letter-writing, leaflet, or poster campaign, public demonstration, or other advocacy campaign. All applications should be carried out in a thoughtful, professional manner, and are limited only by your creativity and assessment of feasibility.

Organization/program selection. Within the first few weeks of the semester decide what social and economic development organization/program you will study. Due: Week 3.

Part A. This assignment is designed for the student to gain an understanding of the overall organizational mission, goals, and scope of activities. This will provide the basis for an in-depth examination of the organization's social and economic development efforts (see Section XII). Due: Week 6.

Part B. This part of the study is aimed at understanding the social and economic development effect of the organization. In other words, what and how effective is policy "on the ground" (see handout)? A draft plan for Parts B and C will be discussed with the instructor midway through the semester. Due: End of semester.

Part C. This part of the study is an application of what you have learned. Due: End of semester.

VIII. CLASS SESSION DATES, TOPICS, AND READING ASSIGNMENTS

Part I: Understanding SED Policy: Introduction and Theoretical Foundation

Week 1: What is Social and Economic Development Policy?

*   Become familiar with the following Web pages: United Nations Development Program: http://www.undp.org/; United Nations Economic and Social Development: http://www.un.org/esa/; World Bank poverty page: http://www.worldbank.org/poverty/sitemap.htm; One World.net: http://www.oneworld.net/article/frontpage/10/3; Third World Network: http://www.twnside.org.sg/; Praxis: http://caster.ssw.upenn.edu; Welfare Information Network: http://www.welfareinfo.org/index.html; 2000 Census, U.S. Census Bureau: http://www.census.gov/; World Wide Web Resources for Social Workers: http://www.nyu.edu/socialwork/wwwrsw

*   Quiz: World Bank quiz on poverty: http://www.worldbank.org/poverty/quiz/

*   Video: Richter, Z (Producer). (1997). *The new urban renewal: Reclaiming our neighborhoods*. [Videorecording]. Part one. Rebuilding neighborhoods from the ground up. Alexandria, VA: South Carolina ETV; Corporation for Educational Radio and Television; Distributed by PBS Video.

Week 2: U.S. and International Perspectives on Poverty: Voices of the Poor and Statistical Interpretations

*   Nayaran. D., & Petesch, P. (2001). *Voices of the poor: From many lands*. New York: Oxford University Press. (Conclusion: An Empowering Approach to Poverty Reduction, pp. 461–493)

*   United Nations. (2003). *Report on the world social situation: Social vulnerability*. New York: United Nations. (Executive summary and vulnerability: An overview, available online: http://www.un.org/esa/socdev/rwss/tocrwss2003.htm#tocrwss2003)

- Kozol, J. (1991). Life on the Mississippi. New York: Crown. (chapter 1, Children in American schools, pp. 7–39)
- Blank, R. M. (2001). An overview of trends in social and economic well-being, by race. In N. J. Smelser, W. J. Wilson & F. Mitchell (Eds.), *America becoming: Racial trends and their consequences* (Vol. 1, pp. 21–39). Washington, DC: National Academy Press.
- *Video:* Jim Kirchherr (Producer). (2003). *Made in USA: The East St. Louis Story.* [Videorecording] St. Louis: KETC St. Louis, Distributed by KETC St. Louis (PBS affiliate), 60 minutes.
- *Video:* Yoon, Kyung (Producer). (2001). *Hear our voices—The poor on poverty.* [Videorecording]. Washington, DC: World Bank, 1818 H Street, NW, 20443, 60 minutes.

Week 3: Theories of Economic Development and Poverty

- Meier, G. M.(2001). The old generation of development economists and the new. In G. M. Meier & J. E. Stiglitz (Eds.), *Frontiers of development economics: The future in perspective* (pp. 13–50). Washington, DC: Oxford University Press.
- Sen, A. (1999). *Development as Freedom.* New York: Anchor. (Poverty as a capability deprivation, pp. 87–110).
- Estes, R. (1999). The poverties: Competing definitions and alternative approaches to measurement. *Social Development Issues, 21*(2), 11–21.
- Putnam, R. D. (1995). Bowling alone: America's declining social capital. *Journal of Democracy, 6,* 65–78.
- *Video:* CBS (2004, July 18,). Alice Coles of Bayview, Virginia. *60 minutes,* CBS News, 15 minutes. Available: http://www.cbsnews.com/stories/2003/11/26/60minutes/main585793.shtml?CMP = ILC-SearchStories

Week 4: Social and Economic Development Policy in Communities

- Midgley, J. (1996). Toward a developmental model of social policy: Relevance of the Third World experience. *Journal of Sociology and Social Welfare, 23,* 59–74.
- Murphy & Cunningham: chapter 1, Introduction; chapter 2, Potency of community power; chapter 3, Community development corporations/resurgence of organizing; chapter 4, The small community.

Part II: Basic Needs in SED Policy

Week 5: Health and Gender Issues in SED

- Beverly, S., & Sherraden, M. (1995). Investment in human development as a strategy for social development. *Social Development Issues, 19*(10), 1–18. (Also available as a working paper (95–1), Center for Social Development, Washington University: http://gwbweb.wustl.edu
- Chen, L. C., Evans, T. G., & Cash, R. A. (1999). Health as a global public good. In I. Kaul, I. Grunberg, & M. A. Stern (Eds.), *Global public goods: International cooperation in the 21st century* (pp. 284–304). New York: Oxford & United Nations Development Program.
- Alderson, L., Conn, M., Donald, J., & Kemp, L. (1994). Making communities work: Women and community economic development. In B. Galaway & J. Hudson (Eds.), *Community economic development: Perspectives on research and policy* (pp. 120–128). Toronto, Canada: Thompson Educational Publishing.

Week 6: Education

- Murphy & Cunningham: chapter 10, Maximizing Social Strength.
- Stone, C., Doherty, K., Jones, C., & Ross, T. (1999). Schools and disadvantaged neighborhoods: The community development challenge. In R. F. Ferguson & W. T. Dickens (Eds.), *Urban problems and community development* (pp. 339–380). Washington, DC: Brookings Institution.
- Duncan, C. M. (2001). Social capital in America's poor communities. In S. Saegert, J. P. Thompson, & M. Warren (Eds.), *Social capital and poor communities* (pp. 60–86). New York: Russell Sage.
- Noguera, P. A. (2001). Transforming urban schools through investments in the social capital of parents. In S. Saegert, J. P. Thompson, & M. Warren (Eds.), *Social capital and poor communities* (pp. 189–212). New York: Russell Sage.

- Portes, A., & Landolt, P. (1996). The downside of social capital. *The American Prospect, 7*(26), pp. 20. (Recommended. Available at: http://www.prospect.org)
- Guest Speaker: Refugee Relief Organization
- Part A due

Week 7: Employment Development and Human Rights

- Murphy & Cunningham: chapter 15, Workforce development.
- National Council of La Raza. (2000, April). Hispanic families and the Earned Income Tax Credit. Available at http://www.nclr.org
- Carr, M., Chen, M. A., & Tate, J. (2000). Globalization and home-based workers. *Feminist Economics, 6*(3), 123–142.
- The Missouri Department of Economic Development. (2000). The Missouri self-sufficiency standard: Necessary wages for essential needs. http://www.ded.state.mo.us
- United Nations Children's Fund. (1999). *UNICEF humanitarian principles training: A child rights protection approach to complex emergencies*, Session 5—Human rights instruments: Limitations, remedies, mechanisms. http://coe-dmha.org/Unicef/UNICEF2FS.htm (In class)
- Guest speaker: Workforce Investment/employment

Week 8: Building Household and Community Assets

- Meet individually this week with instructor to discuss plan for Part B (Bring draft plan for Part B)
- Sherraden, M. (2001). Asset-building policy and programs for the poor. In T. M. Shapiro & E. N. Wolff (Eds.), *Assets for the poor: The benefits of spreading asset ownership* (pp. 302–323). New York: Russell Sage.
- Friedrich, A., & Rodriguez, E. (2001, August). Financial insecurity amid growing wealth: Why healthier saving is essential to Latino prosperity. Available at http://www.nclr.org
- Regan, S., & Paxton, W. (2001, May). *Assets-based welfare: International comparisons*. London: Institute for Public Policy Research.
- National Endowment for Financial Education, The Corporation for Enterprise Development, and the Fannie Mae Foundation. (2001). *Finding paths to prosperity*. (Review, introduction, and chapter 1, pp. 6–12)
- Corporation for Enterprise Development Web page. Available at http://www.cfed.org/ (Review) (See: State Asset Development Report Card)
- Center for Social Development Web page. Available at http://gwbweb.wustl.edu/csd/
- Guest Speaker: IDAs and financial education

Week 9: Housing Development

- Murphy & Cunningham: chapter 13, Neighborhood Preservation Through Affordable Housing.
- Campen, J. (1997, November-December). The Community Reinvestment Act: A law that works. *Dollars & Sense, 214*, pp. 34–39. (Available at Expanded Academic ASAP)
- Pugh, C. (2001). The theory and practice of housing sector development for developing countries, 1950–99. *Housing Studies, 16*(4), 399–423.
- Jackson, K. (1987). Crabgrass frontier: The suburbanization of the United States. New York: Oxford University Press. (chapter 11, Federal subsidy and the suburban dream: How Washington changed the American housing market, pp. 190–218)
- Green, R. K., & Malpezzi, S. (2003). *A primer on U.S. housing markets and housing policy*. Washington, DC: The Urban Institute Press. (chapter 3, A brief review of housing policies and programs, pp. 85–133) (Recommended)
- Guest Speaker: Grassroots housing organization

Week 10: Community Resource Development

- Murphy & Cunningham: chapter 11, Tapping Essential Resources; chapter 12: Capital Formation: Building Community Financial Assets.
- Federal Reserve Bank of St. Louis. (2003). Community development financing: Coming up with the money. http://www.stls.frb.org/community/selfstudy
- Familiarize yourself with and bookmark these Web sites on your computer:

  - Neighborhood Funders Group: Grantmakers Supporting Community Change. http://www.nfg.org/
  - New Markets Tax Credits, in *Bridges*, Spring 2002, Federal Reserve Board: http://www.stls.frb.org
  - Neighborhood Funders Group: http://www.nfg.org
  - Discover total resources: A guide for nonprofits: http://www.mellon.com/communityaffairs/guide.html
  - NewTithing Group: http://www.newtithing.org/
  - National Federation of Community Development Credit Unions: http://www.natfed.org/i4a/pages/index.cfm?pageid=1
  - Tools for Organizations. http://www.Idealist.org/tools.html

- Guest Speaker: Federal Reserve Bank of St. Louis

Week 11: Business Development

- Murphy & Cunningham: chapter 14, Business District Renewal.
- Porter, M.(1995). The competitive advantage of the inner city. *Harvard Business Review* (May-June), 55–71. (Reprint No. 95310)
- Schreiner, M., & Morduch, J. (2002). Opportunities and challenges for microfinance in the United States. In J. H. Carr & Z. Y. Tong (Eds.), *Replicating microfinance in the United States* (pp. 19–61). Washington, DC: Woodrow Wilson Center Press
- Roberts, B. (2002) New markets tax credits. *Bridges*, Spring. Available at www.stls.frb.org (Review)
- Video: Rooy, R. (Producer/Director) with Access to Credit Media Project (1998). *To our credit*. Part Two: Bootstrap Banking in America. Available from PBS online, http://www.pbs.org/toourcredit/home.htm).

Part III: Global Issues Influencing SED Policy

Week 12: Globalization and Social and Economic Development Policy

- Cahn, M. A. (1995). The players: Institutional and noninstitutional actors in the policy process. In S. Z. Theodoulou & M. A. Cahn (Eds.), *Public policy: The essential readings* (pp. 201–211). Englewood Cliffs, NJ: Prentice-Hall.
- Mills, C. W. (1995). The power elite. In S. Z. Theodoulou & M. A. Cahn, *Public policy: The essential readings* (pp. 72–85). Englewood Cliffs, NJ: Prentice-Hall.
- Prigoff, A. (2000). *Economics for social workers*. Belmont, CA: Wadsworth. (chapter 9, Global trade policy sets the framework for a new world order, pp. 129–149)
- Draut, T., Callahan, D., Hawkes, C. (2002). Crossing divides: New common ground on poverty and economic security. New York. http://www.demos-usa.org/pubs/Crossing_Divides.pdf
- Economic Affairs Bureau. (2000). ABCs of the global economy. *Dollars and Sense, 228*(March-April). Available at http://www.dollarsandsense.org/archives/2000/0300collect.html

Part IV: Policy and Evaluation on a Smaller Scale

Week 13: Social and Economic Development Policy Evaluation

- Rossi, P. H. (1999). Evaluating community development programs: Problems and prospects. In R. F. Ferguson & T. Dickens (Eds.), *Urban problems and community development* (pp. 521–567). Washington, DC: Brookings Institution.

- Nachmias, D. (1995). The role of evaluation in public policy. In S. Z. Theodoulou & M. A. Cahn (Eds.), *Public policy: The essential readings* (pp. 173–180). Englewood Cliffs, NJ: Prentice-Hall.
- Case study: Beyond housing: The comprehensive community rental program in the South Bronx. Kennedy School of Government, Harvard University, Cambridge, MA. (In class)

Week 14: Student Presentations

Week 15: Student Presentations

Week 16: Parts B and C due (no class)

IX. SOCIAL AND ECONOMIC DEVELOPMENT POLICY STUDY

Part A: Organization Description

This assignment is designed to help students gain an understanding of the SED organizational mission, goals, and scope of activities. This will provide the basis for an in-depth examination of the organization's social and economic development efforts.

1. Name of organization and relevant contact information
2. Mission and goals of the organization
3. Brief history of the organization
4. What does the organization do? How do SED programs interface with other programs in the organization?
5. Who is covered by the organization's programs?
6. What is the service area?
7. Key staff responsible for SED?
8. Key collaborating organizations and agencies?
9. What is the source(s) of the organization's funding?
10. What values guide the delivery of these services?
11. Knowledge base or scientific grounding (theoretical and empirical explanations) for the organization's approach
12. What are the policy origins of the organization's programs?
13. Have any evaluations been done? Can these be shared with you?

You will need to gain "entry" into the organization by calling and/or e-mailing a contact person and explaining the assignment. (If they have questions, you may have them contact me.)

Gathering this information will require collecting written materials, looking at Web information, and at least one face-to-face interview with someone fairly knowledgeable about the organization. Most of the time people will be helpful—but you must be very clear about what you want and why. Furthermore, think about what the organization has to gain from this and how you might present yourself so that your contacts are more willing to give you their time, and what you might do for them that would be helpful (i.e., what kind of data/information do they need?).

The project should be informed by course readings, as well as additional relevant materials, with citations where appropriate. Avoid lengthy quotations; use APA citation style; 4–5 pages; typed.

Part B: Social and Economic Development Policy Study: Analysis

This assignment is designed to help students gain an understanding of the SED organizational mission, goals, and scope of activities. This will provide the basis for an in-depth examination of the organization's social and economic development efforts.

1. Choose one program within the organization to examine in more depth.

   a. Brief history and goals. What does the program do? How does it interface with other programs in the organization?

   b. Who are the "clients" or "participants" in the program? Service area?

    c.   Who are the key staff and what is their professional or nonprofessional experience?

    d.   Who/what funds the program and what are the key policies that affect the program?

    e.   Who are the key collaborating organizations and agencies and stakeholders, including nonsocial service organizations?

2.   To what extent does this program meet social and economic development goals?

    a.   What is your question? (Why is this question relevant to SED?)

    b.   How will you get information about this program (your method of inquiry) and why are you choosing this approach?

    c.   What are your principal findings?

    d.   How do you interpret these findings, particularly the effect on social and economic development in the target area/population?

    e.   Based on these findings, how do you assess the ability of the program to achieve social and economic development?

    f.   How does the program meet key and relevant criteria set forth in the National Association of Social Workers' Code of Ethics?

This paper is analytic and is based on your exploratory research.

Your approach to research can take a number of different forms, such as interviews, surveys, focus groups, secondary data analysis, informant interviewing, and so forth. Select your method based on the best way to get the information you need to answer your question and the practicality/feasibility of the approach. Your method and any research instruments used must be approved by the appropriate administrative head of the organization. You may not collect or disclose any identifying information about any of the individual research participants.

The project should be informed by course readings as well as additional relevant materials, with citations where appropriate. Avoid lengthy quotations. Use APA citation style; 8–10 pages; typed.

Part C: Social and Economic Development Organization and Policy Study: Application

1.   How do your findings further inform development of the organization's programs?

2.   What are the policy implications of your findings? In other words, what changes or new policies are needed to meet the goal of social and economic development for the target area/population?

3.   Are there implications for development of other social and economic development organizations and services in the area? 3-5 pages; typed.

International Social Work

BSSW 480

COURSE DESCRIPTION

This undergraduate elective course presents a broad overview of the history and effects of globalization and the implications for social work. Issues will include human rights, animal rights, voluntary and involuntary migration, and world health, including the environmental health of the planet. The focus will be on developing a global and local awareness of our interdependence in terms of economics, gender, spirituality, politics, technology, culture, and values. We will learn about the micro and macro service delivery systems of other places in the world by creating relevant links with individuals, groups, international communities, and nongovernmental and world organizations. We will explore a critical analysis of the history of international social work and of the United Nations. Current opportunities and challenges for international social work practice, policy, and research will be addressed.

LEARNING OBJECTIVES

Students will be able to:

1. Improve their practice locally through knowledge of social work as practiced in other parts of the world and by situating local social issues in a larger context. Students will develop an understanding of the social effects of global interdependence and more accuracy about world geography.

2. Broaden their knowledge of human behavior through exposure to unfamiliar cultures. Students will understand the effect of transnational inequalities and conflicts and issues of power and domination, especially as they relate to women.

3. Understand major forces of human oppression internationally, (including poverty and economic oppression as violence), and major instruments of human rights, primarily the Universal Declaration of Human Rights, the Nuremberg Code, the Convention on the Elimination of All Forms of Violence Against Women (CEDAW), and the International Social Work Code of Ethics.

4. Struggle with values of universal versus cultural relativism and concepts such as development and sustainability.

5. Critically analyze the history, models, and structures of international social work practice, policy, and research.

TEXTS

Berry, Wendell. (2001). *In the presence of fear: Three essays for a changed world*. Great Barrington, MA: The Orion Society.

Ramanathan, C., & Link, R. (1999). *All our futures, principles and resources for social work practice in a global era*. Belmont, CA: Brooks/Cole.

PLEASE NOTE that a copy of each of these books is on reserve in the library.

ASSIGNMENTS

If you could travel anywhere in the world, where would you go and WHY? This is one way to begin thinking about your postcards and your projects. Always keep in mind that you are exploring social work practices from other perspectives. This "reciprocal" or mutual learning model is the foundation of the course. This course will give you opportunities for collaborative, interdependent, and self-directed learning. Your grade will be dependent on the quality of work, not the type of project you choose or the outcome, as in the case of grant funding.

"Postcards from . . ."

Starting Week 3, a student will present a 20-minute "postcard" from any place outside of the United States that she or he chooses. Each postcard should be a short, written paper (or it could be a small poster) and a presentation that includes information on the geographical location of the area, the political climate, the form of government, the structure of social services, prominent social issues, economic development, and environmental resources. Choose a country other than the one you will choose for your final project.

Case Study

At the end of chapter 8 in *All Our Futures*, there are six case studies. Choose one and answer the questions that follow: For cases 8.1 and 8.2, what would your assessment be and what interventions would be appropriate? You can choose to write your response or present it orally in class.

Project Possibilities

The outline of the where, what, and how and a time line of your project is due by week 3 (or 4 at the latest). Please feel free to schedule an appointment with me to clarify your ideas. We will also spend some class time discussing ideas and projects as they progress.

A real life example of a creative/experiential project from the Feminist class was a group presentation of an altar/shrine with representations of Afghan culture from a female perspective. The group played a short video along with ethnic music of the culture, shared ethnic food, and had the class dress in sheets similar to a burka (the traditional dress for women in Afghanistan).

Another possibility would be to use foreign film as a vehicle to explore tradition, culture, and social work practice. Two recent films that are excellent examples for comparative cultural analysis are "Monsoon Wedding" and "My Big Fat Greek Wedding." For instance, using "Monsoon Wedding" as a reference, the issue of child abuse in India could be examined at micro and macro levels of intervention.

A more traditional paper might reflect comparative social work practices in other countries from the perspective of a client, a worker, and an administrator. This project would involve Internet communications with individuals, agencies, and organizations in other countries. In other words, you would create narratives or tell the stories of those in other places. Stories open doors, tear down walls, and change lives. Try to write with the intention of a wider audience, with the potential for publication. Ideally you would share your written perspective with those you will write about.

You could study communications or mass media by following a particular international issue for critical analysis. What is the source, how fairly is the issue presented, and what are the implications for social workers locally and abroad, clients, and the public? For example, watch or listen to the British Broadcasting Corporation (BBC) and compare the news of the day with a U.S. version.

Students interested in hunger issues could present a poverty banquet, which is an experiential exercise in which a percentage of students would be dining in style with filet, candles, and wine while the rest would eat beans and drink water. This would all take place in the same venue and the percent of students in each group, who are randomly selected, would reflect the actual percentages of those living in hunger and plenty. This is a powerful opportunity to dialogue about facts and feelings related to the distribution of wealth worldwide.

A policy-focused project might investigate the U.S. policy toward a particular country in relationship to a social issue and the subsequent social and economic effects. How could the policy be changed to be more helpful to that country? Ideally, this project would also include interviews with people from this country.

The entire class could focus together on one project, perhaps a campuswide consciousness-raising effort or an organized social action. For example, a group of high school students recently staged a day of silence to protest opprepression around the world. Students did not speak for 24 hours and wore surgical masks with this statement "Oppression is a widely spread disease." A class project might incorporate aspects of some of the other projects presented here. Collaboration with the Social Work Club is strongly recommended if a campuswide project is undertaken. A fund-raising component could take place in conjunction with a community action. Personally I like the idea of a dance marathon. Students at the University of Chicago recently did this and raised $5,000 for an AIDS project. Responsibilities and expectations would need to be clearly defined by the group, which would need to create a time line to keep it on track. Peer-grading would be incorporated for project evaluation.

Another option would be grant writing to obtain funds for travel abroad for field credits. I am exploring a sabbatical leave in Geneva, Switzerland, and the possibility of supervising students who could be placed at organizations with international headquarters there, such as the Women's International League for Peace and Freedom, the

United Nations, and the World Health Organization. Grant funding is always an uncertainty, and I would encourage you to be open to the experience of the grant writing itself but not to the outcome (not easy to do).

Your grade on the project will be dependent on how well you present the cultural conflicts, value dimensions, the structure of social service delivery systems, and what we can learn from others. Each project will need to include a written paper with at least five references.

The following is a short list of UN Web sites to get you started. I have a longer list that is available for you to choose what may be more specific to your interests.

- UN homepage: http://www.un.org
- Peace and Security: http://www.un.org/peace
- Economic and Social Development: http://www.un.org/ecosocdev/
- Human Rights: http://www.un.org/rights/
- UN News: http://www.un.org/News
- UN Documents: http://www.un.org/Docs
- WomenWatch: http://www.un.org/womenwatch
- World Health Organization: http://www.who.org/
- International Federation of Social Workers: www.ifsw.org

CALENDAR

Week 1: Introduction to International Social Work

History of international social work from Jane Addams and Women's International League for Peace and Freedom (WILPF) to current issues in globalization; local and global interdependence; the concept of reciprocity and the role of students abroad.

Week 2: The Health of the Planet

Post-9/11 commentary from a contemporary philosopher; issues of community and the environment: How do we build sustainable communities? What is the effect of technology on our world? What are the roles of interspecies dependency and animal rights? What are the implications for social work?

- Berry, *In the Presence of Fear: Three Essays for a Changed World.*

Week 3: Issues, Innovations, and a Framework for Assessment of a Global Perspective

What are the barriers to and elements of a global practice?
- Chapter 13, Future Visions for Global Studies in Social Work, in Ramanathan & Link.
- Project outline due

Week 4: Global Values and Ethics

Cultural relativism and universal values; comparing codes of ethics; the culture of war and violence; world health and spirituality.
- Chapter 5, Infusing Global Perspectives into Social Work Values and Ethics, in Ramanathan & Link.

Week 5: The Effects of Globalization on Human Behavior

Case studies explore environmental and ecological factors that affect the human condition.
- Chapter 3, Understanding the Human Condition and Human Behavior, in Ramanathan & Link.

Week 6: From Cultural Conflicts to Creative Strategies

History of human migration, voluntary and involuntary; economic power and gender politics; local history of indigenous communities.
- Chapter 8, A Global Model of Ethnic Diversity Conflict: Implications for Social Work with Populations at Risk, in Ramanathan & Link.
- Case reflection due

Week 7: Micro and Macro Examples of Global Social Work Practice

Social development theory; barriers and benefits to practice.

- Chapter 4, Infusing Global Perspectives into Social Work Practice, in Ramanathan & Link.

Week 8: Who Benefits from Policy? Issues of Distributive Justice

Connecting values, practice, policy and research.

- Chapter 6, Global Approaches to Learning Social Welfare Policy, in Ramanathan & Link.

Week 9: Research for Social and Economic Development

Revolutions in technology and information.

- Chapter 7, Informational Tools for Social Workers: Research in the Global Age, in Ramanathan & Link.

Week 10: The New World Order

Economic development: the World Bank and International Monetary Fund.

- Chapter 9, Global Social and Economic Justice Issues, in Ramanathan & Link.

Week 11: What's It Like to Go Abroad?

Examples of international internships from the field and exchange programs.

- Chapter 10, Models of Field Practice in Global Settings, in Ramanathan & Link.

Week 12: More on Social Development Theory

Understanding the history and concept of social development; the role of theory in social change; what to learn from the past and implications for the future.

- Chapter 11, Social Development in Social Work: Learning from Global Dialogue, in Ramanathan & Link.

Week 13: Projects due/class presentations

Week 14: Projects due/class presentations

Week 15: Course review and evaluation

Week 16: Finals week

- International Holiday Celebration
- Traditional Food and World Music

BIBLIOGRAPHY

You will need to have at least five reference for your project. Almost all of these books are in my personal library and available for loan.

World Issues

Barley, N. (1995). *Grave matters: A lively history of death around the world*. New York: Henry Holt.

Bello, W., Cunningham, S., & Rau, B. (1999). *Dark victory: The United States and Global poverty*. Oakland, CA: Foodfirst.

Flavin, C., French, H., & Gardner, G, et al. (2002). *State of the world 2002*. New York: W.W. Norton.

McLaughlin, C., & Davidson, G. (1994). *Spiritual politics: Changing the world from the inside out*. New York: Ballantine Books.

Schultz, J. (2002). *The democracy owner's manual: A practical guide to changing the world*. New Brunswick, NJ: Rutgers University Press.

van Wormer, K. (1997). *Social welfare: A world view*. Chicago: Nelson-Hall.

Yunus, M. (1999). *Banker to the poor, micro-lending and the battle against world poverty*. New York: Public Affairs.

War and Peace

Houston, J. (1995). *Manual for the peacemaker: An Iroquois legend to heal self and society.* Wheaton, IL: Quest Books.

Vidal, G. (2002). *Perpetual war for perpetual peace: How we got to be so hated.* New York: Thunder's Mouth Press. *International Journal on World Peace,* Professors World Peace Academy, NY.

Values and Ethics

Dalai L. (1999). *Ethics for the new millennium.* New York: Riverhead Books.

Pearsall, M. (1999). *Women and values: Readings in recent feminist philosophy.* Belmont, CA: Wadsworth.

International Social Work

Van Soest, D. (1997). *The global crisis of violence: Common problems, universal causes, shared strategies.* Washington, DC: NASW Press.

Reisch, M., & Gambrill, E. (1997). *Social Work in the 21st Century.* Thousand Oaks, CA: Pine Forge Press.

Hokenstad, M., & Midgley, J. (1997). *Issues in international social work: Global challenges for a new century.* Washington, DC: NASW Press.

Healy, L. (2001). *International social work: Professional action in an interdependent world.* New York: Oxford University Press.

International Social Work (journal), Sage Publications.

Human Rights

Pereira, W. (1997). *Inhuman rights, the western system and global human rights abuse.* Goa, India: The Other India Press.

Bender, D., et al. (1998). *Human rights, opposing viewpoints.* San Diego, CA: Greenhaven Press.

Schulz, W. (2001). *In our own best interest: How defending human rights benefits us all.* Boston: Beacon.

Diversity and Social Justice

Goodman, D. (2001). *Promoting diversity and social justice, educating people from privileged groups.* Thousand Oaks, CA: Sage.

Biography

Elshtain, J. (2002). *Jane Addams and the dream of American democracy.* New York: Basic Books.

Billups, J. (2002). *Faithful angels: Portraits of international social work notables.* Washington DC: NASW Press.

Novel

Edgell, Z. (1982). *Beka Lamb.* Portsmouth, NH: Heinemann Publishers.

Gender/Culture/Ethnicity

Heizer, R, & Mills, J. (1991). *The four ages of Tsurai: A documentary history of the Indian village on Trinidad Bay.* Trinidad, CA: Trinidad Museum Society.

Kerns, V., & Brown, J. (1992). *In her prime: New views of middle aged women.* Urbana: University of Illinois Press.

Spott, R., & Kroeber, A. L. (1997). *Yurok narratives.* Trinidad, CA: Trinidad Museum Society.

Sullivan, R. (2002). *A whale hunt: How a Native American village did what no one thought it could.* New York: Touchstone.

Middlebrook, D. W. (1998). *Suits me: The double life of Billy Tipton.* Boston: Houghton Mifflin.

Fonseca, I. (1995). *Bury me standing: The Gypsies and their journey.* New York: Vintage Books.

Julia, M. (2000). *Constructing gender: Multicultural perspectives in working with women*. Belmont, CA: Brooks/Cole.

Balgopal, P. (2000). *Social work practice with immigrants and refugees*. New York: Columbia University Press.

Potocki-Tripodi, M. (2002). *Best practices for social work with refugees and immigrants*. New York: Columbia University Press.

Ragan, K. (1998). *Fearless girls, wise women & beloved sisters: Heroines in folktales from around the world*. New York: W.W. Norton & Co.

Women's Studies International Forum [journal]

Economics

O'Rourke, P. J. (1998). *Eat the rich: A treatise on economics*. New York: Atlantic Monthly Press.

Goff, B., & Fleisher, A. (1999). *Spoiled rotten: Affluence, anxiety and social decay in America*. Boulder, CO: Westview Press.

International Social Work and Human Rights
MSSW 688

I. COURSE DESCRIPTION

This course examines the contemporary relevance of international social work and the lived meaning of the social construct of "human rights." The National Association of Social Workers' recent reference to human rights as the "theoretic foundation" of the profession and the International Federation of Social Work's (IFSW) calling of social work a "human rights profession" underscore the importance of this idea, which has become a legal mandate to fulfill human need. With an emphasis upon the interface between social work, primarily international social work, and human rights, this course will examine the implications of human rights for macro, mezzo, and micro levels of intervention with particular emphasis upon an educated layperson's perspective on human rights and the development of collaborative partnerships among disciplines.

Please note that this course is an elective in the MSW Program.

II. COURSE TEXT AND READINGS

Required Reading

Healy, L. (2001). *International social work: Professional action in an interdependent world.* New York: Oxford University Press.

International Federation of Social Workers. (2002). *Social work and the rights of the child: A professional training manual.* Berne, Switzerland: Author.

Reichert, E. (2003). *Social work and human rights: A foundation for policy and practice.* New York: Columbia University Press.

Steiner, H., & Alston, P. (2000). *International human rights in context: Law, politics, morals.* New York: Oxford University Press.

Wronka, J. (1998). *Human rights and social policy in the 21st century.* (Rev. ed.). Lanham, MD: University Press of America.

Recommended

Ife, J. (2001). *Human rights and social work.* Port Chester, NY: Cambridge University Press.

International Federation of Social Workers. (1994). *Social work and human rights.* New York: United Nations.

International Human Rights Internship Program. (2000). *Circle of rights: A training and resource manual for economic, social, and cultural rights.* Washington, DC: Author.

Kly, Y., & Kly, D. (2001). *In pursuit of the right to self-determination.* Atlanta, GA: Clarity.

Lifton, R. (2003). *The superpower syndrome: America's apocalyptic confrontation with the world.* New York: Thunder's Mouth Press/Nations Books.

Mann, J. (1999). *Health and human rights.* New York: Routledge.

United Nations. (2002). *International human rights documents* (Vols. 1, 2). New York: Author.

UNESCO. (1986). *The ABC's of teaching human rights.* New York: United Nations.

van Wormer, K. (1997). *Social welfare: A world view.* New York: Nelson-Hall.

Weissbrodt, F., Fitzpatrick, J., & Newman, F. (2001). *International human rights: Law, policy, and process.* Cincinnati, OH: Anderson.

Weissbrodt, D., Fitzpatrick, J., Newman, F., Hoffman, M., & Rumsey, M. (2001). *Selected international human rights instruments and bibliography for research on international human rights law* (3rd ed.). Cincinnati, OH: Anderson. (Strongly recommended; an excellent guide also to electronic resources)

Wronka, J. (2002). *Creating a human rights culture: The Dr. Ambedkar Memorial Lectures*. Bhubanaswar, Orissa, India: National Institute of Social Work and Social Sciences.

III. COURSE OBJECTIVES

Upon completion of this course, the students should be able to:

1. Understand the history of the idea of human rights with particular attention to the historical-philosophical underpinnings of the Universal Declaration of Human Rights and some of its progeny, such as the Convention on the Rights of the Child (CRC); International Covenant on Civil and Political Rights (ICCPR); and International Covenant on Economic, Social, and Cultural Rights (ICESCR); the Convention on the Elimination of Discrimination Against Women (CEDAW); the Convention on the Elimination of Racial Discrimination (CERD); and the Convention Against Torture (CAT).

2. Understand and demonstrate applications of how human rights can be integrated into micro, mezzo, and macro dimensions of international social work policy and practice.

3. Be aware of what governments and nongovernmental organizations are doing to advance human rights.

4. Have a thorough knowledge of the current state of international human rights law in the UN, including implementation mechanisms and, to some extent, the regional systems, in particular the inter-American system.

5. Understand U.S. jurisprudence and social policy in the context of international human rights law.

6. Be aware of issues pertaining to cultural relativism and universalism, particularly as they relate to social work, and demonstrate ways to resolve ethical dilemmas as they arise.

7. Demonstrate knowledge of social action strategies to advance the creation of a human rights culture, which is a "lived awareness" of human rights principles, including, but not limited to, moral education, conflict resolution, and a commitment to nonviolent strategies, the proposal of human rights bills, and the development of monitoring mechanisms in general.

8. Understand the major dimensions of international social work in general, including, but not limited to, the importance of internationally related domestic practice and advocacy, professional exchange, international practice, and international policy development and advocacy, with particular attention to the interface between human rights and social work ethical codes.

IV. COURSE OUTLINE AND READING ASSIGNMENTS

Module 1: Toward the Creation of a Human Rights Culture

Introduction to Human Rights; A Human Rights Culture as a "Lived Awareness" of Human Rights Principles; The Interrelationship Between Human Rights and Social Policy; A History of the Idea of Human Rights; Toward the Integration of Human Rights and the Micro, Mezzo and Macro Levels with Particular Attention to the Profession of Social Work; The Interdependence and Indivisibility of Human Rights; The Interconnectedness Between Rights, Duties and a Social and International Order; The Relationship Between International Social Work and Human Rights; A History of International Social Work and the Relevance of International Social Work Today.

Readings

- Wronka, chapters 1 and 2 (The historical-philosophical context: A history of the idea of human rights).
- Healy, chapters 1–4 (International social work; History and development of social work; International professional action; social work around the world today).

Module 2: A Continuing History of the Idea of Human Rights and Implications for Social Policy and Practice

The Debates Prior to the Signing of the Universal Declaration of Human Rights; The Human Rights Triptych; The Universal Declaration as Customary International Law; A Comparison of the Universal Declaration with U.S.

COURSE OUTLINES | INTERNATIONAL SOCIAL WORK AND HUMAN RIGHTS   95

Federal and State Constitutions; International Social Welfare Organizations and Their Functions; Values and Ethics of International Social Work; The Interface Between International and Domestic Practice and Policy; Influencing Global Policy.

Readings

- Wronka, chapters 3–5 (The United Nations and beyond; Comparison of the United States Constitution with the Universal Declaration of Human Rights; Comparison of state constitutions with the Universal Declaration of Human Rights).
- Healy, chapters 6–10 (International social welfare organizations; Values and ethics for international professional action; International relief and development practice; international/domestic practice interface; Understanding and influencing global policy.)
- View film: *Eleanor—First lady of the world*. (1982). Burbank, CA: Columbia Tristar Home Video.

Module 3: Beyond the Universal Declaration of Human Rights in the Global Community

Ratification and Implementation of Human Rights Treaties; The International Covenant on Economic, Social and Cultural Rights and Other Major Human Rights Conventions; International Implementation and Enforcement Mechanisms; The U.N. Human Rights Committees; State Reporting Under the International Human Rights Treaties with Particular Attention to the United States; The Initial U.S. Report to the U.N. Committee on Civil and Political Rights; Suggested Social Action Strategies; Education for International Professional Action; Social Work as a Force for Humane Global Change and Development

Readings

- Wronka, chapters 6–8 (Strategies to modify U.S. constitution; Essays toward the creation of a human rights culture; Social action in the struggle for human dignity).
- Healy, chapters 11–12 (Education for international professional action; Social work as a force for humane global change and development).
- View original film footage of Malcolm X in: *Malcolm X: Death of a prophet*. Fort Mill, SC: Sterling entertainment group.

Note: By this module, you will need to hand in a paragraph or two that briefly discusses your topic of interest paper and how you plan to go about researching it. Please see the attached guidelines for what is required in this assignment.

Module 4: Building Upon the Universal Declaration With Particular Emphasis on the Profession of Social Work

The International Covenant on Civil and Political Rights and Its Implication for Social Work Practice; The International Covenant on Economic, Social and Cultural Rights and Its Implication for Practice

Reading

- Reichert, chapters 2–4 (Universal Declaration of Human Rights; Building upon the Universal Declaration; International Covenant on Economic and Social Rights).

Module 5: Working With Vulnerable Groups as a Human Rights Concern

Women, Children, Persons with Disabilities, and/or HIV/AIDS, Gays and Lesbians, Older Persons and Victims of Racism as Cases in Point

Reading

- Reichert, chapters 5–7 (Vulnerable groups; Other vulnerable groups; International aspects of social work)

Module 6: Applying Human Rights to the Social Work Profession

Redux

Readings

- Reichert, chapter 8 (Applying Human Rights to Social Work).

- International Federation of Social Work, Professional Training Module on the Rights of the Child.

Students should also go over Wronka and Healy to engage in the class discussion today that would basically summarize the essential points in regard to the application of human rights to social work theory, policy, and practice.

Module 7: The Contemporary Situation of Human Rights in the World

Background and Content With Particular Attention to an Interdisciplinary Framework; The Judgment of Nuremberg in Context; The Public/Private Divide with Particular Attention to the Convention on the Elimination of Discrimination Against Women; Toward Effective Monitoring Mechanisms

Reading

- Steiner and Alston, chapters 1–4 (Introduction to human rights issues and discourse from an interdisciplinary perspective; Up to Nuremberg; Civil and political rights; Economic and social rights).

Module 8: The Problem of Cultural Relativism

Illustrations from Different Cultures; Gender and Culture; Universalism Versus Cultural Relativism; Comparative Religious Perspectives; International Law Perspectives; Proselytism; Children; East Asian Perspectives

Reading

- Steiner and Alston, chapters 5–6 (Rights, duties, and cultural relativism; Conflicting traditions and rights).

Module 9: The United Nations System

Charter-Based Institutions; Fact Finding; The 1503 and 1235 Procedures; Case Studies in Iran, China; The Thematic Mechanisms; The Evolving Role of the Security Council; East Timor as a Case in Point

Reading

- Steiner and Alston, chapters 7–9 (The need for international institutions and their challenge to notions of sovereignty; Treaty organs).

Module 10: Regional Public Access Arrangements With International "Regimes"

The European Convention System; The Inter-American System; The African System; The Role of NGOs, The UN Declaration on Human Rights Defenders of 1998; NGO's Access to the UN

Reading

- Steiner and Alston, chapters 10–11 (Regional arrangements; Civil society: Human rights NGOs and other groups).

Module 11: The Interpretation of International and National Systems

The Spread of State Constitutions and the Liberal Model; Human Rights Treaties Within States Legal and Political Orders; Illustrations From Different States; State Judicial Enforcement; The Enforcement by States Against Violator States

Reading

- Steiner and Alston, chapters 12–13 (Interpretation of international and national systems; Enforcement by states against violator states).

Module 12: Select Topics of Burgeoning Interest in the Global Community

Truth Commissions; The International Criminal Court; Pinochet Legislation; Self-Determination and Autonomy Regimes

Reading

- Steiner and Alston, chapters 14–15 (Massive human rights tragedies: Prosecutions and truth commissions; Self-determination and autonomy regimes)

Module 13: Globalization, Development, and Human Rights

The Role of Development, International Aid and Debt; The Role of the World Bank, The International Monetary Fund and Multinational Corporations

Reading

- Alston, chapter 16 (Globalization, development and human rights)

Note: Your topic of interest paper is due when this module meets.

Module 14: Summary and Conclusions

Presentations on reseach action projects begin.

Module 15: Presentations on Reseach Action Projects Continued

V. METHODS OF INSTRUCTION

Students are taught to reflect critically upon the relevance of human rights theory and praxis to promote social justice. This reflection ought to be "dragged into" one's "vital labors," as the phenomenologist Merleau-Ponty called it, in such a way that should not be merely cognitive (occurring in the mind), but may also require changes in the heart (the spirit) and conduct (the body) roughly consistent with the humanics mission of this School of Social Work and Springfield College. To facilitate such an inquiry, this class will emphasize, in part, didactic methods of teaching, yet also rely largely on group discussion in seminar format, coupled with experiential exercises, videos, and debates designed to foster a lived sense of the meaning of human rights.

This course, therefore, works on the assumption that "information is power," especially when people do not know that their human rights are being violated. This information, however, must be "lived" in the sense that this knowledge leads a person to social action. The instructor, furthermore, will act primarily as a resource to facilitate learning within the broad area of human rights, hoping to act as a "catalyst" to assist in igniting students' passions to pursue human rights research-action projects that are directly relevant to the world situation today and to the profession of social work.

It is important to point out, finally, that this outline and corresponding topics and readings are extensive and comprehensive. Students, in concert with the professor, may wish to determine what aspects of the curriculum and readings they wish to emphasize. Or, they may wish to do the entire curriculum, in essence sacrificing depth for breadth. In either case both options are equally viable and this exercise of dialogue between students and professor, a major teaching style throughout this course, ought to illustrate the true dialogical nature of human rights work, which is so important in the creation of a human rights culture.

VI. COURSE ASSIGNMENTS AND CRITERIA FOR GRADING

1. Students are to hand in one paper on their particular area of interest in the broad field of human rights, roughly between 7 and 12 pages. This paper ought to be in the form of a research-action project as discussed in class. In other words, you will research your particular areas of interest and based upon your findings, you will pose various interventions. You will be required to hand in in written form what you plan to do by the third module. You will also need to present your findings toward the end of the class (30% of the grade), beginning on the 14th module. The paper itself is due the week of the 12th module.

    The paper must be well written and in APA format, demonstrating a thorough understanding of a particular topic that ought to be related to any aspect of human rights as discussed in class. If, for example, you do a study of welfare benefits to children born in or out of wedlock, you will note how this pertains to articles of the Universal Declaration or any of the other human rights conventions studied, as well as human rights reports and comments from the human rights committees.

2. Students are also required to hand in a final paper on the last day of class, roughly between 7 to 12 pages, which discusses the relevance/irrelevance of human rights and international social work for dealing with contemporary social problems. In that final paper, I will be looking primarily for an understanding of the readings and course lectures. You needn't agree that human rights and international social work are relevant; if they are not relevant, please feel free to tell me. However, to reemphasize, it is important that you demonstrate an un-

derstanding of the readings and base your opinion on the materials read to support your "human voice," that is your assessment of the materials. This paper is due the last day of class. It is worth 50% of your grade. This paper also must be well written and in APA format.

3. In addition to your presentation on the topic of interest paper, you will be required to do another presentation that summarizes a particular portion of the readings yet also enhances the reading by bringing in outside material. Thus, you may be responsible for summarizing a chapter in one of the books, such as chapter 7 in Healy on Values and Ethics. Then, you may wish to further discuss an aspect of the chapter, such as the debates between cultural relativism and universalism, by bringing in outside materials pertaining to an issue in the area of human rights, such as female genital mutilation in certain nonindustrialized countries or the issue of anorexia nervosa in predominantly Western countries. Thus, you may wish to examine in brief if in this particular case it is fair to condemn one practice while living in a culture that also has its human rights. This presentation is worth 10% of your grade.

4. You are also required to attend class, be prepared for the class lectures and discussions by having done the readings, and participate accordingly. Attendance and class participation thus counts for the remaining 10% of the grade.

If you come to class, participate, do the readings, and obviously, work on the assignments, I wouldn't worry about a grade.

VII. BIBLIOGRAPHY

Alston, P. (1990). U.S. ratification of the covenant on economic, social and cultural rights: The need for an entirely new strategy. *American Journal of International Law, 84,* 365–393.

Amnesty International. (1991). *Amnesty International report 1991.* New York: Author.

Anelauskas, V. (1998). *Discovering America as it is.* Atlanta: Clarity Press.

Aspalter, C. (2002). *Discovering the welfare state in East Asia.* Westport, CT: Praeger.

Auslander, G. (Ed.). (1997). *International perspectives in social work in health care.* New York: Haworth Press.

Beigher, Y. (2002). *New challenges for UNICEF; Children, women, and human rights.* Desoto, TX: Palgrave Macmillan.

Briar-Lawson, K. (2001). *Family centered policies and practices: International perspectives.* New York: Columbia University Press.

Brownlie, I. (Ed.). (1971). *Basic documents on human rights.* Cary, NC: Clarendon Press.

Buergenthal, T. (1999). *International human rights in a nutshell.* St. Paul, MN: West.

Chomsky, N. (2000). *Case studies in hypocrisy.* San Francisco, CA: AK Press.

Claude, R. P., & Weston, B. (Eds.). (1992). *Human rights in the world community.* Baltimore, MD: University of Pennsylvania Press.

Colton, M., & Casas, F. (1997). *Stigma and social welfare: An international comparative study.* Brookfield, VT: Avebury.

Coyle, A., Campbell, A., & Neufeld, R. (2003). *Capitalist punishment: Prison privatization and human rights.* Atlanta: Clarity.

Donnelly, J. (1989). *Universal human rights in theory and practice.* Ithaca, NY: Cornell University Press.

Donnelly, J., & Howard R. (1987). *International handbook of human rights.* Westport, CT: Greenwood.

Drinan, R. (1987). *Cry of the oppressed: The history and hope of the human rights revolution.* San Francisco: Harper and Row.

Edie, A. (1987). *United Nations Commission on Human Rights: Report on the right to adequate food as a human right* (E/CN.4/SUB.2/1987/23). New York: United Nations.

Fellmeth, R. (2002). *Child rights and remedies: How the U.S. legal system affects children.* Atlanta, GA: Clarity.

Ferrero, R. (1986). Subcommission on prevention of discrimination and protection of minorities: *The new international economic order and the promotion of human rights* (E/CN.4/SUB.2/1983/24/Rev.1). New York: United Nations.

Flanz, G., & Blaustein, A. (1997). *Constitutions of the countries of the world.* Dobbs Ferry, NY: Oceana.

Fourth World Movement. (1990). *The Wresinski report.* Landover, MD: Author.

Friedman, J., & Wiseberg, L. (1981). *Teaching human rights.* Washington, DC: Human Rights Internet.

Gil, D., & Gil, E. (Eds.). (1985). *The future of work.* Rochester, NY: Schenkman.

Gil, D. (1998). *Confronting social injustice.* New York: Columbia University Press.

Green, J. F. (1956). *The U.N. and human rights.* Washington, DC: Brookings Institution.

Hartmann, T. (2002). *Unequal protection: The rise of corporate dominance, the theft of human rights.* Gordonsville, VA: Rodale Press.

Harvey, P. (1989). *Securing the right to employment.* Princeton, NJ: Princeton University Press.

Health and Human Rights. Cambridge, MA: Harvard University Press. (journal)

Hokenstad, M. (1992). *Profiles in international social work.* Washington, DC: NASW Press.

Human Rights Internet (1991). *For the record: Indigenous peoples and slavery in the United Nations.* Ontario, Canada: Author.

Human Rights Quarterly. Baltimore, MD: John Hopkins University Press. (journal)

International Journal of Children's Rights. Boston: Martinus Nijhoff.

Kly, Y. (1986). *The true political philosophy of Malcolm X (El Hajj Malik El Shabazz).* Atlanta, GA: Clarity.

Kyle, D., & Koslowski, R. (2001). *Global human smuggling: Comparative perspectives.* Baltimore, MD: John Hopkins University Press.

Lappe, F., Collins, J., & Rosset, P. (1998). *World hunger: Twelve myths.* New York: Grove.

Laqueur, W., & Rubin, B. (Eds.). (1990). *The human rights reader* (Rev. ed.). New York: New American Library.

Lauren, P. (1998). *The evolution of international human rights law.* Baltimore, MD: University of Pennsylvania Press.

Lauterpacht, H. (1950). *International law and human rights.* London: Stevens and Sons.

Lesnik, B. (Ed.) (1998). *Countering discrimination in social work.* Brookfield, VT: Ashgate.

Lifton, Ro. (2003). *Superpower syndrome: America's apocalyptic confrontation with the world.* New York: Thunder's Mouth Press.

Lillich, R. (1989). The Constitution and international human rights. *American Journal of International Law, 83,* 851–862.

Lyons, K. (1999). *International social work: Themes and perspectives.* Brookfield, VT: Ashgate.

Macarov, D. (2003). *What the market does to people: Privatization, globalization and poverty.* Atlanta, GA: Clarity.

Maddex, R., Robinson, M., & Tutor, D. (2000). *International encyclopedia of human rights.* Washington, DC: Congressional Quarterly.

Maydas, N., Watts, T., & Elliott, D. (Eds.). *International handbook of social work theory and practice.* Westport, CT: Greenwood.

Meron, T. (1989). *Human rights and humanitarian norms as customary law.* Cary, NC: Clarendon.

Neil, G. (1997). *Combating child abuse: International perspectives and trends.* Cary, NC: Oxford University Press.

Paust, J. (1983). Human dignity as a constitutional right: A jurisprudentially based inquiry into criteria and content. *Howard Law Journal, 27*, 144–225.

Rosenfeld, J., & Tardieu, B. (2000). *Artisans of democracy: How ordinary people, families in extreme poverty, and social institutions become allies to overcome social exclusion.* Lanham, MD: University Press of America.

Rosenweig, M. (1988). Psychology and United Nations human rights efforts. *American Psychologist, 43*, 79–86.

Roy, A. & Vecchiolla, F. (2004). *Thoughts on an advanced generalist education: Models, readings, and essays.* Peosta, Il: Eddie Bowers.

Tomasevski, K. (1993). *Women and human rights.* Boston: Zed Books.

Sacquet, A. (2002). *World atlas of sustainable development.* Paris: Éditions Autrement.

Schabas, W. (2000). *Genocide in International law.* New York: Cambridge University Press.

Shelton, D. (2001). *Remedies in international human rights law.* Cary, NC: Oxford University Press.

Schoenberger, T. (2001). *Levi's children: Coming to terms with human rights in the global marketplace.* Emeryville, CA: Grove Press.

Solomon, C. (1999). *Active learning exercises for social work and the human services.* Boston: Allyn & Bacon.

Steiner, H., & Alston, P. (2000). *International human rights in context: Politics, law, and morals.* Cary, NC: Oxford University Press.

Toebas, B. (1999). *The right to health as a human right in international law.* Antwerpen: Intersentia/Hart Press.

United Nations. (1999). *World survey of the role of women in development.* New York: Author.

United Nations Development Program. *Human development report* (Issued annually). New York: W.W. Norton.

United Nations. (2000). *A compilation of international human rights instruments.* New York: Author.

United Nations. (2001). *Basic facts about the United Nations.* New York: Author.

United States Government Printing Office (1997). *Human rights report of foreign countries.* Washington, DC: Author.

Van Soest, D. (1997). *The global crisis of violence.* Washington, DC: National Association of Social Work.

Warren-Adamson, C. (2002). *Family centers and their international role in social action.* Brookfield, VT: Ashgate.

Worldwatch Institute. *State of the world* (Issued annually). New York: W.W. Norton.

Wronka, J. M. (1995). Human rights. In R. Edwards (Ed.), *Encyclopedia of Social Work* (19th ed.) (pp. 1404–1418). Washington, DC: NASW Press.

Wronka, J. (1998). A little humility please: Human rights and social policy in the United States, *Harvard International Review*, Summer, 1998, 92–96.

Wronka, J. (2001). *The Dr. Ambedkar Memorial Lectures on the theme creating a human rights culture:* Bhubenaswar, India: National Institute for Social Work and the Social Sciences.

SELECT ELECTRONIC RESOURCES

It is important to subscribe to the international listserv of human rights educators at hr-education@hrea.org. It alerts subscribers to the latest human rights developments and circulates worldwide requests for information pertaining to human rights.

In addition, please pay attention to the bibliography for research in the recommended reading by Weissbrodt et al. However, the following Web sites are fundamental enough to act as portals from which to navigate for human rights information, education, research, and social action in general:

* www.humanrightsculture.org: Human Rights Action International
* www.aaas.org: American Association for the Advancement of Science
* www.africa-union.org: African Union

- www.amnesty.org: Amnesty International
- www.atd-fourthworld.org/accueil-uk.html: International fourth world movement
- www.business-humanrights.org/Home: Center for Resources for Business and Human Rights
- www.cesr.org: Center for Economic and Social Rights
- www.etc-graz.at/: European training and research center for human rights
- www.childpolicyintl.org: Portal sponsored by Columbia University
- www.crin.org : Child rights information network
- www.fxb.org: Francois-Xavier Bagnoud Center for Human Rights at Harvard University
- www.globalexchange.org: Organization dedicated to international distributive justice
- www.hrea.org: Human Rights Education Associates
- www.hri.ca: Human Rights Internet, a major portal for human rights information.
- www.humanrightsculture.org: Human Rights Action International
- www.iassw.soton.ac.uk: International Association of Schools of Social Work
- www.icsw.org: International Council on Social Welfare
- www.ifsw.org: International Federation of Social Workers
- www.ilo.org: International Labor Organization
- www.library.yale.edu/un/un3b4.htm: Portal sponsored by Yale University
- www.narf.org: Native American Rights Foundation
- www.ngocongo.org: The Conference of Non-Governmental Organizations in Consultative Relationship with the United Nations (CONGO)
- www.nyu.edu/socialwork/wwwrsw/: A World Wide Web resource for social work sponsored by New York University
- www.oas.org: Organization of American States
- www.pdhre.org: People's Decade for Human Rights Education
- www.strongun.org: Coalition for a Strong United Nations
- www.unhchr.ch/: United Nations High Commissioner for Human Rights
- www.unicef.org: UNICEF
- www.who.int/en/: World Health Organization
- www.wilpf.org/main.html: Women's International League for Peace and Freedom
- www.worldcitizen.org: World Citizen Foundation

Bonne chance!

Human Rights in Global Perspective
SOWK 3800

This elective course is intended for second- and third-year undergraduates. It is also open to students outside the social work major as a general studies course. This exposes nonmajors to social work values and sometimes recruits students to the social work program.

COURSE DESCRIPTION AND PURPOSE

This course raises consciousness about global human rights issues. Students explore the historical, philosophical, and legal foundations of the concept of human rights, while becoming acquainted with current human rights debates. They learn about the role of the United Nations, governmental, and nongovernmental organizations in protecting human rights. They examine current and emerging human rights issues in one region of the world, while gaining an overview of such issues globally. By participating in a service-learning experience, they reflect on human rights in our own country. Students discover that human rights are the bedrock of the social work profession internationally.

BACKGROUND

The Council on Social Work Education's Educational Policy and Accreditation Standards require that "programs integrate social and economic justice content grounded in an understanding of distributive justice, human and civil rights, and the global interconnections of oppression." This course addresses that standard.

METHOD

Material is presented through readings, videos, oral reports, lectures, in-class exercises, class discussion, debates, writing assignments, and guest speakers. A service-learning experience is a course requirement.

COURSE OBJECTIVES

By the completion of the course, students will be able to:

1. Understand the origins of the concept of universal human rights.

2. Understand the role that historical events, culture, and public sentiment play in the development of support for the concept of universal human rights on a national and international level.

3. Understand the role of the United Nations in delineating and working toward the protection of human rights.

4. Understand what governmental and nongovernmental organizations are doing to advance human rights.

5. Understand the similarities and differences that exist among human rights issues in various regions of the world.

6. Have a more in-depth understanding of the rights of women, minorities, indigenous peoples, and children as specific examples of human rights issues.

7. Understand that human rights violations occur not just in other nations but right here in the United States.

8. Identify ways to become involved in the global struggle to protect human rights.

9. Understand the linkages between the human rights movement and the social work profession internationally.

READINGS AND COURSE RESOURCES

- Achebe, C. (1959). *Things fall apart*. New York: Anchor Books.
- Lauren, P. G. (1998). *The evolution of international human rights: Visions seen*. Philadelphia, PA: University of Pennsylvania Press.
- Tomasevski, K. (1995). *Women and human rights*. London: Zed Books.

- Williams, M. (Ed.). (1998). *Human rights: Opposing viewpoints*. San Diego, CA: Greenhaven Press.
- Human Rights in Global Perspective Web site: http://www.stockton.edu/ ~ falkd/hr-site.htm (Contains links to readings, lecture notes, related Web sites, and Web Caucus conference.)
- Additional readings as indicated in the course calendar.

STUDENT RESPONSIBILITIES

A considerable amount of material for this course will be presented in class. In addition, there will be in-class exercises that cannot be made up. Therefore, you are expected to attend, participate in, and be on time for all scheduled classes. If you are unable to attend class due to an emergency, please call the instructor and leave a voice-mail message. If you miss more than two classes, a substantial grade reduction may result.

You are responsible for handing in all assignments by the scheduled deadline.

ASSIGNMENTS

1. Readings: from the textbooks, the course Web site, and materials distributed in class.
2. Quizzes: Several brief quizzes will be given on the readings and lectures.
3. Web Caucus journal: You are expected to keep a journal on Web Caucus and to read regularly the journals of other students. The primary purpose of the journal is to discuss the service-learning experience, but you are also encouraged to discuss readings, current events, human rights Web sites, and class experiences (videos, exercises, discussions, debates).
4. Participation in class discussions and in-class exercises and debates.
5. Oral report: You will research a particular human rights issue in one region of the world, make a 10-minute presentation to the rest of the class on that issue, and turn in a 1–2 page outline of your report and a list of sources used. Information for the report should be obtained from at least three sources. If Web sites are used as a source, a printout of the first page of each site used must be turned in with the report.
6. Service learning: You are expected to participate in Stockton's Service Learning Program, which requires 30 hours of community service that is related to the course material.

CALENDAR

Week 1/Session 1

Orientation to course; What are human rights? Three generations of human rights: (1) civil and political rights; (2) economic, social, and cultural rights; (3) right to peace, development, and clean environment

- Video and discussion: *The power of human rights* (Voices of human rights, Human rights high school, Peace watch)

Week 1/Session 2

Social work as a human rights profession

- NASW international policy on human rights (course Web site: readings)
- IFSW human rights policy (course Web site: readings)
- Wronka, Human rights

Week 2/Session 1

History of development of concept of human rights: early visions of human rights

- Lauren, chapter 1: My Brother's and Sister's Keeper: Visions and the Birth of Human Rights
- Miscellaneous excerpts from original texts: Hammurabi, Jewish and Christian Bible, Mahayana Buddhism, the Koran (available on the course Web site: readings)
- Time line (on course Web site: linked to homepage)

Week 2/Session 2

Philosophical and value basis underlying concept of human rights

- Miscellaneous excerpts from original texts: Magna Carta, Beccaria, U.S. Declaration of Independence, U.S. Bill of Rights, Douglas (available on the course Web site: readings);
- Locke, Rousseau (handouts)
- Lauren, chapter 2: To Protect Humanity and Defend Justice: Early International Efforts

Week 3/Session 1

Human rights "hot spots" around the world; history of development of concept of human rights: World War I and revolutions

- Video and discussion: *Around the world* (China and free trade, Sarajevo under siege, intervention in Somalia)
- Lauren, chapter 3: Entering the Twentieth Century: World Visions, War, and Revolutions

Week 3/Session 2

Introduction to Service Learning

- Guest speaker from Service Learning office: Interview procedures, agencies available, how to work with the agency to design a learning experience that addresses human rights issues, philosophy of learning through service, importance of civic engagement

Week 4/Session 1

History of development of concept of human rights: human rights between World Wars I and II; case discussion: learning to identify human rights issues in service learning and social work internship settings

- Lauren, chapter 4: Opportunities and Challenges: Visions and Rights Between the Wars

Week 4/Session 2

QUIZ 1 (on Lauren, chapters 1–4 and on miscellaneous excerpts from original texts discussed in class); social work as an international profession—its mission and purpose, how the profession relates to the international human rights movement

- Further discussion of service-learning cases, and Web Caucus journal assignment

Week 5/Session 1

History of development of concept of human rights: World War II

- Lauren, chapter 5: A "People's War": The Crusade of World War II

Week 5/Session 2

History of development of concept of human rights: Founding of the United Nations; UN Charter; the role and structure of the United Nations

- Lauren, chapter 6: A "People's Peace": Peace and a Charter with Human Rights

Week 6/Session 1

History of the development of the concept of human rights: *The Universal Declaration of Human Rights;* overview of *The Universal Declaration of Human Rights* and of other declarations and conventions of the United Nations

- Lauren, chapter 7: Proclaiming a Vision: The Universal Declaration of Human Rights

Week 6/Session 2

History of the development of the concept of human rights: The years since the Universal Declaration

- Lauren, chapter 8: Transforming Visions into Reality: Fifty Years of the Universal Declaration

Week 7/Session 1

QUIZ 2 (on Lauren, chapters 5–8 and on The Universal Declaration of Human Rights); history of the development of the concept of human rights: ongoing evolution of international human rights

- Lauren, Conclusion: Visions and the Evolution of International Human Rights

Week 7/Session 2

The role of national human rights institutions and of nongovernmental organizations

- Debate: The effectiveness of nongovernmental organizations. Guest speaker from campus chapter of Amnesty International
- Williams, *Human rights: Opposing viewpoints,* chapter 3-1 and 3-2 (pp. 118–26)

Week 8/Session 1

Cultural relativism

- Debate: Universal standards versus cultural diversity
- Achebe, *Things fall apart*
- Williams, *Human rights: Opposing viewpoints,* chapter 1-1 and 1-2 (pp. 17–24)

Week 8/Session 2

QUIZ 3 (on Achebe, *Things fall apart*); cultural relativism (role play)

- Class members take on roles of cultural groups as described in Achebe novel

Week 9/Session 1

Women and human rights

- Debate: Women's rights are human rights?
- Video: *Women under attack* (female genital mutilation, rape and war, world women's movement)
- Tomasevski, chapters 1–3; Williams, *Human rights: Opposing viewpoints*, chapter 1-5 and 1-6 (pp. 44–56)

Week 9/Session 2

Women and human rights (student panel discussion)

- Debate: Political asylum for women?
- Tomasevski, chapters 6–8; Rasekh, et al., Women's health and human rights in Afghanistan;
- Williams, *Human rights: Opposing viewpoints*, chapter 3-5 and 3-6 (pp. 135–48)

Week 10/Session 1

Children's rights; case discussion focusing on parallels between children's rights issues in developing nations and those of children living in Atlantic City, NJ; the role of social work in enhancing the lives of children

- Video: *The world's children*
- Reichenberg & Friedman, *Traumatized children: Healing the invisible wounds of children in war: A rights approach*

Week 10/Session 2

The rights of minorities and indigenous peoples

- Video: U.S. and Canada civil rights segment
- King, Address at March on Washington for jobs and freedom (Web page)
- Video: *Tibet in Exile*
- Dalai Lama, Nobel Prize acceptance speech

Week 11/Session 2

QUIZ 4 (on readings from women, children, and minorities/indigenous peoples); case discussion, focusing on parallels between the rights of minorities and indigenous peoples in other parts of the world and those occurring today in the United States; the role of social work in working to protect human rights of minorities and indigenous peoples

- Debate: Tibet
- Williams, *Human rights: Opposing Viewpoints,* chapter 4-5 and 4-6 (pp. 187–200)

Week 11/Session 2

Oral report: Group Reporting on Human Rights Issues in Asia

- Debate: Asian values
- Williams, *Human rights: Opposing viewpoints,* chapter 1-3 and 1-4 (pp. 25–43)

Week 12/Session 1

Oral report: Group Reporting on Human Rights Issues in Australia, New Zealand, and the Pacific Islands

Week 12/Session 2

No class/Thanksgiving Day

Week 13/Session 1

Oral report: Group Reporting on Human Rights Issues in Africa

- Debate: Refugees and political asylum
- Williams, *Human rights: Opposing viewpoints*, chapter 2-5 and 2-6 (pp. 88–107)

Week 13/Session 2

Oral reports: Group Reporting on Human Rights Issues in the Middle East

- Video: *Beyond the Veil*

Week 14/Session 1

Oral reports: Group Reporting on Human Rights Issues in Europe

- Debate: International criminal court?
- Williams, *Human rights: Opposing viewpoints*, chapter 4-1 and 4-2 (pp. 165–180)

Week 14/Session 2

Oral reports: Group Reporting on Human Rights Issues in Central and South America

- Debate: Factory standards
- Williams, *Human rights: Opposing viewpoints*, chapter 3-3 and 3-4 (pp. 127–134)

Week 15/Session1

Summary discussion of social work as a human rights profession; evaluation, QUIZ 5 (course overall)

BIBLIOGRAPHY

Human Rights in General

An-Na'im, A. A.(1994). State responsibility under international human rights law to change religious and customary laws. In R. J. Cook (Ed.), *Human rights and women: National and international perspectives*. Philadelphia: University of Pennsylvania Press.

International Federation of Social Workers. (2002). *Social work and the rights of the child: A professional training manual on the UN Convention*. Berne, Switzerland: International Federation of Social Workers.

Ishay, M. R. (Ed.). (1997). *The human rights reader: Major political essays, speeches, and documents from the Bible to the present.* New York: Routledge.

Leary, V. A. (1996). The paradox of workers' rights as human rights. In L. A. Compa & S. F. Diamond (Eds.), *Human rights, labor rights, and international trade.* Philadelphia: University of Pennsylvania Press.

National Association of Social Workers. (2000). International policy on human rights. In, *Social work speaks: National Association of Social Workers policy statements: 2000—2003* (5th ed.) (pp. 178–186). Washington, DC: NASW Press.

United Nations. (1994). *Human rights and social work: A manual for schools of social work and the social work profession* (Professional Training Series No 1). New York: United Nations.

United Nations. (1995). *National human rights institutions* (Professional Training Series No. 4). New York: United Nations.

United Nations. (1995). *Report of the Fourth World Conference on Women.* New York: United Nations. (This document is available on the Internet.)

United Nations. (1995). *The United Nations and human rights: 1945–1995.* New York: United Nations.

Wronka, J. M. (1992) *Human rights and social policy in the 21st century: A history of the idea of human rights and comparison of the United Nations Universal Declaration of Human Rights with United States federal and state constitutions.* Lanham, MD: University Press of America.

Wronka, J. M. (1995). Human rights. In R. Edwards (Ed.), *Encyclopedia of social work* (19th ed.) (pp. 1405–1418). Washington, DC: NASW Press.

Children's Rights

Daniele, Y., Rodley, N. S., & Weisaeth, L. (1996). *International responses to traumatic stress: Humanitarian, human rights, justice, peace and development contributions, collaborative actions and future initiatives.* Amityville, NY: Baywood Publishing Co.

Desjarlais, R, Eisenberg, L., Good, B., & Kleinman, A. (1995). *World mental health: Problems and priorities in low-income countries.* New York: Oxford University Press (chapter 7, Children and youth).

Kozol, J. (1995). *Amazing grace: The lives of children and the conscience of a nation.* New York: Harper Perennial.

McCourt, F. (1996). *Angela's ashes.* New York: Scribner.

Reichenberg, D., & Friedman, S. (1996). Traumatized children: Healing the invisible wounds of children in war: A rights approach. In Y. Daniele, N. S. Rodley, & L. Weisaeth (Eds.), *International responses to traumatic stress: Humanitarian, human rights, justice, peace and development contributions, collaborative actions and future initiatives.* Amityville, NY: Baywood Publishing Co.

UNICEF. (1999). State of the world's children (Annual report). Available at http://www.unicef.org/

The Rights of Minorities

Kly, Y. N. (Ed.). (1995). *A popular guide to minority rights.* Atlanta, GA: Clarity Press.

Mankiller, W. P. (1993). *Mankiller: A chief and her people.* New York: St. Martin's Press.

Paton, A. (1948). *Cry, the beloved country.* New York: Charles Scribner's Sons.

Women's Rights

Brooks, G. (1995). *Nine parts of desire: The hidden world of Islamic women.* New York: Anchor Books.

Bhugra, D. (1996). *Homelessness and mental health.* Cambridge, England: Cambridge University Press. (chapter 5, Homeless women)

Chan, C. L. (1995). Gender issues in market socialism. In L. Wong & S. MacPherson (Eds.), *Social change and social policy in contemporary China* (pp. 188–215). Hong Kong: City University of Hong Kong.

Chang, J. (1993). *Wild swans: Three daughters of China*. London: Harper Collins.

Cook, R. J. (Ed.). (1994). *Human rights and women: National and international perspectives*. Philadelphia: University of Pennsylvania Press.

Corrin, C. (ed.) (1996). *Women in a violent world: Feminist analyses and resistance across "Europe."* Edinburgh, Scotland: Edinburgh University Press.

Desjarlais, R., Eisenberg, L., Good, B., & Kleinman, A. (1995). *World mental health: Problems and priorities in low-income countries.* (chapter 8, Women)

Kassindja, F. (1998). *Do they hear you when you cry?* New York: Delacourt Press.

Mladjenovic, L., & Matijasevic, D. (1996). SOS Belgrade July 1993–1995: Dirty Streets. In C. Corrin (Ed.), *Women in a violent world: Feminist analyses and resistance across "Europe."* (pp. 119–132). Edinburgh: Edinburgh University Press.

Rasekh, Z., Bauer, H. M., Manos, M. M., & Iacopino, V. (1998). Women's health and human rights in Afghanistan. *Journal of the American Medical Association, 290*, 449–455.

Reichert, E. (1998). Women's rights are human rights: Platform for action. *International social work, 41*(3), 371–84.

Tomasevski, K. (1993). *Women and human rights*. London: Zed Books.

United Nations. (1995). *The United Nations and the advancement of women: 1945–96*. New York: United Nations.

U.S. Department of State, President's Interagency Council on Women. (1997). *America's commitment: Federal programs benefiting women and new initiatives as follow-up to the UN Fourth World Conference on Women.* Washington: Author.

Walker, Alice. (1992). *Possessing the secret of joy*. New York: Pocket Books.

Videos

Hunter-Gault, C., Masters, H., Ortiz, E. (Authors). (1993). *Rights and Wrongs Series* [Videorecording]. Global Vision.

- *The Power of Human Rights*
- *U.S. and Canada*
- *Around the World*
- *The World's Children*
- *Women under Attack*

Banks, B., and McLogan, M. (Producers). (1991). *Tibet in Exile* [Videorecording]. The Video Project.

Gregg, A. (Producer). (1997). *Beyond the Veil: Are Iranian Women Rebelling?* [Videorecording]. Canadian Broadcasting Corporation.

CLEVELAND STATE UNIVERSITY
DEPARTMENT OF SOCIAL WORK | CLEVELAND, OH
BETH CAGAN

Women and International Social Development
FST 359 SWK

COURSE DESCRIPTION

This undergraduate course draws from three overlapping fields of research and professional activity: international social work, women's studies, and social development. Their common goal is to improve the well-being of people around the world, with a special emphasis on poor women in poor nations. While drawing from different academic and professional roots, the three fields share common values based on concern for social justice and human rights.

International social work applies social work theory and methodology to global issues of social welfare policy and practice, such as how nations around the world organize and deliver social services. Women's studies is an interdisciplinary academic field that explores the role and significance of gender to understand and challenge women's oppression. Social development integrates ideas and strategies from many disciplines to address the many forms of social inequality facing people throughout the world, including those based on gender.

The field of social development, the primary intellectual home of this course, emerged in the 1960s from the recognition that neither social welfare nor economic growth alone would improve the quality of life for most people in postcolonial nations. According to this perspective, economic development must be linked with improvements in other areas of life—for example, health care, education, housing—so that the broader goal of *social* development can be reached. A new international field of research and practice was established that promoted increased social well-being through policy and planning, with an emphasis on sustainable growth and grassroots participation. In the 1970s, this field was introduced to social work programs in the United States, and now enjoys its own international professional organization, the Inter-University Consortium for International Social Development (IUCISD), and its own journal, *Social Development Issues* (SDI). Social development is strongly influenced by feminist theory and, although interdisciplinary, reflects its social work origins and values.

This course addresses not only the problems faced by women in the developing world, but also the efforts of these women to create social and economic institutions that are responsive to their needs and the needs of their families. Through readings, films, discussions, individual and group research projects, and class presentations, students will gain an understanding of what needs to be done to improve the lot of women—particularly in poorer nations, but also in more economically advantaged areas. Wherever possible, case studies will be used to give voice to women so that they are understood as subjects of their own lives and purposes, rather than as objects of the viewpoints and judgments of outsiders. The instructor's field research on the efforts of a revolutionary peasant community in El Salvador to promote women's participation will be used as an illustration of some of the complexities of promoting long-term social change.

COURSE OBJECTIVES

This course has two main objectives: (1) to examine problems facing poor women in poor countries around the world in meeting their needs for economic resources and access to human rights, and (2) to consider various strategies for overcoming those problems. While many poor men also suffer from these problems, the situation for women is generally more serious. This is because culture and tradition have historically confined women to the domestic sphere and excluded them from participation in public life. As a result, they have less power than men of their class and community, and their needs are often overlooked even in the context of development projects such as building a dam or extending low-interest credit. For this reason, scholars and activists in the field strongly believe that social development must address directly women's disempowerment and exclusion from participation.

Because these issues are so complex, they are often studied only on the graduate level. However, this course is designed for undergraduate students, including those without any background in women's studies, international relations, social work, or other relevant fields. Every effort will be made to bring beginning-level students on board, so that the whole class will soon become comfortable with the vocabulary and conceptual framework of the course.

In addition to the objectives specified above, the course is intended to familiarize students of all majors and interests with the problems and experiences of people in developing nations. This includes exploring cultural, environmental, historical, and social differences among these nations and between the developed and the developing world. Furthermore, students will conduct independent research on specific issues of women's development that are of interest to them and share this research with the rest of the class. Some students may even find that the course opens up new doors and opportunities for further study, and perhaps even leads to a new career focus!

Students who complete this course are expected to:

a. become sensitized to commonalities and differences in experience between women in the developed and developing world;

b. build on what they have learned about women's development through additional coursework, readings, organizational involvement, and personal experiences;

c. demonstrate a commitment to understanding and diminishing the causes of inequities between genders and among nations.

REQUIRED TEXTS

Ba, M. (1980). *So long a letter.* Portsmith, NY: Heinemann Educational Books.

Wilson, M. G., & Whitmore, E. (2000). *Seeds of fire: Social development in an era of globalism.* Croton-on-Hudson, NY: Apex Press.

Karl, M. (1995). *Women and empowerment: Participation in decision making.* New York: Zed Books.

Visnanathan, N., Duggan, L., Nisonoff, L., & Wiergersma, N. (Eds.). (1997). *The women, gender and development reader.* New York: Zed Books.

STUDENT EVALUATION

1. Participation and attendance: This course will be taught as a seminar, with emphasis on discussion and exchange of ideas. For this reason, you need to attend class regularly and read the assigned material on time. Participation and attendance will affect your final grades substantially. If you participate regularly and effectively in class discussions, showing that you have read (and thought about) the readings, your final grade can be raised by as much as one letter; if you are often absent and/or rarely prepared for class discussions, your grade may be lowered by as much as one letter.

2. Written assignments: There are four separate writing assignments for this course:

    • three short papers (2–3 pages each) based on the readings/discussions.

    • research paper (10 + pages), due at the end of the semester

    Since this is a Writing Across the Curriculum (WAC) course, you have to earn a C or better to get credit for the writing requirement. Any of the short papers can be rewritten. The research paper must be submitted in successive drafts so that feedback can be given. All work must be typed or word processed and carefully proofread. Details of each writing assignment are given below. (See appendix)

3. Additional assignment for FST 359: Students taking the course at the 300 level will also be required to hand in a 4–5-page book review of one of the course texts (excluding the novel *So Long a Letter*). A handout on writing a book review will be provided. The review is due on the last day of class.

4. Class presentations: Near the end of the semester, all students will make an informal presentation to the class about what they have learned in their research projects, so that this material can be shared with the rest of the class. See handout for details and schedule of presentations.

COURSE OUTLINE

1. Introduction and overview: Weeks 1–3

    Establishing a feminist framework for examining social development in non-Western cultures.

    We will begin by developing a basic understanding of the nature of the issues concerning women and development. At this point, our focus will be primarily general and descriptive rather than detailed and theoretical.

Many of the themes and ideas raised in this introductory section will be revisited later in more depth. Right now we are interested in these broad questions about women and development:

- What is meant by development and underdevelopment? How are nations classified according to their level of development and the status of women?

- What kinds of problems do women face in developed and developing countries? Why are the concepts of participation and empowerment so critical?

- How can we look at other, especially non-Western, cultures objectively, without bias? What do we do with our own values and goals?

Required reading

- *Women and empowerment:* Introduction and chapter 1, "Obstacles and opportunities" (pp. 1–18), chapter 3, "Women mobilizing and organizing" (pp. 32–58)

- *Women, gender and development reader*: Hoodfar, "Return to the veil: Personal strategy and public participation in Egypt" (pp. 320–325)

- Moyanty, "Under western eyes: Feminist scholarship and colonial discourses" (pp. 79–82, top)

- *So Long A Letter* (whole book: pp. 1–90) Note: This novel provides a glimpse of Senegalese culture and its effect on women's lives.

Recommended reading

- Chant, S. (1995). Gender and development in the 1990s. *Third World Planning Review*, *17*(2), 111–116.

- Chua, P., Bhavnani, K. K., & Foran, J. (2000). Women, culture, development: A new paradigm for development studies? *Ethnic and Racial Studies*, *23*(5), 820–841.

- Deere, C. D. (1995). What difference does gender make? Rethinking peasant studies. *Feminist Economics*, *1*(1), 53–72.

- Julia, M. (2001). Social development and the feminist tradition. *Social Development Issues*, *23*(1), 14–25.

2. Foundations of global inequality: Weeks 4–5

Theories of development: Why some nations are rich and others poor.

In this section we will look at some of the competing theories about economic disparity among nations, focusing especially on modernization theory and its critics. This view underlies the policies of neoliberalism and structural adjustment that have been imposed around the world under the new economic order of "globalism." We will also look at the primary alternatives to modernization theory: dependency theory and Marxism, and consider an Eastern-inspired approach, "Buddhist Economics," described by the British economist E. F. Schumacher in his book, *Small Is Beautiful.*

Required reading

- *Seeds of fire:* Preface (pp. 10–12) chapter 1, "The age of 'disposable humanity'" (pp. 13–29).

- *The women, gender and development reader*: Visvanathan, "General introduction" (pp. 1–6), Charlton, "Development as history and process" (pp. 7–13)

- Class handout (from *Small is beautiful: Economics as if people mattered):* Schumacher, "Buddhist economics"

Recommended reading

- Ghorayshi, P. (1996). Women in developing countries: Methodological and theoretical considerations. *Women & Politics*, 16(3), 89–111.

- Koczberski, G. (1998). Women in development: A critical analysis. *Third World Quarterly*, *19*(3), 395–409.

- Shiva, V., & Shiva, M. (1995). Third world women denied right to development. *Impact*, *30*(6), 19, 27.

3. Gender relations in developing societies: A feminist analysis: Weeks 6–8

Why women have been excluded from the development process.

This section will bring us to a closer examination of gender relations in developing societies and allow us to explore how culture, religion, and tradition intersect with economic factors. Of particular interest is the gendered division of labor and its organization of life into public and private spheres, which is seen by feminists as the primary mechanism of women's oppression.

Required reading

- *Women, gender and development reader*: Sen, "Subordination and sexual control: A comparative view of the control of women." (pp. 142–149)
- Snyder & Tadesse, "The African context: Women in the political economy" (pp. 75–78)
- Kandiyoti, "Bargaining with patriarchy" (pp. 86–92)
- Benería, "Accounting for women's work: The progress of two decades." (pp. 112–118)
- Chant, "Single-parent families: Choice or constraint? The formation of female-headed households in Mexican shanty towns" (pp. 155–162)

Recommended reading

- Hopgood, J. F. (1996). Women of Latin America: Pobreza, marianismo, y coraje. *Journal of Third World Studies*, *13*(1), 362–368.
- Majid, A. (1998). The politics of feminism in Islam. *Signs*, *23*(2), 321–361.
- Oloka Onyango, J., & Tamale, S. (1995). The personal is political, or why women's rights are indeed human rights: An African perspective on international feminism. *Human Rights Quarterly*, *17*(4), 691–731.
- Pettman, J. J. (1997). Body politics: International sex tourism. *Third World Quarterly*, *18*(1), 93–108.

4. Promoting women's development: Weeks 9–11

Women organize around the world for empowerment and participation.

Our attention turns to the steps taken by women around the world to overcome male domination and promote alternative development strategies based on women's needs. These have gone through a historical progression, from Women In Development (WID), to Women And Development (WAD), and finally, Gender And Development (GAD). We shall examine these different perspectives on overcoming obstacles to women's development and promoting gender equity as well as equitable development.

Required reading

- *Women and empowerment*: chapter 4, "Participation in politics and public life" (pp. 59–94), chapter 5, "Women and development" (pp. 94–120)
- *Seeds of fire*: chapter 5, "Gender and international development praxis" (pp. 120–129)
- *The women, gender and development reader*: Tinker, "The making of a field: Advocates, practitioners and scholars" (pp. 33–42), Young, "Gender and development" (pp. 51–54)

Recommended reading

- George, U. (2002). Strategies for social development: Lessons from Kerala's experience. *Social Development Issues*, *23*(1), 15–24.
- Ray, R., & Korteweg, A. C. (1999). Women's movements in the Third World: Identity, mobilization, and autonomy. *Annual Review of Sociology*, *25*, 47–71.
- Rosenfield, A. (Dec. 2000). After Cairo: Women's reproductive and sexual health, rights, and empowerment. *American Journal of Public Health*, *90*(12), 1838–1840.

- Safa, H. I. (1996). Beijing, diversity and globalization: Challenges to the women's movement in Latin America and the Caribbean. *Organization, 3*(4), 563–570.

5. Social work and international social development: Week 12

Identifying meaningful roles for human service professionals in the development process.

This section will explore how social work skills, values, and experiences can be integrated into the field of social development. Ideas about creating new models of social work practice based on North-South partnerships and accompaniment will be examined. We will also discuss how grassroots communities can be mobilized to build social movements and promote social change.

Required reading

- *Seeds of fire:* chapter 6 "Professional contributions: Social work and international development practice" (pp. 130–140) chapter 9 "Challenging the race to the bottom" (pp. 175–185)

Recommended reading

- Meares, A. C., & Sharma, R. R. (1995). From South to North: A new partnership for Development. *Development, 2,* 31–35.
- Lucas, E. (2001). Social development strategies of a non-governmental grassroots women's organisation in Nigeria. *International Journal of Social Welfare, 10*(3), 185–193.
- Mayadas, N. S., & Elliot, D. (1997). Lessons from international social work: Policies and practice. In M. Reisch & E. Gambrill (Eds.), *Social work in the 21st century* (pp. 175–185). Thousand Oaks, CA: Pine Forge Press.

6. Case studies of women's development: Weeks 13–14

Learning from the problems and experiences of women around the world.

I will present my own research on women's development in a repatriated refugee community in El Salvador (in a slide/video presentation) and other aspects of my research. This will bring us to consider the implications for women of the collapse of socialist alternatives and the emergence of a unipolar world. We will also discuss the role of the United Nations and NGOs in promoting women's development.

Reading

- Cagan, B. (1994). A case study in populist community development in rural El Salvador. *Social Development Issues, 16*(2), pp. 36–49—(to be distributed in class)
- *The women, gender and development reader:* Beneria, "Capitalism and socialism: Some feminist questions" (pp. 326–333)
- *Women and empowerment:* chapter 6, "International mobilization of women in and around the United Nations" (pp. 121–148), chapter 7, "Conclusion: The challenges ahead" (pp. 149–150), annexes I and II (pp. 151–158)

Recommended reading

- Alamdari, K. (1994). The Beijing conference: A testimony for women's achievement and reshuffling global alliances. *California Sociologist, 17-18*(1/2), 81–89.
- Gambhir, B. (2001, March). Of geese and ganders: Mainstreaming gender in the context of sustainable human development. *Journal of Gender Studies, 10*(1), 17–32.

7. Student presentations of research projects: Weeks 15–16

Films (dates of showing TBA):

- van Wijk, J., & Molenaar, H. (Producers). (1993). *Daughters of the Nile* [Motion picture]. Amsterdam, The Netherlands: Molenweek Film. (Available from Filmakers Library, 124 E. 40th St, New York, NY 10016)

- Quarengo, P., & Souleymane, M. (Directors/Producers). (1994). *Women of the Sahel* [Motion picture]. Torino, Italy: Dream Film. (Available from First Run/Icarus Films, 153 Waverly Pl., New York, NY 10014)
- Ivarez, M. J., & Hernandez, M. C. (Directors/Producers). (1990). *Lady Marshall* [Motion picture]. Managua, Nicaragua: Luna Films. (Available from Women Make Movies, 462 Broadway, Suite 500x, New York, NY 10013)
- Jhinqan, S., & Masumdar, R. (Directors/Producers). (1995). *The Hidden Story* [Motion picture]. Delhi, India. (Available from Women Make Movies, 462 Broadway, Suite 500x, New York, NY 10013)
- Chasnoff, S. (Producer/Director). (1996). *Beyond Beijing: The international women's movement* [Motion picture]. Evanston, IL : Beyond Media. (Available from Women Make Movies, 462 Broadway, Suite 500x, New York, NY 10013)

BIBLIOGRAPHY (readings relevant to women and international social development)

Books

Bose, C. E., & Acosta-Belén, E. (Eds.). (1995). *Women in the Latin American development process*. Philadelphia, PA: Temple University Press.

de Bruyn, M. (Ed.). (1995). *Gender, society & development: Advancing women's status, women and men together?* Amsterdam, The Netherlands: Royal Tropical Institute.

Croll, E. (2000). *Endangered daughters: Discrimination and development in Asia*. New York: Routledge.

Eade, D. (1999). *Development with women: Selected essays from development in practice*. Oxford, England: Oxfam.

Flood, T. (1997). *Women in South Africa*. Bellville, South Africa: University of Western Cape, Gender Equity Unit.

Heyzer, N., Kapoor, S., & Sandler, J. (Eds.). (1995). *A commitment to the world's women: Perspectives on development for Beijing and beyond*. New York: UNIFEM.

House-Midamba, B., & Ekechi, F. K. (Eds.). (1995). *African market women and economic power: The role of women in African economic development*. Westport, CT: Greenwood Press.

Jackson, C., & Pearson, R. (1998). *Feminist visions of development: Gender, analysis and policy*. New York: Routledge.

Jahan, R. (1995). *The elusive agenda: Mainstreaming women in development*. Atlantic Highlands, NJ: Zed Books.

Midgley, J. (1995). *Social development: The developmental perspective in social welfare*. Thousand Oaks, CA: Sage.

Momsen, J. H., & Kinnaird, V. (Eds.). (1993). *Different places, different voices: Gender and development in Africa, Asia, and Latin America*. New York: Routledge.

Moon, G. (Ed.). (1996). *Making her rights a reality: Women's human rights and development*. Fitzroy Vic.: Law Foundation of New South Wales.

Moser, C. O. (1993). *Gender planning and development: Theory, practice, and training*. New York: Routledge.

Nuket, K. (1990). *Bringing women in: Women's issues in international development programs*. Boulder, CO: Rienner.

O'Connell, H. (1996). *Equality postponed: Gender, rights and development*. Oxford, England: WorldView.

Perry, S., & Schenck, C. (2001). *Eye to eye: Women practising development across cultures*. New York: Zed Books.

Porter, M., & Judd, E. (1999). *Feminists doing development: A practical critique*. New York: Zed Books.

Ramanathan, C. S., & Link, R. (1999). *All our futures: Principles and resources for social work practice in a global era*. Belmont, CA: Wadsworth.

Reichert, E. (2003). *Social work and human rights: A foundation for policy and practice*. New York: Columbia University Press.

Sittarak, S. (1998). *The daughters of development: Women and the changing environment*. New York: Zed Books.

Stephen, L. (1997) *Women and social movements in Latin America: Power from below*. Austin: University of Texas Press.

Stoez, D., Guzzetta, C., & Lusk, M. (1999). *International Development.* Needham Heights, MA: Allyn & Bacon.

Townsend, J. G., & Zapata, E. (Eds.). (1999). *Women and power: Fighting patriarchies and poverty.* New York: Zed Books.

Wallace, T., & March, C. (Eds.). (1991). *Changing perceptions: Writings on gender and development.* Oxford, England: Oxfam.

Wetzel, J. W. (1993). *The world of women: In pursuit of human rights.* London: McMillan.

Articles

Alamdari, K. (1994). The Beijing conference: A testimony for women's achievement and reshuffling global alliances. *California Sociologist, 17-18*(1/2), 81–89.

Bertone, A. M. (2000). Sexual trafficking in women: International political economy and the politics of sex. *Gender Issues, 18*(1), 4–22.

Chant, S. (1995). Gender and development in the 1990s. *Third World Planning Review, 17*(2), 111–116.

Chua, P., Bhavnani, K. K., & Foran, J. (2000). Women, culture, development: A new paradigm for development studies? *Ethnic and Racial Studies, 23*(5), 820–841.

Deere, C. D. (1995). What difference does gender make? Rethinking peasant studies. *Feminist Economics, 1*(1), 53–72.

Hopgood, J. F. (1996). Women of Latin America: Pobreza, marianismo, y coraje. *Journal of Third World Studies, 13*(1), 362–368.

Koczberski, G. (1998). Women in development: A critical analysis. *Third World Quarterly, 19*(3), 395–409.

Lucas, E. (2001). Social development strategies of a non-governmental grassroots women's organisation in Nigeria. *International Journal of Social Welfare, 10*(3), 185–193.

Majid, A. (1998). The politics of feminism in Islam. *Signs, 23*(2), 321–361.

Meares, A. C., & Sharma, R. R. (1995). From South to North: A new partnership for development. *Development, 2,* 31–35.

Oloka Onyango, J., & Tamale, S. (1995). The personal is political, or why women's rights are indeed human rights: An African perspective on international feminism. *Human Rights Quarterly, 17*(4), 691–731.

Pettman, J. J. (1997). Body politics: International sex tourism. *Third World Quarterly, 18*(1), 93–108.

Ray, R., & Korteweg, A. C. (1999). Women's movements in the Third World: Identity, mobilization, and autonomy. *Annual Review of Sociology, 25,* 47–71.

Rosenfield, A. (2000, December). After Cairo: Women's reproductive and sexual health, rights, and empowerment. *American Journal of Public Health, 90*(12), 1838–40.

Safa, H. I. (1996). Beijing, diversity and globalization: Challenges to the women's movement in Latin America and the Caribbean. *Organization, 3*(4), 563–570.

Shiva,V., & Shiva, M. (1995). Third World women denied right to development. *Impact, 30*(6), 19, 27.

APPENDIX: WRITTEN ASSIGNMENTS

Paper 1 (2–3 pages)

Marilee Karl's book, *Women and Empowerment,* focuses on two interrelated concepts that are key to women's social development: participation and empowerment. Your assignment is to use these concepts to analyze the barriers facing women in developing countries to improve their status and well-being. Specifically, I want you to apply one or both of these concepts to Mariama Ba's novel, *So Long a Story.* Although this is a work of fiction, it was written by a Senegalese woman to convey the conditions of life for women in her society, and we shall treat it as a sociocultural document.

Your paper should demonstrate that (1) you have read and understood Karl's discussion of the meaning and significance of participation and empowerment for women's development, and (2) that you are able to use these concepts (one or both) as analytic tools to examine the world of Senegalese women as presented in the novella. Remember, we are using Senegal as an example of the situation faced by women in many developing societies.

I expect a close reading of the novella so that you can give specific examples of situations that can be analyzed by the concepts of participation and/or empowerment. You will not have time to discuss the whole story; just focus on those characters, events, or circumstances that lend themselves to your analysis. For example, you might choose to focus on one character, or compare two or more characters, or look more broadly at the various ways in which Senegalese culture affects women's participation and empowerment.

The paper should be about three pages in length, double-spaced. Please proofread carefully and correct mistakes before you hand it in. Your style can be informal, but make sure it focuses on the assigned topic.

Paper 2 (2–3 pages)

This assignment looks at the various competing theories about development that we have discussed in class. These are modernization theory, dependency theory, and three theories that focus on women: Women In Development (WID), Women And Development (WAD), and Gender And Development (GAD).

The purpose of theory is to help make sense out of confusing events by identifying the important elements and providing a structure for understanding cause and effect. To test the usefulness and validity of these theories, this assignment will ask you to apply them to real-life situations and compare how they would explain what has happened and what needs to be done.

Listed below are five hypothetical scenarios based on actual conditions facing women in developing societies. You are to choose *one* of these scenarios and compare how it would be handled by either:

A. modernization theory and dependency theory, or

B. all three of the women's development theories (WID, WAD, GAD).

In addition to explaining how these different theories would come up with different interpretations of the scenario, you are also encouraged to evaluate the theories you are discussing. Remember, your choices of which theories to compare are limited; you are to compare modernization theory with dependency theory, or you are to compare WID, WAD, and GAD. Refer to the texts where appropriate.

There are three objectives for this assignment:

• to assess your understanding of the readings and class discussions about development theory.

• to give you practice in applying theoretical perspectives to real-life problems.

• to encourage you to develop and express your own views about the usefulness of development theory for understanding the problems of women's development.

Scenarios (choose one):

1. Maria Mathai, a 28-year-old Kenyan mother of four young daughters, lives and works on the family's five-acre farm 250 kilometers from Nairobi. Her husband, a sound recording specialist with an audiovisual company, is killed in an explosion while working on location in Ethiopia. After his death, Maria finds she has no rights to the farm since by tribal tradition only sons can inherit land. She must move to the city to find a means of supporting her family, leaving her children to stay with her mother.

2. Halima, 49, sells traditional Sudanese bread in a market in Khartoum. She persuades a local trader to lend her money, which she uses to set up five small cafés. These are so successful that she is able to repay the loan within one year, and take out another loan to build a bakery, so that she doesn't have to buy bread and cake from other producers. With her profits Halima can move into a more comfortable house with her mother and her adult son and his wife.

3. Five peasant women in Honduras are given small loans from a development bank to learn how to sew and to purchase sewing machines. At first, the women are pleased with their new skills and the opportunity to earn money, but after a year they find that few people are buying the clothes they made because cheaper, mass-produced, and imported goods are sold in the markets.

4. Villagers in West Bengal, India, are resisting plans to build a fertilizer factory, even though it would bring jobs and revenue to this poor community. Opposition stems from concerns over environmental destruction, particularly in light of the 1984 Bhopal incident, where several thousand people died from a gas leak in the Union

Carbide pesticide plant. Women are especially concerned, since they would have the burden of nursing the sick and bringing up crippled children if another disaster were to strike.

5. To promote enthusiasm and loyalty among their female work force, American companies in Malaysia organize beauty contests and other kinds of competitions. Prizes include free courses in grooming, overseas trips, and overnight hotel reservations for two in the capital city. At the same time, wages for these workers are not enough to keep their families out of poverty.

Paper 3 (2–3 pages)

Many of the writers we encountered in this course argue that although women around the world have many things in common, there are also significant differences in their lives due to nationality, race, culture, and class. It is this last factor, social class that is the subject for this paper.

You are to look through the assigned readings for evidence of the effect and significance of social class (i.e., defined loosely as economic level) on women's experience. What does social class do for—or to—women? Does being in a higher class generally free women from gender restrictions? Or does it impose different kinds of restrictions? Are upper-class women better off than their poorer counterparts, not just economically, but socially as well? How do gender and class interact? Are there any generalizations or patterns that you can see from the evidence in the readings? Do they apply to our own society?

Research project (10+ pages)

The purpose of this project is to encourage you to probe more deeply into a particular topic of your own choosing that is relevant to the general subject of women and international social development. In this way, you will develop greater familiarity with the literature in this area and become an "expert" on your topic. You will share what you have learned with other students through an informal oral presentation given at the end of the semester and hand in a written research report by the first day of finals week.

Here are the specifics:

*   The project can be carried out singly or in pairs. Presentations can be joint, but each student has to hand in her/his own research paper (with an explanation of how the work was divided).

*   Both the presentations and written reports should relate your research to what you have learned in class. That is, course readings and discussions should become part of your research material.

*   Internet sources are good (and easy), but they are not sufficient by themselves. I want you to go to the library and look at real books and journals. You must include at least two books and five journal articles in your bibliography. (If the journal is published online, that is acceptable.)

*   The research paper should be clearly organized, with different section headings to provide structure. You can write in the first person and offer your own views, but be careful to follow standard research format. Most important, be careful not to plagiarize. Basically, this means you must give credit to your sources so that you don't pass off someone else's words or ideas as your own. (See handout on the mechanics of writing a research paper.)

*   Your presentation should aim for effectiveness in communicating what you have learned to the class. Don't read your paper but instead talk to us—about why you took on this topic, what questions you started with, what you found out, what questions remain, and so forth. Think of ways to engage us in a discussion so you are not doing all the talking. This is meant to be an informal sharing of learning, and may help shape the direction and content of the final report.

Timetable:

*   By Week 4, you must choose a research topic. Hand in a brief, written description of what your research will focus on, why you have chosen that topic, possible sources, and so forth.

*   By Week 8, you must hand in an outline of your research paper. Identify the main sections of your paper, giving enough specifics to make it clear that you have really begun looking at the literature and planning what topics and issues the paper will focus on.

*   By Week 12, you must hand in a draft of your research paper. This draft will be reviewed and handed back with suggestions.

- By Week 15, you must hand in the final research paper.

Suggested topics:

The topic must focus on women and development in a non-Western society. Here are some suggestions:

- The impact of AIDS on women's development in sub-Saharan Africa.
- The role of social workers in promoting gender equality in ____ (choose a country or region)
- Women in the informal economy in Central America.
- Can single-parent families empower women?
- Controlling fertility as a means of promoting women's economic and social development.
- The role of women's health clinics in Muslim nations in improving women's status.
- The effect of education on gender equality in the Third World.
- Are arranged marriages a barrier to women's development?

Violence Against Women: A Global Perspective
SOW5109.0W62

COURSE DESCRIPTION

This course offers an introduction to the types of violence that affect women from a global perspective. Community, political, and economic issues that support violence against women will be discussed by country, ethnic group(s) within countries, and religious principles. Attention will be paid to marital customs, social traditions, and legal sanctions that support violence directed at women. Critical thinking will be used to develop macro strategies that take into account individual and society strengths while seeking economic and social justice. This course meets CSWE's Educational Policy and Accreditation Standards that encourage the integration of international content into all social work courses. This has been taught as a Web-based course and is open to graduate and undergraduate social-work and non–social-work students.

COURSE LEARNING OBJECTIVES

By the end of the course the student will:

1. understand the different types of violence that are directed at women;
2. understand how violence impairs the development of women economically, physically, and emotionally;
3. be able to discuss the stratification (positioning) of women from a global perspective;
4. be able to discuss the appropriateness of several theories that seek to explain factors that contribute and/or condone violence directed at women;
5. be able to discuss cultural mandates that foster the economic, psychological, and physical control of women;
6. develop community-based strategies aimed at dislodging physically, psychologically, and emotionally violent techniques that are used to reduce a woman's effectiveness and viability;
7. understand how individual perceptions of a situation determine survival and resistance; and
8. develop skills that will enable them to empower women experiencing violence.

REQUIRED TEXTS AND MATERIALS

Stout, K. D., & McPhail, B. (1998). *Confronting sexism and violence against women: A challenge for social work.* New York: Longman.

American Psychological Association. (2001). *Publication manual of the American Psychological Association* (5th ed.). Washington, DC: Author.

Reserved Readings. This material can be assessed either through checking out a binder that is housed at UCF's library, or online (an icon is positioned before each Reserved Reading section for each Module).

EVALUATION OF LEARNING AND GRADING

1. Paper (20 points). Write a 10-page paper that discusses your personal experiences with violence. The focus of this paper is gender-based violence. That is, violence directed toward you because of your gender. Included in this paper must be how you dealt with the experiences, who was (were) involved, and how has (have) this/ these experience(s) shaped your current views. Include what you believe we as a country can do to ensure others do not share your experiences. Also include a section that identifies how your topic affects your gender internationally. This paper must be sent to my e-mail account (bturnage@mail.ucf.edu). Make sure your name, class information, and so forth are listed on your cover page. Remember, the cover page does not count as a page of text, nor does the reference page(s).

2. Group Presentation and Paper (30 points). Write a 10-page paper that discusses a type of violence that is directed only at women. This paper must present the form of violence chosen from a global perspective. You must include information about the population (perpetrators and victims/survivors) involved, cultural and political mandates that support/allow the violent behaviors, theories that explain the violence, and strategies that are culturally and personally viable to alleviate the violence. This paper must be sent to my e-mail account (bturnage@mail.ucf.edu). Make sure all group members' names, class information, and so forth are listed on your cover page. Remember, the cover page does not count as a page of text, nor does the reference page(s).

    The presentation part of this assignment will be presented via WebCT. Five group accounts have been established for this course. After you have selected your group members, e-mail me (bturnage@mail.ucf.edu) your topic and group members' names. These names will be used to establish your group account. This account (discussion room) will be accessible only to group members and myself. Students will select a group of five members. As there are 27 students registered for this course, only two groups may have 6 members. Assigned presentation dates will coordinate with course schedule.

3. Response to Course Readings (8 points). This assignment is required for Modules 1, 2, 4, and 6. These entries are to present your thoughts and feelings related to course readings. Be sure to discuss the national and international effect of the issue presented. To receive full credit for items 4 and 6, responses must meet all of the assessment criteria.

4. Module Discussion Items (32 points). There is a discussion item associated with each module. These items (questions, statements) are to intensify and support your critical thinking skills. Each module will be accessible for one week. A time line will be provided. This time line will provide the module's name, discussion topic item, discussion title that is to be used to post to the correct discussion board, open and close dates, and the total number of points available for each item.

5. Response to Fellow Students (3 points). Modules 5, 9, and 13 require you to respond to another student's discussion item posting. All responses must be presented respectfully and possess a national and international focus. Refer to course protocols for information that outlines respectful student interactions. Students who ridicule, discount, insult, or shame another student in this form will lose 5 points from their total course points. This assignment is to spur thinking and not to prove who's right and who's wrong.

6. Demographics (2 points). This information was requested to be able to contact students when the server is down or not responding.

7. Remaining 5 points. There will be 4 to 5 options presented to satisfy (obtain) these points. To obtain these points, you must write a one-page opinion paper discussing your impression of the chosen event and submit proof of attendance (ticket stub, etc.). Include in your paper how this material affects women nationally and internationally, along with how your experience affected you.

    A. One option is *The Vagina Monologues*. This play will be presented February 15, 20, and 21, 2002. The play will start at 7 pm each night. Student ticket prices are $10.50 (with an ID). You can purchase tickets at the UCF Arena Box Office (407-823-6006) or Ticketmaster (located at UCF 407-839-3900, there is a handling charge when you use Ticketmaster). Proceeds will benefit local antiviolence organizations. To find out more about this play, check out www.angelfire.com/fl5/vdayucf. The UCF Bookstore carries the book.

    B. Option two is The Tunnel of Oppression (The Tunnel). The Tunnel is scheduled for April 17 and 18, 2002. A flyer adverting this free event will be e-mailed to all students. Several University of Central Florida entities are hosting this experience. The Tunnel will provide you an opportunity to view eight types of oppression through participant observation.

    C. Other options will be presented.

    A final course grade will be based on the total number of points accumulated from assignments.

COURSE OUTLINE

Below is the outline for the weekly assignments. Pay particular attention to the open and close dates for each module. Module 1 will close January 17, 2002, at 12 noon. Starting with Module 2, each module will open on a Wednesday at 12 AM and close the following Wednesday at 12 noon. After the module has closed, future access will be denied. Be sure to print this material and complete all parts of each module prior to its closing. All modules are worth two points.

Module 1

- Item: In America, What cultural methods are employed to keep women in submissive roles?
- Discussion title: America and Violence
- Item: E-mail demographics
- Discussion title: bturnage@mail.ucf.edu
- Item: View of readings
- Discussion title: Module 1 reading

Module 2

- Item: How does one normalize violence against women?
- Discussion title: Normalize Violence
- Item: View of readings
- Discussion title: Module 2 reading

Module 3

- Item: How does the use of the Third Way impact women's access to the major institutions in their society?
- Discussion title: Third Way

Module 4

- Item: Where do women get the message that they can fix their relationship/partner?
- Discussion title: Fix Relationship/Partner
- Item: View of readings
- Discussion title: Module 4 reading

Module 5

- Item: What commonalities can you identify among the three typologies?
- Discussion title: Commonalities
- Item: Respond to 1 posting

Module 6

- Item: How does the quality of males' lives differ from the quality of females' lives?
- Discussion title: Quality of Life
- Item: View of readings
- Discussion title: Module 6 reading

Module 7

- Item: Put yourself in the position of a woman who has experienced female circumcision. What would you like for us to know about you?
- Discussion title: FGM Woman
- Item: Put yourself into the position of a man who has just married a woman who has experienced female circumcision. What would you like for us to know about you?
- Discussion title: FGM Man

Module 8

- Item: What similarities do you see between the practice of footbinding and the U.S.'s current standards of beauty?
- Discussion title: Footbinding

Module 9

- Item: What price do you believe that women, who stand their ground, respect other women, and live productive lives, pay for their decision?
- Discussion title: Price
- Item: Respond to 1 posting

Module 10

- Item: Discuss a recent incident when you saw a woman being subjected to emotional violence (cursed at, browbeaten, called names, threatened, etc.). Include how you felt as you viewed this incident.
- Discussion title: Saw Emotional Violence

Module 11

- Item: What methods can you suggest to be used to improve women's economic position in two countries?
- Discussion title: Women's Economic Position

Module 12

- Item: Identify three beliefs and customs that perpetuate sexual violence against women. What can be done to erase/amend these practices?
- Discussion title: Sexual Violence

Module 13

- Item: How can we make the world safe for women and girls to fulfill their potential?
- Discussion title: Make World Safe
- Item: Respond to 1 posting

Module 14

- Item: What actions have you participated in that have contributed to violence against women?
- Discussion title: Contributing to Violence

Module 15

- Item: How has your view of gendered-based violence changed?
- Discussion title: Current View

READING LIST BY MODULE

Unit 1: Overview of Violence Toward Women

Module 1: Types of Violence

- Stout & McPhail, chapter 1: Presenting the continuum: A brief overview, pp. 1–12.
- Hosken, F. P. (1994). Male violence against women: A growing global cancer. *WIN News*, *20*(3), 1–3. Retrieved June 9, 2004, from http://www.feminist.com/win.htm
- A global view of violence against women. (1996). *WIN News*, *22*(2), 1–2. Retrieved June 9, 2004, from http://www.feminist.com/win.htm
- Heise, L. (1995/1996). The global war against women. *Annual Editions: Sociology*, *24*, 147–149.
- Abuse by men "not considered a crime" in many countries. (1999). *WIN News*, *25*(4), 1–2. Retrieved December 3, 2001, from http://www.feminist.com/win.htm
- Heise, L. (1993). Violence against women. *World Health*, *46*(1), 1–2.

Module 2: Global Status of Women

- Stout & McPhail, chapter 2: Women's institutional status, pp. 13–43.
- Cartwright, S. (1998). Bridging national policies and international commitments: The question of the status of women. *UN Chronicle, 35*(1), 1–3.
- Layng, A. (1990/1991). What keeps women "in their place?" *Annual Editions: Anthropology,* 148–151.
- Swanson, L. (2000). Task force recommends screening females for abuse beginning at age 12. *Canadian Medical Association Journal, 163*(11), 1–2. Retrieved December 3, 2001, from http://www.cmaj.ca/cgi/re-print/163/11/1492

Module 3: Women & Social Policies

- McRobbie, A. (2000). Feminism and the Third Way. *Feminist Review, 64,* 1–13.
- Edwards, M. L. (1991). Toward a Third Way: Women's politics and welfare policies in Sweden. *Social Research, 58*(3), 1–18.
- Hargreaves, S. (2001). Rape as a war crime: Putting policy into practice. *Lancet, 57*(9258), 1–2.
- Kaplan, K. W. E. (2001, March 5). A verdict against rape: War crimes convictions. *U.S. News & World Report, 130*(9), 1.

Unit 2: Battering

Module 4: What Is Battering?

- Stout & McPhail, chapter 9: Women who are battered, pp. 211–250.
- Haniff, N. Z. (1998). Male violence against men and women in the Caribbean: The case of Jamaica. *Journal of Comparative Family Studies, 29*(2), 1–8. Retrieved June 13, 2004, from http://infotrac.galegroup.com/itw/infomark/916/303/76846593w3/purl=rc1_ITOF_0_A57
- Kahn, M. (2001). Suffering in silence: Domestic violence in Pakistan. *British Medical Journal, 322*(7283), 1–2. Retrieved June 13, 2004, from http://bmj.bmjjournals.com/cgi/content/full/322/7283/425
- Booth, L. (2000). As a child, I saw my mother's boyfriend regularly smash her face and body: Police intervention and attitudes toward domestic violence. *New Statesman, 129*(4512), 1–2.
- "Domestic violence in Sri Lanka: Police still reluctant to arrest men." (1999). *WIN News, 25*(4), 1. Retrieved June 13, 2004, from http://www.feminist.com/win.htm

Module 5: Batterers and Causes

- Fernandeze, M. (1997). Domestic violence by extended family members in India: Interplay of gender and generation. *Journal of Interpersonal Violence, 12*(3), 433–455.
- Ehrenreich, B. (1995, April 3). Battered welfare syndrome: Welfare reforms will cause many women to stay in abusive relationships. *Time, 145*(14), 1–2.
- National Research Council. (1999). The causes of violence against women: An overview. In J. D. Torr & K. L. Swisher (Eds.), *Violence against women* (pp. 78–85). San Diego, CA: Greenhaven Press.
- Berg, M. H. (1999, June 7). Child's play—or something more? *Newsweek, 133*(23), 1–2.
- Editorial. (1997, November 3). One in four American women has experienced domestic violence. *Women's Health Weekly,* pp. 1–3.

Unit 3: Women's Bodies

Module 6: Controlling Women's Bodies

- Stout & McPhail, chapter 6: Controlling women's bodies: Health and reproductive freedom, pp. 134–158
- Francome, C. (1980). Abortion policy in Britain and the United States. *Social Work, 25*(1), 5–9.
- Survey shows women want a say in their health care. (1997, September 1). *Women's Health Weekly,* pp. 1–4.

- Brimelow, P. (1999, October 18). Who has abortions. *Forbes, 164*(10), 1.
- Kirsch, J. D., & Cedeno, M. A. (1999). Informed consent for family planning for poor women in Chiapas, Mexico. *Lancet, 354*(9176), 419.
- Saving women's lives. (1999). *Population Reports, 27*(2), 1–5.
- Ewig, C. (1999.) The missing element. *Hemisphere: A magazine of the Americas, 9*(1), 1–5.

Module 7: Genital Mutilation

- Stout & McPhail, chapter 6: Controlling women's bodies: Health and reproductive freedom, pp. 147–149
- Jones, W. K. (1997). Female genital mutilation/female circumcision: Who is at risk in the U.S. *Public Health Reports, 112*(5), 368–377.
- Baleta, A. (2001). Women's groups in Kenya win small victory against female circumcision. *Lancet, 357*(9253), 371.
- Ford, N., & Frontiers, M. S. (2001). Tackling female genital cutting in Somalia [Electronic version]. *Lancet, 358*(9288), 1179.
- Bosch, X. (2001). Female genital mutilation in developed countries [Electronic version]. *Lancet, 358*(9288), 1177.
- Tanzania: Thousands to undergo FGM despite prohibition. (2001). *WIN News, 27*(4), 1–2. Retrieved June 13, 2004, from http://www.feminist.com/win.htm
- Hadis, E. (2001). Austria: Discussing FGM: Days for African men—July 26–28, 2001. *WIN News, 27*(4), 1–3. Retrieved June 13, 2004, from http://www.feminist.com/win.htm
- German Bundestag: Major inquiry—female genital mutilation. (2001). *WIN News, 27*(4), 1–2. Retrieved June 13, 2004, from http://www.feminist.com/win.htm
- International Colloquium: Female genital mutilation in Africa and France—Paris, June 14, 2001. (2001). *WIN News, 27*(4), 1–3. Retrieved June 13, 2004, from http://www.feminist.com/win.htm

Module 8: Footbinding and Religion

- Broadwin, J. (1997). Walking contradictions: Chinese women unbound at the turn of the century. *Journal of Historical Sociology, 10*(4), 1–23.
- Gates, H. (2001). Footloose in Fijian: Economic correlates of footbinding. *Society for Comparative Study of Society and History 43*(1), 130–148.
- Griswold, E. (2001, February 26). Honor killings vs. Islam: Faith of her fathers. *The New Republic 224*(9), 1–3.

Unit 4: Psychological, Emotional, and Economic Violence

Module 9: Psychological Violence

- Stout & McPhail, chapter 3: Psychological wounds, pp. 44–78.
- Schumacher, J. A., Smith Slep, A. M., & Heyman, R. E. (2000). Risk factors for male-to female partner psychological abuse. *Aggression and Violent Behavior, 6*(2-3), 255–268.
- Marshall, L. L. (1996). Psychological abuse of women: Six distinct clusters. *Journal of Family Violence, 11*(4), 379–409.

Module 10: Emotional Violence

- Stout & McPhail, chapter 4: Gendered communication, pp. 79–100.
- O'Hagan, K. P. (1995). Emotional and psychological abuse: Problems of definition. *Child Abuse & Neglect, 19*(4), 449–461.
- O'Hearn, F. E., & Davis, K. E. (1997). Women's experience of giving and receiving emotional abuse: An attachment perspective. *Journal of Interpersonal Violence, 12*(3), 375–391.
- Hamamrman, S., & Bernet, W. (2000). Researchers offer an operational definition of emotional abuse. *Boston University Child & Adolescent Behavior Letter, 16*(12), 1–3.

Module 11: Economic Violence

- Stout & McPhail, chapter 5: Economic assault on women, pp. 101–133.
- Cooper, B. M. (1995). Women's worth and wedding gift exchange in Maradi, Niger, 1907–1989: Wealth in people, wealth in things. *The Journal of African History*, *36*(1), 121–140.
- The unwelcome wedding guest. (2000). *The Wilson Quarterly*, *24*(1), 96–97.
- Women and the globalization of the world economy. (1997). *WIN News*, *23*(4), 1–3. Retrieved June 13, 2004, from http://www.feminist.com/win.htm
- Japan: Status of women and work. (1996). *WIN News*, *22*(1), 1–2. Retrieved June 13, 2004, from http://www.feminist.com/win.htm
- Dinerman, M. (2001). Counting, costs, and the value of caring work. *Affilia*, *16*(2), 133–137.
- Koretz, G. (2001, May 7). She's a woman, offer her less: A game sheds light on the pay gap. *Business Week*, (3731), 1.

Unit 5: Physical Acts of Violence

Module 12: Rape and Burning

- Stout & McPhail, chapter 8: Sexual harassment: Assaults on women at work and at school, pp. 184–210.
- Bogert, C., & Dufka, C. (2001). Sexual violence in Sierra Leone. *Lancet*, *357*(9252), 304.
- Baby gang raped. (2001). *Maclean's*, *114*(48), 304.
- Baleta, A. (2001). Alleged rape of 9-month-old baby shocks South Africa. *Lancet*, *358*(9294), 1707.
- Editorial. (1998, January 17). Acid horrors: Bangladesh. *The Economist 346*(8051), 1–2.
- Bangladesh: More acid attacks on women. (1999). *WIN News*, *25*(4), 1–2. Retrieved June 13, 2004, from http://www.feminist.com/win.htm
- Pakistan: Four women burned every day by husbands. (2000). *WIN News*, *26*(2), 1. Retrieved June 13, 2004, from http://www.feminist.com/win.htm

Module 13: Sexual Assaults and Murder

- Stout & McPhail, chapter 10: Sexual assault, pp. 251–287.
- Dussich, J. P. J. (2001). Decisions not to report sexual assault: A comparative study among women living in Japan who are Japanese, Korean, Chinese, and English-speaking. *International Journal of Offender Therapy and Comparative Criminology*, *45*(3), 278–301.
- Jordan, J. (1996). Where is the sisterhood? Gender genocide against females. *The Progressive*, *60*(6), 20–21.
- Violence against women in the military. (2001). *USA Today Magazine*, *130*(2675), 1–2.
- Hegde, R. S. (1999). Marking bodies, reproducing violence: A feminist reading of female infanticide in South India. *Violence Against Women*, *5*(5), 1–14.
- Turkey: Honor killings exposed as more families move to cities. (2001). *WIN News*, *27*(4), 1–2. Retrieved June 13, 2004, from http://www.feminist.com/win.htm
- Prusher, I. R. (2000, August 10). One woman tackles "honor" crimes in Jordan. *Christian Science Monitor*, pp. 1–3.

Unit 6: What Can Be Done?

Module 14: Social Workers and Governmental Response

- Stout & McPhail, chapter 12: Personal and professional implications: A conversation with social workers, pp. 312–328.
- Ending violence against women. (2000). *WIN News*, *26*(2), 1–4. Retrieved June 13, 2004, from http://www.feminist.com/win.htm

- Country reports on human rights practices for 1993. (1994). *WIN News*, *20*(2), 1–20. Retrieved June 13, 2004, from http://www.feminist.com/win.htm

- Shanks, L., Ford, N., Schull, M., & Jong, K. D. (2001). Responding to rape. *Lancet*, *357*(9252), 304.

- Japan: Proposals to eradicate violence against women. (1999). *WIN News*, *25*(4), 1. Retrieved June 13, 2004, from http://www.feminist.com/win.htm

- Thailand: Towards a gender violence-free society. (1999). *WIN News*, *25*(94), 1–2. Retrieved June 13, 2004, from http://www.feminist.com/win.htm

- Bosch, X. (2001). Spain's government puts domestic violence protection plan as top priority. *Lancet*, *357*(9269), 1682.

Module 15: Public

- Durham, H., & Loff, B. (2001). Japan's "comfort women." *Lancet*, *357*(9252), 302.

- Corelli, R. (1993). An apology for degrading acts: Japan apologizes for sexual enslavement of women during the 1930s. *Maclean's*, *106*(33), 1–2.

- Ostrowski, C. J. (1996). The clothesline project: Women's stories of gender-related Violence. *Women and Language*, *19*(1), 1–7. Retrieved June 13, 2004, from http://bess.fcla.edu

- Domestic violence in Cambodia: A study of health care providers perceptions and response. (2000). *WIN News*, *26*(1), 1–2. Retrieved June 13, 2004, from http://www.feminist.com/win.htm

EXAMPLE MODULE

There are four separate areas (screens) in each module. For example, the appearance of each centered Module Two below represents a separate area within the module. For each module, the first area outlines the layout of the module. Area two provides the module's learning objectives and a brief introduction. Area three contains each module's Assignments, and area four provides the assessment tools, along with the point allocation. Starting with Module Four, weekly points were allocated based on posting to the correct board and clarity of posting.

Module Two: Global Status of Women

Table of Contents

- Module 2: Global Status of Women
- Introduction
- Assignments
- Assessment

Module Two: Global Status of Women

Learner Objectives:

- What you will learn in this module? You will:

    a. become familiar with the concept of institutional status

    b. become familiar with women's structural position

    c. be exposed to strategies that can be used to advocate for gender equality

Introduction to Module:

Women throughout the world continue to experience human rights violations. These violations against women surround their institutional status throughout the world and in their home countries. Stout and McPhail (1998, p. 6) define institutional status as "the status of women within major systems: political, economic, [education, social], religions, and family systems." Although each can be viewed as a separate institutional system, they can also be viewed as overlapping barriers that govern a women's life.

Understandably, and as a direct result of their institutional status, women face different life chances (Cartwright, 1998). The term life chances refers to the opportunities that are afforded an individual. These opportunities can be educational, social, economic, physical/mental health, and/or sexual. When women are stripped of the opportunities required to fully develop their potential, their gifts to our global communities are blocked.

This week's readings define and discuss the concept of institutional status and the many ways women have been subjected to human rights violations.

References:

Cartwright, S. (1998). Bridging national policies and international commitments: The question of the status of women. *UN Chronicle, 35*(1), 1–3.

Stout, K. D., & McPhail, B. (1998). *Confronting sexism and violence against women: A challenge for social work.* New York: Longman.

Module Two: Global Status of Women

Assignments:

- Read this week's material:

    - Stout, & McPhail, chapter 2, pp. 13–43
    - Cartwright, S. (1998). Bridging national policies and international commitments: The question of the status of women. *UN Chronicle, 35*(1), 1–3.
    - Layng, A. (1990/1991). What keeps women "in their place?" *Annual Editions: Anthropology*, 148–151.
    - Swanson, L. (2000). Task force recommends screening females for abuse beginning at age 12. *Canadian Medical Association Journal, 163*(11), 1–2. Retrieved December 3, 2001, from http://www.cmaj.ca/cgi/reprint/163/11/1492

- Post Journal Entry

    - Your response/view to this week's readings.

- Post response to question:

    - How does one normalize violence against women?

Module Two: Global Status of Women

Assessment:

- Participants were to:

    - Read this week's material
    - Post journal entry—Response/view of this week's readings.
    - Post response to "How does one normalize violence against women?"

Task	0	1	2
Journal entry	Did not post	Posted to wrong discussion board	Correct Post
Response to question	Did not post	Posted to wrong discussion broad	Correct Post

SELECTED BIBLIOGRAPHY

Abramson, J. (Ed.). (1996). *Postmortem: The O. J. Simpson case: Justice confronts race, domestic violence, lawyers, money, and the media.* New York: Basic Books.

Adams, C. J., & Fortune, M. N. (Eds.). (1995). *Violence against women and children: A Christian theological sourcebook.* New York: Continuum.

Aguilar-San Juan, L. (Ed.). (1994). *The state of Asian America: Activism and resistance in the 1990s.* Boston, MA: South End Press.

American Nurses Association. (1998). *Culturally competent assessment for family violence.* Washington, DC: American Nurses Publication.

Arat, Z. F. (1994). Kemalism and Turkish women. *Women & Politics, 14*(4), 57.

Arthur, L. B. (Ed.). (1999). *Religion, dress, and the body.* New York: Oxford.

Averill, A. S. (1997). *Older battered women's project microform: Final report.* Montpelier, VT: Vermont Network Against Domestic Violence and Sexual Assault.

Barnett, O. W., Miller-Perrin, C. L., & Perrin, R. D. (1997). *Family violence across the lifespan: An introduction.* Thousand Oaks, CA: Sage.

Bell, L. S. (1994). For better, for worse: Women and the world market in rural China. *Modern China, 20*(2), 180.

Bellesiles, M. A. (1999). *Lethal imagination: Violence and brutality in American history.* New York: New York University Press.

Berry, D. B. (1998). *The domestic violence sourcebook: Everything you need to know.* Los Angeles: Lowell House.

Blake, C. F. (1994). Foot-binding in neo-Confucian China and the appropriation of female labor. *Signs, 19*(3), 676–699.

Biddulph, S., & Cook, S. (1999). Kidnapping and selling women and children: The state's construction and response. *Violence Against Women, 5*(12), 1437–1450.

Bosch, X. (2000). Report reveals extent of domestic violence in Spain. *Lancet, 355*(9203), 20.

Bowker, L. H. (Ed.). (1998). *Masculinities and violence.* Thousand Oaks, CA: Sage.

Brandwein, R. A. (Ed.). (1999). *Battered women, children, and welfare reform: The ties that bind.* Thousand Oaks, CA: Sage.

Bridgeman, J., & Millns, S. (Eds.) (1995). *Law and body politics: Regulating the female body.* Brookfield, VT: Dartmouth.

Burstyn, L. (1995). Female circumcision comes to America. *The Atlantic Monthly, 276*(4), 28.

Busch, N. B., & Valentine, D. (2000). Empowerment practice: A focus on battered women. *Affilia, 15*(1), 82–95.

Buzawa, E. S., & Buzawa, C. G. (Eds.). (1993). *The impact of arrest on domestic assault.* Newbury Park, CA: Sage.

Buzawa, E. S., & Buzawa, C. G. (Eds.). (1996). *Do arrests and restraining orders work?* Thousand Oaks, CA: Sage.

Byatt, A. S. (1996). *Babel tower.* New York: Random House.

Clinton, H. R. (1996). Women's rights are human rights: Address delivered at the Fourth UN Conference on Women, Beijing 1995 (transcript). *Women's Studies Quarterly, 24*(1-2), 98.

Coale, A. J., & Banister, J. (1994). Five decades of missing females in China. *Demography, 31*(3), 459.

Cohen, A. (2000). Excess female mortality in India: The case of Himachal Pradesh. *American Journal of Public Health, 90,* 1369–1371.

Congress, E. P. (Ed.). (1997). *Multicultural perspectives in working with families.* New York: Springer Publishers.

Cooks, P. W. (1997). *Abused men: The hidden side of domestic violence.* Westport, CO: Praeger.

Cooks, S., & Davies, S. (Eds.). (1999). *Harsh punishment: International experiences of women's imprisonment.* Boston: Northeastern University Press.

Cox, E. S. (1992). Central American and Caribbean conference on violence against women: Encuentro Centroamericano y Caribe sobre Violencia contra la Mujer. *Off our backs, 22*(3), 10-25.

Cronk, L. (1993). Parental favoritism toward daughters. Kenyan Mukogodo people. *American Scientist, 81*(3), 272-284.

Cummings, S. R. (1998). Consequences of foot binding among older women in Beijing, China. *The Journal of the American Medical Association, 279*(2), 96E.

Curran, C. E., Farley, M. A., & McCormick, R. A. (Eds.). (1996). *Feminist ethics and the Catholic moral tradition.* New York: Paulist Press.

Curti, L. (1998). *Female stories, female bodies: Narrative, identity, and representation.* New York: New York University Press.

Daire, V. (2000). The case against mandatory reporting of domestic violence injuries. *Florida Bar Journal, 74*(1), 78-89.

Daniels, C., & Kennedy, M. V. (1999). *Over the threshold: Intimate violence in early America.* New York: Routledge.

Dare, S. (1995, April 23). A passage to Hawaii: The picture brides' tale. Asian women who were mail-order brides between 1908 to 1924 discuss their experiences, which are the subject of forthcoming film, *Picture Bride* by director Kayo Hatto. *The New York Times,* pp. H13(N), H13(L).

Decker, D. J. (1999). *Stopping the violence: A group model to change men's abusive attitudes and behaviors.* New York: Haworth Maltreatment and Trauma Press.

DeKeseredy, W. S., & Schwartz, M. D. (1998). *Woman abuse on campus: Results from the Canadian national survey.* Thousand Oaks, CA: Sage.

Donovan, J. M. (1991). Infanticide and the juries in France, 1825-1913. *Journal of Family History, 16*(2), 157-179.

Dorkenoo, E. (1994). African women speak out on FGM. *National NOW Times, 26*(4), 11.

Dube, R., & Bhatnagar, R. (1999). Women without choice: Female infanticide and the rhetoric of overpopulation in postcolonial India. *Women's Studies Quarterly, 27*(1/2), 73-88.

Dugger, C. W. (1996, September 11). Woman betrayed by loved ones mourns a double loss. Togo native Mariam Razak was betrayed by both her family and her fiancé when they neglected to warn her of their decision to subject her to genital mutilation. *The New York Times,* pp. A9(N), B7(L).

Durham, H., & Loff, B. (2001). Japan's "comfort women." *Lancet, 357*(9252), 302.

Editorial. (1992). 100 million women missing. Violence against women and female infanticide. *WIN News, 18*(1), 80.

Editorial. (1993). Female infanticide growing in India. *WIN News, 19*(4), 61.

Editorial. (1994, February 19). Born female—and fettered. Department of State focuses human rights report on female genital mutilation. *The New York Times,* pp. 12(N), 18(L).

Editorial. (1994, August 22). Too much yang, not enough yin. In both China and India, female infanticide and prejudice against girls still accepted. *The New York Times,* pp. A10(N), A12(L).

Editorial. (1998a). Globalization: Displacement, commodification and modern-day slavery of women. *WIN News, 24*(3), 51.

Editorial. (1998b). India: Child marriage especially popular in Rajasthan. *WIN News, 24*(3), 54.

Editorial. (1998b). Poland: The Catholic family life—male violence rules. *WIN News, 24*(3), 32.

Ellison, C. G. (1999). Are there religious variations in domestic violence? *Journal of Family Issues, 20*(1), 87-99.

Ellsberg, M., Heise, L., Pena, R., Agurto, S., & Winkvist, A. (2001). Researching violence against women, methodological considerations from three Nicaraguan studies. *Studies in Family Planning, 32,* 1–16.

Eriksson, M. K. (2000). *Reproductive freedom: In the context of international human rights and humanitarian law.* Boston: The Hague.

Fall, K. A. (1999). *Alternatives to domestic violence: A homework manual for battering intervention groups.* Philadelphia, PA: Accelerated Development.

Feather, N. T. (1996). Domestic violence, gender, and perceptions of justice. *Sex Roles, 35*(7/8), 507–519.

Feder, L. (Ed.). (1999). *Women and domestic violence: An interdisciplinary approach.* New York: Haworth Press.

Fenster, T. (Ed.). (1999). *Gender, planning, and human rights.* New York: Routledge.

Foote, J. (1991, May 27). From Russia—with love? Mail-order brides for lonely British bachelors. *Newsweek,* pp. 38–40.

Francus, M. (1997, May). Monstrous mothers, monstrous societies: Infanticide and the rule of law in Restoration and eighteen-century England. *Eighteenth Century Life, 21*(2), 133–148.

French, S. G., Teays, W., & Purdy, L. M. (Eds.). (1998). *Violence against women: Philosophical perspectives.* Ithaca, NY: Cornell University Press.

Ginsburg, F. D., & Rapp, R. (Eds.). (1995). *Conceiving the new world order: The global politics of reproduction.* Berkeley: University of California Press.

Girshick, L. B. (1999). *No safe haven: Stories of women in prison.* Boston: Northeastern University Press.

Goodwin, J. (1997). Prisoners of biology: In Nepal, there's no abortion debate, just a life sentence. *Utne Reader, 79,* 66–74.

Gordon, J. S. (1998). *Helping survivors of domestic violence: The effectiveness of medical, mental health, and community services.* New York: Garland Publication.

Green, D. (1999). *Gender violence in Africa: African women's responses.* New York: St. Martin's Press.

Haj-Yahia, M. M. (1999). Wife abuse and its psychological consequences as revealed by the First Palestinian National Survey on Violence Against Women. *Journal of Family Psychology, 13*(4), 642–653.

Hargreaves, S. (2001). Rape as a war crime: Putting policy into practice. *Lancet, 357*(9258), 737.

Hall, H. V. (Ed.). (1999). *Lethal violence: A sourcebook on fatal domestic, acquaintance, and stranger violence.* Boca Raton, FL: CRC Press.

Hall, K., & Bucholtz, M. (Eds.). (1995). *Gender articulated: Language and the socially constructed self.* New York: Routledge.

Hamos, J. E. (1980). *State domestic violence laws and how to pass them: A manual for lobbyists.* Rockville, MD: National Clearinghouse on Domestic Violence.

Hansen, K. V., & Garey, A. I. (Eds.). (1998). *Families in the US: Kinship and domestic politics.* Philadelphia, PA: Temple University Press.

Harrowitz, N. A., & Hyams, B. (Eds.). (1995). *Jews and gender: Responses to Otto Weininger.* Philadelphia, PA: Temple University Press.

Harway, M., & O'Neil, J. M. (Eds.). (1999). *What causes men's violence against women?* Thousand Oaks, CA: Sage.

Henshall Momsen, J., & Kinnaird, V. (Eds.). (1993). *Different places, different voices: Gender and development in Africa, Asia, and Latin America.* New York: Routledge.

Hijab, N. (1988). *Womanpower: The Arab debate on women at work.* Cambridge, England: Cambridge University Press.

Hong, F. (1997). *Footbinding, feminism, and freedom: The liberation of women's bodies in modern China.* Portland, OR: F. Cass.

Horn, P. (1992, December). Beating back the revolution: Domestic violence's economic toll on women. *Dollars & Sense*, 12.

Hosken, F. B. (1994). The facts about FGM in Egypt—an overview. Female genital and sexual mutilations. *WIN News*, 20 (4), 30. Retrieved June 13, 2004, from http:/bess.fcla.edu

Hoyle, C. (1998). *Negotiating domestic violence: Police, criminal justice, and victims*. New York: Oxford University Press.

Jennings, P. J., & Swiss, S. (2001). Health and human rights: Women and sexual violence. *Lancet, 351*, 302–304.

Kadioglu, A. (1994). Women's subordination in Turkey: Is Islam really the villain? *The Middle East Journal, 48*. (Available at http:/bess.fcla.edu)

Kashani, J. H., & Allan, W. D. (1998). *The impact of family violence on children and adolescents*. Thousand Oaks, CA: Sage.

Kim, E. H., & Choi, C. (Eds.). (1998). *Dangerous women: Gender and Korean nationalism*. New York: Routledge.

Kord, S. (1993). Women as children, women as childkillers: Poetic images of infanticide in eighteenth-century Germany. *Eighteenth-Century Studies, 26*(3), 449–467.

Kramer, E. J., Ivey, S. L., & Ying, Y. W. (Eds.). (1999). *Immigrant women's health: Problems and solutions*. San Francisco, CA: Jossey-Bass.

Lee, L. C., & Zane, N. W. S. (Eds.). (1998). *Handbook of Asian American psychology*. Thousand Oaks, CA: Sage.

Leventhal, B., & Lundy, S. E. (Eds.). (1999). *Same-sex domestic violence: Strategies for change*. Thousand Oaks, CA: Sage.

Levi, L., & Roses, L. E. (1993). La mano vuelta. Letter from Lillian Levi on being a woman in Nicaragua. *The Women's Review of Books, 10*(10-11), 15–23.

Lobel, K. (Ed.). (1986). *Naming the violence: Speaking out about lesbian battering*. Seattle, WA: Seal Press.

Locke, L. M. (1999). Attitudes toward domestic violence: Race and gender issues. *Sex Roles, 40*(3-4), 227–245.

Loeb Adler, L., & Denmark, F. L. (Eds.). (1995). *Violence and the prevention of violence*. Westport, CO: Praeger.

Madanes, C., Keim, J. P., & Smelser, D. (1995). *The violence of men: New techniques for working with abusive families: A therapy of social action*. San Francisco, CA: Jossey-Bass.

Maschke, K. J. (Ed.). (1997). *The legal response to violence against women*. New York: Garland Publishers.

Mayer, T. (Ed.). (1994). *Women and the Israeli occupation: The politics of change*. New York: Routledge.

McClenne, J., & Gunther, J. (Eds.). (1999). *A professional's guide to understanding gay and lesbian domestic violence: Understanding practice interventions*. Lewiston, NY: E. Mellen.

McCue, M. (1994). *No punching Judy: Curriculum for the prevention of domestic violence*. Huntington, NY: The Bureau for At-Risk Youth.

McGillivray, A., & Comaskey, B. (1999). *Black eyes all of the time: Intimate violence, aboriginal women, and the justice system*. Toronto, Canada: University of Toronto Press.

Meer, K. D., Bergman, R., & Kusner, J. S. (1993). Socio-cultural determinants of child mortality in southern Peru: Including some methodological considerations. *Social Science & Medicine, 36*(3), 317–335.

National Institute of Justice. (1996). *Domestic violence, stalking, and antistalking legislation: An annual report to Congress under the Violence Against Women Act*. Washington, DC: U.S. Department of Justice.

Nerenberg, L. (1997). *Final report to the Administration on Aging for restructuring aging and domestic violence services for elderly battered women microform*. San Francisco, CA: Goldman Institute on Aging.

Peled, E. (1999). Barriers to children's domestic violence counseling: A qualitative study. *Families in Society, 80*(6), 578–585.

Pradelles de Latour, C. H. (1994). Marriage payments, debt and fatherhood among the Bangoua: A Lacanian analysis of a kinship system. *Africa, 64*(1), 21–29.

Preboth, M. (2000). Routine screening for domestic violence. *American Family Physician, 61*(1), 242–248.

Pryke, J., & Thomas, M. (1998). *Domestic violence and social work.* Aldershot, England: Ashgate.

Ramirez, R. L. (1999). *What it means to be a man: Reflections on Puerto Rican masculinity.* New Brunswick, NJ: Rutgers University Press.

Rao, V. (1993). The rising price of husbands: A hedonic analysis of dowry increases in rural India. *Journal of Political Economy, 101*(4), 666–676.

Renteln, A. D. (1992). Sex selection and reproductive freedom. *Women's Studies International Forum, 15*(3), 405–413.

Salber, P. R., & Taliaferro, E. (1995). *The physician's guide to domestic violence: How to ask the right questions and recognize abuse another way to save a life.* Volcano, CA: Volcano Press.

Sales, R. (1997). *Women divided: Gender, religion, and politics in Northern Ireland.* New York: Routledge.

Schlege, A., & Eloul, R. (1988). Marriage transactions: Labor, property, status. *American Anthropologist, 90*(2), 291–298.

Seager, J. (1997). *The state of women in the world atlas.* New York: Penguin.

Shepard, M. F., & Pence, E. L. (1999). *Coordinating community responses to domestic violence: Lessons from Duluth and beyond.* Thousand Oaks, CA: Sage.

Sipe, B., & Hall, E. J. (1996). *I am not your victim: Anatomy of domestic violence.* Thousand Oaks, CA: Sage.

Smith, F. (1998). *American body politics: Race, gender, and black literary renaissance.* Athens, GA: University of Georgia Press.

Spatz Widom, C. (1992). *The cycle of violence.* Washington, DC: National Institute of Justice.

Spaulding, J. (1992). The value of virginity on Echo Island, 1860–1866. *International Journal of African Historical Studies, 25*(1), 67–98.

Spender, D. (1998). *Man-made language.* New York: New York University Press.

Spilka, M. (1997). *Eight lessons in love: A domestic violence reader.* Columbia: University of Missouri Press.

Tambiah, S. J. (1989). Bridewealth and dowry revisited: The position of women in sub-Saharan Africa and North India. *Current Anthropology, 30*(4), 413–420.

Thobaben, R. G., Schlagheck, D. M., & Funderburk, C. (1991). *Issues in American political life: Money, violence, and biology.* Englewood Cliffs, NJ: Prentice Hall.

Toubia, N. (1993). *Female genital mutilation: A call for global action.* New York: Women, Ink.

Van Soest, D. (1997). *The global crisis of violence: Common problems, universal causes, shared solutions.* Washington, DC: NASW Press.

Van Soest, D., & Crosby, J. (1997). *Challenges of violence worldwide: A curriculum module.* Washington, DC: NASW Press.

Walder, R. (1995). Why the problem (female genital mutilation) continues in Britain. *British Medical Journal, 310*(6994), 1593–1598.

Wallace, B. C. (1996). Adult children of dysfunctional families: Prevention, intervention, and treatment for community mental health promotion. Westport, CO: Praeger.

Websdale, N. (1999). *Understanding domestic homicide.* Boston: Northeastern University Press.

Weitz, R. (Ed.). (1998). *The politics of women's bodies: Sexuality, appearance, and behavior.* New York: Oxford University Press.

White, M. (1995). Protecting the human rights of women. *Human Rights, 22*(4), 5.

WHO. (2001). *WHO multi-country study on women's health and domestic violence progress report.* Geneva: WHO/WHD.

Wilson, S. (1988). Infanticide, child abandonment, and female honour in nineteenth-century Corsica. *Comparative Studies in Society and History, 3*(4), 762–777.

Wolkenstein, B. H., & Sterman, L. (1998). Unmet needs of older women in a clinic population: The discovery of possible long-term sequelae of domestic violence. *Professional Psychology, 29*(4), 341–347.

Women, Law, & Development International. (1998). *Gender violence: The hidden war crime.* Washington, DC: Women, Law, & Development International.

Woodward, K. (Ed.). (1999). *Figuring age: Women, bodies, generations.* Bloomington, ID: Indiana University Press.

Youngs, G. (Ed.). (2000). *Political economy, power and the body: Global perspectives.* New York: St. Martin's Press.

Civil Society, NGOs, and Social Work
SW 652

COURSE DESCRIPTION

This MSW course will address the historical, philosophical, and theoretical underpinnings of philanthropy, charity, civil society, and nongovernmental organizations. Through 1960, social services were delivered almost exclusively by public and voluntary organizations. However, inclusion of nongovernmental organizations (NGOs) in the service delivery system raises both positive and negative global concerns. Issues will be discussed related to the debate about the future of the public sector, NGOs, and Civil Society Organizations (CSO) in terms of service delivery and how these sectors fit with the social work profession.

RATIONALE

The importance of understanding the public, private, and civil society sectors in social work, how these arenas are different, and how they work together is of critical importance to social workers entering the workforce with an MSW degree. Students in the international and community development and practice with families and children concentrations will be working with public, private, and civil society organizations. Therefore, competencies are needed for social workers to understand the dynamics of these service delivery systems.

COURSE OBJECTIVES AND EDUCATIONAL OUTCOMES

This MSW course will prepare students:

1. To understand the differences between and among for-profit, nonprofit, civil society, and public organizations in the United States and abroad.
2. To understand how the history, values, and principles of social work and social welfare fit with the history and intent of the nongovernmental organizations.
3. To develop a beginning understanding of the use of supervision in nongovernmental organizations.
4. To understand the concepts of nongovernmental organizations and civil society and their growth and importance today and into the future.
5. To explore local, regional, and global strategies with regard to service delivery systems.
6. To gain familiarity with the NGO program planning and management process.
7. To develop and systematically apply professional social work knowledge, values, and skills in working with NGOs, CSOs, and public organizations at local through international levels.
8. To develop, articulate, analyze, implement, and evaluate a practice paradigm in working with these organizations that emerges from a human rights and social justice perspective.
9. To apply, analyze, and evaluate the knowledge and skills of advanced social work practice with both public and private sectors both locally and globally.
10. To explore and understand the implications and consequences of inequality, justice, and oppression in serving vulnerable populations through NGOs, CSOs, and government organizations.

REQUIRED READING

Eade, D. (Ed.). (2000). *Development, NGOs, and civil society*. Great Britain: Oxfam Publications.

Smillie, I., & Hailey, J. (2001). *Managing for change: Leadership, strategy, and management in Asian NGOs*. London, England and Sterling, VA: Earthscan Publications Ltd.

RECOMMENDED READING

Campfens, H. (1997). *Community development around the world: Practice, theory, research, training.* Toronto, Canada: University of Toronto Press.

Midgley, J. (1995). *Social development: The developmental perspective in social welfare.* Thousands Oaks, CA: Sage.

Stoesz, D., Guzzetta, C., & Lusk, M. (1999). *International development.* Boston: Allyn & Bacon.

DESCRIPTION OF ASSIGNMENTS

1. **Midsemester Exam (30% of final grade)**

   In-class exam on first six classes. This exam will demonstrate students' understanding of concepts, theories, models, techniques, paradigms, and other related terms as discussed in the first six classes before the exam.

2. **Seminar Presentation (30% of final grade)**

   Plan and conduct a one-and-one-half-hour seminar session focusing on a nongovernmental organization in your area with reference to its institutional capabilities serving the population it is working with. The presentation should focus on the history, mission, vision, goals, objectives, modus operandi, organizational structure, leadership, and outlay of funds, plans, budget, supervision, and monitoring process of the selected NGO.

3. **Institutional Analysis Paper (30% of final grade)**

   Research paper using primary or secondary data that will demonstrate advanced application of field of practice knowledge and theory related to social service delivery systems from the perspective of nongovernmental organizations (not to exceed 18 pages, including appendices and references). Outline or summary of institutional analysis paper is to be briefly presented to colleagues in class (maximum one-half hour, including discussion) for the purpose of obtaining feedback for incorporation into the final draft of the paper before submission. This assignment will focus more on institutional capabilities of nongovernmental organizations in social service delivery. The paper will also focus on problems that are affecting vulnerable segments of the population and communities in developed countries like the United States and in developing countries across the world.

COURSE OUTLINE

Class 1. Introduction

Review of course syllabus and assignments; Nonprofit and philanthropy: history, mission, vision and values; Missionaries and development; History and philosophy of social welfare: from charity to development.

Readings

- Campfens, part 1: Introduction to the international study, pp. 3–10
- Stoesz, Guzzetta, & Lusk, chapter 5: Missionaries and development, pp. 85–101
- Midgley, introduction and chapter 1: A definition of social development, pp. 1–35.

Class 2. Understanding Social Service Delivery Systems

Nongovernmental organizations: Definitions and origins; What is a civil society organization? NGOs and development: The debate and its future; The Grameen Development Bank.

Readings

- Eade, Development, NGOs, and civil society: The debate and its future, pp. 15–43
- Stoesz, Guzzetta & Lusk, chapter 12: The Grameen Development Bank, pp. 209–222.

Class 3. Scaling Up NGO Impact on Development: Learning from Experience

Scaling up via cooperation with governments, operational expansion, lobbying and advocacy, supporting local initiatives; International relief and development practice.

Readings

- Eade, Scaling up NGO impact on development: Learning from experience, pp. 44–63
- Healy, chapter 8: International relief and development practice, pp. 170–192.

Class 4. Symbols and Systems: Elements of Organizational Culture

Organizational culture: Values and assumptions, mission, rituals and stories; Organization age and maturity, teams and team working, human resources development, gender policies.

Reading

- Smillie and Hailey, Symbols and symptoms: Elements of organizational culture, pp. 49–68.

Class 5. Leadership and Management

Leaders and leadership; Leadership: background, success, a development perspective; Founder leaders: Exemplars from international development field; Principles for leadership development; The leadership development process; Guideline for leadership maintenance and growth; Leaders and organizers.

Readings

- Smillie and Hailey, chapter 7: Leadership and the Thoroughly Modern Manager, pp. 133–158
- Bobo, Kendall, & Max, chapter 11: Organizing for social change, pp. 86–93.

Class 6. Corporate Governance for NGOs

The structural growth problem, the accountability problem, the evaluation problem, the economies of scale problems; Solutions; Help yourself by helping the poor; Development is business; NGOs: Ladles in the global soup kitchen?

Readings

- Eade, Corporate governance, pp. 80–90, Help yourself by helping the poor, pp. 64–74.

Class 7. Strengthening Civil Society Organizations

NGOs and the state; Political theory; Participatory action research; Civil society in comparative perspective.

Readings

- Eade. Let's get civil society straight: NGOs, the state, and political theory, pp. 124–141, Strengthening civil society, 175–189
- Salamon, et al., in Global civil society: Dimensions of the non-profit sector, pp. 1–40.

Class 8. Midsemester Exam

Class 9. NGOs, the Poor, Local Government and the State

A case study from Uganda: Responsibility for the health sector, NGO support for the health sector and decentralization and NGOs; The NGO approach, working with the poor, channeling food aid, food-for-work experience, letting government off the hook, getting job done; People's Bank People's Movement.

Readings

- Eade, NGOs and the state: A case study from Uganda, pp. 109–123
- Fuglesang & Chandler, Book: Participation as Process—Process as growth, pp. 31–86.

Class 10. Depoliticizing Development: Developmental Social Work

International social development and social work; Social work, social welfare and social and economic development; Uses and abuses of participation; Participation as process—process as growth.

Readings

- Hokenstad & Midgley, International social development and social work, pp. 74–91
- Estes, Social work, social welfare, and social and economic development, pp. 1–25
- Eade, Depoliticizing development: the uses and abuses of participation, pp. 142–155
- Fuglesang & Chandler, Book: Participation as Process—Process as growth, pp. 87–100.

(Student presentations on institutional analysis begins)

Class 11. NGOs: Learning for Change

The process for organizational learning; Consensual learning; Institutional learning; Formal learning process; The reality of learning

Reading

- Smillie and Hailey, chapter 4: Learning for change, pp. 69–90.

(Student presentations on institutional analysis)

Class 12. NGO Strategy: Fads and Fancies

Approaches: strategy, mission and catharsis; Influence on strategy development: strategy and ambition, donors and strategy development, strategy and the board of directors; The accidental NGOs; Governance, structures and participation

Reading

- Smillie and Hailey, chapter 5: Strategy: Fads and Fancies, pp. 91–132.

(Student presentations on institutional analysis)

Class 13. Dancing with the Prince

NGOs survival strategies in the Afghan conflict; Collaboration with south: Agent's aid or solidarity? Conflict and cooperation: Dynamics in development.

Readings

- Eade, Collaboration with south: agents of aid or solidarity, pp. 75–79, 91–108
- Mathbor, (1997). The importance of community participation in coastal zone management: A Bangladesh perspective, *Community Development Journal*, Oxford University Press, *32*(2), pp. 124–133.

(Student presentations on institutional analysis)

Class 14. A Dangerous Sea: Managing the External Environment

Poverty; Government: The political and regulatory environment; Working with government; Donors, consortia and NGO relationship: Birds of a feather? UNDP and Action Aid implementation of sustainable human development

Readings

- Smillie & Hailey, chapter 2: A dangerous sea: Managing the external environment, pp. 17–48
- Eade, Birds of feather? UNDP and Action Aid implementation of sustainable human development, pp. 156–174.

(Student presentations on institutional analysis)

Final paper due today

Class 15. Exam Schedule

BIBLIOGRAPHY

Alinsky, S. (1971). *Rules for radicals*. New York: Random House.

Barker, J. (1999). *Street-level democracy*. Toronto, Canada: Between the Lines.

Bobo, K., Kendall, J., S. Max. (1991). *Organizing for social change: A manual for activists in the 1990s*. Santa Ana, California: Seven Locks.

Beer, M., & Spector, B. (1984). *Managing human assets*. New York: Free Press.

Blackburn, J. (1998). *Who's voice? Participatory research and policy change*. London: IT Publications.

Brym, Robert J., and R. J. Sacouman, (Eds.). (1979). *Underdevelopment and social movements in Atlantic Canada*. Toronto, Canada: New Hogtown.

Campfens, H. (1997). *Community development around the world: Practice, theory, research, training*. Toronto, Canada: University of Toronto Press.

Caroroll, T. F. (1992). *Intermediary NGOs: The supporting link in grassroots development*. West Hartford, CT: Kumarian Press.

Carver, J. (1990). *Boards that make a difference*. San Francisco, CA: Jossey-Bass.

Chamber, R. (1997). *Whose reality counts: Putting the first last*. London: IT Publications.

Chandoke, N. (1995). *State and civil society: Explosions in political theory*. New Delhi, India: Sage.

Clark, J. (1991). *Democratizing Development: The role of voluntary organizations*. West Hartford, CT: Kumarian Press.

Cohen, J. M. (1999). *Administrative decentralization: Strategies for developing countries*. West Hartford, CT: Kumarian Press.

Drucker, P. (1992). *Managing the non-profit organization: Principles and practice*. New York: Harper Business.

Eade, D. (2000). *Development, NGOs, and civil society*. Great Britain: Oxfam Publications.

Estes, R. J. (1998). *Resources for social and economic development: A guide to the scholarly literature*. Philadelphia: University of Pennsylvania.

Fisher, J. (1998). *Non-governments, NGOs and the political development of the Third World*. West Hartford, CT: Kumarian Press.

Fisher, R., & Ury, W. (1983) *Getting to yes. Negotiating agreements without giving in*. New York: Penguin Books.

Freire, P. (1972). *Pedagogy of the oppressed*. Harmondsworth, England: Penguin Books

Fuglesang, A., & Chandler, D. (1993). *Participation as process process as growth*. Dhaka, Bangladesh: Grameen Trust.

Healy, L. M. (2001). *International social work: Professional action in an independent world*. New York: Oxford University Press.

Hokenstad, M. C., & Midgley, J. (1997). *Issues in international social work: Global challenges for a new century*. Washington, DC: NASW Press.

Hokenstad, M. C., Khinduka, S. K., & Midgley, J. (1992). *Profiles in international social work*. Washington, DC: NASW Press.

Holloway, R. (1998). *Supporting citizens' initiatives: Bangladesh NGOs and society*. London: IT Publications.

Horwitt, S. (1989). *Let them call me rebel. Saul Alinsky: His life and legacy*. New York: Alfred Knopf.

Hudson, M. (1995). *Managing without profit*. London: Penguin.

Kahn, Si. (1970). *How people get power: Organizing oppressed communities for action*. New York: McGraw-Hill.

Khan, M. H. (1998). *Climbing the development ladder with NGO support*. Karachi, India: Oxford University Press.

Korten, D. (1990). *Getting to the 21st century: Voluntary action and the global agenda*. West Hartford, CT: Kumarian Press.

Korten, D. (1995). *When corporations rule the world*. West Hartford, CT: Kumarian Press.

Krishna, A. (1996). *Reasons for hope: Instructive experience in rural development*. West Hartford, CT: Kumarian Press.

Mathbor, G. M. (1997). The importance of community participation in coastal zone management: A Bangladesh perspective. *Community Development Journal, 32* (2), 124–133.

Mathbor, G. M. (2003). Conflict and cooperation: Dynamics in development. *Canadian Journal of Development Studies, 24*(2), 204–207.

Mies, M., & Bennholdt-Thomsen, V. (1999). *The subsistence perspective: Beyond the globalized economy.* New York: Zed Books.

Midgley, J. (1995). *Social development: The developmental perspective in social welfare.* Thousands Oaks, CA: Sage.

Mondros, J. B., & Wilson, S. (1994). *Organizing for power and empowerment.* New York: Columbia University Press.

Ndegwa, S. N. (1996). *The two faces of civil society: NGO and politics in Africa.* West Hartford, CT: Kumarian Press.

Rahman, A. (1999). *Women and microcredit in rural Bangladesh.* Boulder, CO: Westview Press.

Ramanathan, S. R., & Link, R. J. (1999). *All our futures: Principles and resources for social work practice in a global era.* Belmont, CA: Brooks/Cole.

Rey, C., Duncan, N., Shefer, T & Niekerk, A. V. (1997). *Contemporary issues in human development.* New York: International Thompson Publishing.

Rubin, H., & Rubin, I. (1986). *Community organizing and development.* New York: Allyn and Bacon.

Salamon, L. M., Anheier, H. K., List, R., Toepler, S., & Sokolowski, S. W. (1999). *Global civil society: Dimensions of the nonprofit sector.* Baltimore, MD: Johns Hopkins Center for Civil Society Studies.

Smillie, I., & Hailey, J. (2001). *Managing for change: Leadership, strategy, and management in Asian NGOs.* London and Sterling, VA: Earthscan Publications Ltd.

Stoesz, D., Guzzetta, C., & Lusk, M. (1999). *International development.* Boston: Allyn & Bacon.

Swift, J. (1999). *Civil society in question.* Toronto, Canada: Between the Lines.

Tropman, J. E. (1997). *Successful community leadership: A skills guide for volunteers and professionals.* Washington, DC: NASW Press.

Twaine, D. (1983). *Creating change in social settings. Planned program development.* New York: Praeger.

Uphoff, N., & Esman, M. J. (1998). *Reasons for success: Learning from experiences in rural development.* West Hartford, CT: Kumarian Press.

White, S. (1992). *Arguing with the crocodile: Gender and class in Bangladesh.* Dhaka, Bangladesh: University Press.

Wolf, T. (1999). *Managing a non-profit organization in the 21st century.* New York: Simon & Schuster.

Yunus, M. (1999). *Banker to the poor: Micro-lending and the battle against world poverty.* New York: Public Affairs.

UNIVERSITY AT ALBANY
SCHOOL OF SOCIAL WELFARE | ALBANY, NY
WILLIAM ROTH AND KATHARINE BRIAR-LAWSON
OSCAR BEST, NANCY CLAIBORNE, SHIRLEY JONES, AND BLANCA RAMOS (COLLABORATING FACULTY)

Globalization and Sweatshops
SSW 705–SSW 499

In many respects, globalization is an old phenomenon. However, in the past few years globalization has burst upon our consciousness and consciences. Something new is afoot. The World Trade Organization, International Monetary Fund, World Bank, North America Free Trade Association, along with other treaties, signal that globalization has taken a new form and has new importance.

Sweatshops, which are substantially a women's and children's issue, challenge consumers, producers, activists, and others. This course will examine sweatshops, anti-sweatshop movements, the perspectives of sweatshop workers, and the political and economic consequences of sweatshops and anti-sweatshop social activism. Sweatshops are a focal point where globalization is apparent. They occur within the United States, within other countries, and along borders between countries. Connected to the rest of their local, national, and global environments, sweatshops are visible evidence of oppression and lack of social justice.

The difference between rich and poor within countries and between countries has never been greater. Human labor is one casualty, as revealed by sweatshops. The environment is polluted, defiled, and destroyed. Social policy crumbles as the need for it increases. Corporations merge, restructure, and reemerge with an increasingly global reach. English becomes the language of international culture and commerce. The earth becomes ever more homogenized. The globe shrinks with telecommunications, television, the Internet, automation.

Social policy is ever more privatized, and privatization is becoming more corporate. Globalization shreds the safety net in the United States and abroad. Social policy, labor, the poor, and the earth itself are in significant peril.

Globalization affects our work lives and our private lives. Social welfare and social work are changing rapidly in consonance with globalization. It is imperative that we learn more about the globalization occurring around us and affecting us in many diverse, concrete ways.

GOALS OF COURSE

Students will be expected to be able to think about or take action concerning numerous interrelated issues including the following:

- The connection of globalization to local social change.

- Economies and their strong relationship with our lives.

- The relationship between governments, organizations, and economic factors.

- The growing difference between rich and poor.

- Are sweatshops better than destitution and starvation? Ought people in our country make decisions for people in other countries? Are new forms of global governance required for a new era of globalization? What is the role of nongovernmental organizations?

- The influence of telecommunications on just-in-time inventories, information technology, and other new technologies.

- State intervention in globalization and, more generally, questions of politics and economics in a global era.

- The claims of labor unions, corporations, national and international treaties, and citizens on the globe.

- The nature of student interventions and anti-sweatshop work after graduation in relationship to globalization, environmental change, and technological change.

- The effects of globalization on policy and practice in our welfare state.

- The effects of globalization on professions and careers such as social work.

COURSE FORMAT

The course will be team-taught and frequently will have outside speakers. Class days will be devoted to formal class presentations by members of the faculty, with outside speakers. Students will be expected to complement the formal part of the class with study and writing with a faculty member of their choice. The formal class sessions will concern topics such as sweatshops, nongovernmental organizations (NGOs), trade unions, the examples of Africa and South America, changing technologies, wealth and poverty, politics and markets, communities and families, and will illuminate their importance to the comprehension of social welfare policy and practice. Team teaching will be integral to this course, as will be the sometimes different views of outside speakers. It is important that the student experience that civil discourse is possible with opposing views.

ASSIGNMENTS

I.   Paper 60 points

Students will write a paper proposing relevant frameworks, action strategies, and relevant research to address globalization and sweatshops. They may coauthor a paper with a faculty member or choose to undertake their own paper. Length of the paper will be no more than 15 pages unless part of a collaborative product with a faculty member. Parts of the paper may be presented at a forum on globalization and sweatshops.

II. Project 30 points

Students will undertake a project that can include special data gathering, service learning, and product development to advance educational or other initiatives. A description of the project may be presented at a forum on globalization.

III. Participating Class Roles 10 points

Students will be the developers of relevant frameworks, hypotheses, and proposed initiatives, and thus class participation is essential. Debate on essential topics will be encouraged. Students may present their projects at a globalization-and-sweatshops forum.

READINGS

Packet of book excerpts and articles.

WEB SITES

Relevant Web sites include the following:

*   http://www.earthwatch.unep.net
*   http://www.ezln.org/
*   http://www.globalexchange.org/
*   http://www.newschool.edu/cepa/papers/
*   http://www.wedo.org
*   http://www.hrweb.org
*   http://www.zmag.org/museum.htm
*   http://www.globalfundforwomen.org/
*   http://www.monde-diplomatique.fr/
*   http://www.hrw.org
*   http://www.corpwatch.org/
*   http://www.antislavery.org/
*   http://www.theeconomist.com
*   http://www.welfareinfo.org/
*   http://www.amnesty.org

- http://www.worldwatch.org/
- http://www.state.gov/
- http://www.savetherest.org/
- http://www.worldbank.org/poverty/
- http://www.globalfundforchildren.org/
- http://www.usfca.edu/law/globaljustice/

LECTURE SCHEDULE

Week 1

Globalization, Sweatshops, and Social Policy: An Introduction

- Historical nature of problem
- Economic employment, organizational and educational needs of workers
- Role of professions, unions, consumers, advocacy groups, NGOs
- Sweatshops, consumer movements, and the rise of the social work profession

Week 2

An introduction to markets

- Economic frameworks and social consequences of economic challenges
- Markets from below: worker, consumer, community, family, student perspective

Readings

- Roth, W. (2002). *The assault on social policy*. New York: Columbia University Press (Children, pp. 176–200)
- Bernstein, B., Shari, M., & Malkin, E. (2000, November 6). Global labor: A world of sweatshops. *Business Week*, pp. 84–85.
- Roth, B. (2000, July). *Globalization and social welfare*. Paper presented at the International Conference on Social Welfare, Montreal, Canada.
- Epping, R. C. (1992). *A beginner's guide to the world economy: Seventy-one basic economic concepts that will change the way you see the world*. New York: Vintage Books. (Glossary, pp. 155–199).

Week 3

Externalities, public goods, international trade, and the commodification of land and labor.

- Globalization: Why now?
- North–South divides? Why?
- Globalization and technology

Readings

- Lawson, H. A. (2001). Introducing globalization's challenges and opportunities and analyzing economic globalization and liberalization. In K. Briar-Lawson, H. A. Lawson, C. B. Hennon, & A. R. Jones (Eds.), *Family-centered policies and practices: international implications* (pp. 293–337). New York: Columbia University Press.
- Engardio, P., & Belton, C. (2000, November 6). Global capitalism. *Business Week*, pp. 72–76.

Week 4

The effects of globalization on children, women, and families.

- Role of anti-sweatshop movements
- Human costs and benefits

Readings

- Briar-Lawson, K. Lawson, H. A., & Hennon, C. B. (2001). Meaningful gender-equitable work and family well-being. In K. Briar-Lawson, H. A. Lawson, C. B. Hennon, & A. R. Jones (Eds.), *Family-centered policies and practices: international implications* (pp. 76–114). New York: Columbia University Press.
- Lawson, H. A. (2001). Globalization, flows of culture and people, and new-century frameworks for family-centered policies, practices, and development. In K. Briar-Lawson, H. A. Lawson, C. B. Hennon, & A. R. Jones (Eds.), *Family-centered policies and practices: international implications* (pp. 338–376). New York: Columbia University Press.
- Lawson, H. A., & Briar-Lawson, K. (2001). New-century investment strategies and social action agendas for the world's families. In K. Briar-Lawson, H. A. Lawson, C. B. Hennon, & A. R. Jones (Eds.), *Family-centered policies and practices: international implications* (pp. 377–387). New York: Columbia University Press.
- Haspels, N., & Jankanish, M. (Eds.). (2000). *Action against child labour*. Geneva: International Labour Office. (pp. 1–39).

Week 5

Globalization and its effects on South America—Blanca Ramos.

- Videos from the border
- Opportunities for social change
- Justice for maquiladoras
- Anti-sweatshop initiatives
- Legislative initiatives

Readings

- Roth, W., *The assault on social policy*, Poverty, pp. 46–62.
- Indicators (2000, September 23). *The Economist*, pp. 126–128.
- Additional readings to be announced.

Week 6

Africa, African Americans, and social development—Shirley Jones.

- Summit on Africa
- Roles of Universities in social development
- Is reconciliation possible? Development that is humane and culturally responsive
- Anti-sweatshop advocacy and policy

Readings

- Sanders, B., et al. (1999). *Global sustainable development resolution*. [Web page]. U.S. House of Representatives. Available from: http://www.bernie.house.gov
- Additional readings to be announced.

Week 7

Globalization, the environment, sustainable development, and social welfare policy

- Globalization, the environment, and welfare states
- Globalization and rise of sustainable development movements

Readings

- Roth, W., *The assault on social policy*, Welfare, pp. 63–77, Policy, pp. 9–23.
- United Nations Development Programme. (1999). Ten years of human development [Electronic version]. United Nations Development Programme. Retrieved October 9, 1999, from http://gd.tuwien.ac.at/soc/undp/10year.html.
- Death, neglect and the bottom line, [Web page]. *St. Louis Post-Dispatch*. Retrieved November 18, 1999, from http://www.postnet.com/postnet/special_reports/prisoncare.nsf.
- Schlosser, E. (1998, December). The prison industrial complex, [Electronic version]. *The Atlantic Monthly*. (Available at http://www.theatlantic.com)
- Shalom, S. R. (1999, October). The state of the world [Electronic version]. *ZNet*. (Available at http://ww2.wpunj.edu/cohss/polisci/faculty/shalom/ssZse1499.htm)

Week 8

Micro loaning, collateralizing loans, and other alternative approaches—Hal Lawson

- Globalization, social and economic development
- Integrative women and family-centered approaches to economic, employment, and educational need of workers
- Nonmarket/monetary exchanges and new relationships to economics

Reading

- United Nations Development Programme. (1999). Overview. Globalization with a human face. In *Human Development Report 1999*. Oxford: Oxford University Press.

Week 9

Trade unions, nongovernmental organizations—Nancy Claiborne

- Roles of trade unions, collective advocacy, and bargaining
- Role in anti-sweatshop movements
- Monitoring of codes
- Role of NGOs and social policy and reform

Readings

- Fisher, J. (1998). *NGOs, civil society and political development*. West Hartford, CT: Kumarian Press, Inc. (chapter 1, Non-governments: NGOs and the political development of the third world, pp.1–39)
- Moody, K. (1997). *World-class working class*. New York: Verso. (chapter 1, pp. 9–40; chapter 8, pp. 180–200).
- Lee, T. (1993). Happily never NAFTA: There's no such thing as a free trade. In R. Nader (Ed.), *The case against free trade* (pp. 70–78). San Francisco, CA and Berkeley, CA: Earth Island Press and North Atlantic Books.

Week 10

Globalization, global government, sweatshops revisited.

- United Nations, human rights movements, and world labor protection
- United Nations and economic development

Readings

- International Labour Organization. (2000). *ILO mandate.* Geneva, Switzerland: International Labour Organization.
- United Nations. (1994). *Human Rights: A compilation of international instruments.* (Vol. 1/parts 1/2). New York and Geneva: United Nations.

Week 11

Privatization, corporations, transnational corporations, social welfare, and people.

- Models of worker movements to address human rights and economic needs
- International challenges of children and women trafficking
- Downscaling of welfare states and threats to human welfare

Readings

- Nader, R. (1993). Introduction: Free trade and the decline of democracy. In R. Nader (Ed.), *The case against free trade* (pp. 1–13). San Francisco, CA and Berkeley, CA: Earth Island Press and North Atlantic Books.
- Mander, J., Megatechnology, trade, and the new world order, chapter 2, pp. 13–23 in *The case against free trade.*
- Wallach, L., Hidden dangers of GATT and NAFTA, chapter 3, pp. 23–65 in *The case against free trade.*

Week 12

Globalization and social welfare.

- Examining and addressing world disparities
- Toward tax and related demogrants
- Schooling as work?
- New GNP/GDP indices.
- Women and unequal burdens.

  Students' presentations and select readings.

Week 13

The United States and the globe.

- Role of the United States as a spearhead of reform movements or reinforcer of "race to bottom" practices and policies
- Thinking globally, acting locally

  Students' presentations and select readings.

Week 14

The 21st century.

- Progress or regress?
- Foundations for 21st-century welfare states, human rights enforcement tools, anti-sweatshop and related human rights and democratic movements. Beneficial or harmful? Inevitable or changeable?

  Students' presentations and select readings.

SUGGESTED READING

Baudrillard, J., et al. (1999). *The politics of human rights.* New York: Verso.

Bosworth, B. P. (1993). *Saving and investment in a global economy.* Washington, DC: Brookings Institution.

Brecher, J., Childs, J. B., & Cutler, J. (1993). *Global visions: Beyond the New World Order.* Boston: South End Press.

Dixon, J., & Macarov, D. (1998). *Poverty: A Persistent Global Reality.* New York: Routledge.

Henderson, H. (1996). *Building a win–win world: Life beyond global economic warfare.* San Francisco, CA: Berrett-Koehler Publisher.

Ife, J. (1995). *Community development: Creating community alternatives: Vision, analysis and practice.* Melbourne, Australia: Addison Wesley Longman.

Kamerman, S. B. (1998). *Does global retrenchment and restructuring doom the children's cause?* New York: Columbia University.

Kuttner, R. (1996). *Everything for sale: The virtues and limits of markets.* New York: Random House.

Mander, J., & Goldsmith, E. (1996). *The case against the global economy: And for a turn toward the local.* San Francisco, CA: Sierra Club Books.

Rifkin, J. (1995). *The end of work: The decline of the global labor force and the dawn of the post-market era.* New York: G. P. Putnam's Sons.

Sen, A. (1999). *Development as freedom.* New York: Random House.

Shuman, M. (1994). *Towards a global village: International community development initiatives.* London: Pluto Press.

Stoesz, D., Guzzetta, C., Lusk, M. (1999). *International development.* Needham Heights, MA: Allyn & Bacon.

United Nations Development Programme. (2000). *Women's political participation and good governance: 21st century challenges.* New York, NY: United Nations Development Programme.

The United Nations Development Programme. (2000). *Human Development Report, 2000.* New York: Oxford University Press.

The World Bank. (2000). *Entering the 21st century: World development report 1999/2000.* New York: Oxford University Press.

Contemporary Social Welfare: Module on Comparative Social Welfare
SWK 201

COURSE DESCRIPTION

I created a two-week module on Comparative Social Welfare to introduce international content into the Social Work Department's introductory course, Contemporary Social Welfare. Focusing on programs and policies in the advanced welfare states of Western Europe and Canada, the module uses both institutional and conflict theory approaches as its theoretical foundation. Two major objectives are met by the new course content: (1) encouraging students to see beyond the limitations of our own system, and (2) exploring different ways to handle common problems.

This course is part of the social welfare policy sequence of the Department of Social Work and is required of all social work majors. The first course in the sequence, *Introduction to Social Work* (SWK 200), focuses on the profession of social work, while *Contemporary Social Welfare* (SWK 201) looks at the institutional context in which social workers practice—that is, the system of agencies, programs, laws, and policies that social workers deal with to help their clients. SWK 201 provides an overview and conceptual framework for understanding these issues, which will be addressed more fully in the third course in the sequence, *Social Welfare Policy* (SWK 300).

Most people know very little about our social welfare system, despite the fact that it consumes about one-fifth of national wealth and more than one-half of all government spending. Most of this money goes to help the middle class through income maintenance and health programs like Social Security and Medicare, with a much smaller share going to help the poor. Programs aimed at poor people (i.e., public assistance) are stigmatized, often reflecting negative and racist stereotypes. Programs available to all income groups (i.e., social insurance) are more socially acceptable and provide better benefits, although gaps in coverage remain. As most social workers know, finding programs to meet the needs of their clients can be frustrating and difficult.

Other industrialized nations typically offer their citizens a more complete set of benefits and rights, especially in the areas of health care and poverty prevention. For this reason, the United States is really an underdeveloped welfare state: despite our great wealth, we fail to ensure even minimal guarantees of dignity, security, and opportunity for our population. By looking at social welfare in an international and comparative context, we can identify better ways to accomplish these goals.

Social welfare is a controversial and politicized field, reflecting deeply held values and assumptions about basic issues. Why are some people poor and others rich? What obligations do we have toward others? What is the role of government in helping people meet their needs—to promote equality and security or to encourage competition, self-reliance, and individual initiative? How do we balance human rights with the search for profits? While social workers generally share basic values and ideology, they often disagree among themselves about how to answer these questions.

This course will challenge students to think about these issues in a more thoughtful and informed manner so that their views are based on knowledge and analysis rather than unexamined beliefs and prejudices. While providing the intellectual tools for this purpose, the course also conveys the core values of the social work profession: service, social justice, the dignity and worth of the person, and the importance of human relationships. Since social workers are the ones who deal directly with the consequences of poverty, discrimination, and other social ills, they understand how public policy is linked to the everyday needs of real people, and why a more humane society is so essential.

NOTE: While the course is aimed at preparing social work students for beginning-level practice, it should also be of interest to students in other fields.

CONTEMPORARY SOCIAL WELFARE (SWK 201)

Module VI. Comparative Social Welfare Week 14–15

"The United States is more reluctant than any other rich democratic country to make a welfare effort appropriate to its affluence. Our support of national welfare programs is halting; our administration of services for the less privileged is mean. We move toward the welfare state but we do so with ill grace, carping and complaining all the way."
   —Harold Wilensky and Charles Lebeaux

The objective of this section is to view social welfare in the United States from an international perspective to identify strategies for improving our own programs and policies. This final section will:

• Provide an overview of social welfare in other industrialized nations, in the Third World, and in the former Soviet bloc.

• Identify the key historical, social, political, and economic ingredients necessary for successful social welfare policies and programs.

• View the United States as an "underdeveloped" welfare state in comparison to Western Europe and Canada, with special focus on family policy, employee benefits, and health care.

• Explore the implications of current international trends toward privatization and cutbacks for social policy and social justice.

REQUIRED READING

Dolgoff R., & Feldstein, D. (2000). *Understanding social welfare* (5th ed.). Boston: Allyn & Bacon.

• chapter 10 (pp. 232–250): Sustaining the quality of life
• chapter 14 (pp. 343–347): Social trends affecting social welfare

RECOMMENDED READING

Atherton, C. (1997). The changing British welfare state: progress or retreat? *Social Development Issues, 19*(1), 98–108.

Hantrais, L. (1994). Comparing family policy in Britain, France and Germany. *Journal of Social Policy, 23*(2), 135–160.

Gornick, J. C. (2001). Cancel the funeral (European welfare state). *Dissent, 48*(3), 13–16.

Korpi, W. (1995). The position of the elderly in the welfare state: Comparative perspectives on old age care in Sweden. *Social Service Review, 69*(2), 242–273.

Midgley, J. (1995). International and comparative social welfare, in R. L. Edwards (Ed.), *Encyclopedia of social work* (19 ed., Vol. 2) (pp. 1490–1499). Washington, DC: NASW Press.

Myles, J., & Quadrango, J. (2000). Envisioning a "Third Way": The welfare state in the twenty-first century. *Contemporary Sociology, 29*(1), 156–161.

van Wormer, K. (1994). A society without poverty—the Norwegian experience. *Social Work, 39*, 241–336.

ASSIGNMENT

Concept paper (3–4 pages): Choose *one* of the following issues/problems and compare how it is dealt with in the United States and in other industrialized nations. Use at least two of the recommended references.

• Poverty
• Single-parent families
• Health care
• Workplace benefits

Social Exclusion: A New Perspective on Disadvantage
Module

This module is used in an MSW level course: Social Welfare and Social Policy. The module introduces the concept of social exclusion. The term social exclusion represents a rethinking of the philosophical content of social welfare policy that, beginning in the European Union, has spread to Latin America and the United Nations to describe lack of access to mainstream society, be it social, political, or economic. Exploring work on the concept of social exclusion in the European Union provides students with the unique experience of examining the development and use of an alternative theory of status and intervention in the setting of developed countries and in the context of problems (such as child poverty) that they are familiar with.

Social exclusion has its origins in French writings of the 1960s; it has become the major social welfare policy theory of the European Union. It is an important item on the policy agenda as the European Union faces the challenge of adding 15 new member states. The readings include material on the origin of the concept and its theoretical development, the policy process within the European Union, the development of social exclusion into a key European Union policy, and the extension of its use to Latin America and the United Nations.

USE OF THE MODULE

The module is written for a master's level social welfare or policy course. It can be used to cover one week of a 15-week syllabus or adapted for use as a unifying theme in a unit that covers several countries. To use it for a bachelor's level course, I would reduce the number of readings to three and offer assignments 1 and 2.

SOCIAL EXCLUSION: A NEW PERSPECTIVE ON DISADVANTAGE

Module Objectives

1. Become familiar with the philosophical beginnings and background of the development of the concept of social exclusion.
2. Become familiar with the governance structure of the European Union.
3. Become familiar with the policy process through which social exclusion became the preeminent social welfare policy initiative in the European Union.
4. Be able to compare social exclusion policy to United States social welfare policy initiatives.
5. Become familiar with the debate on definitions and dissemination to United Nations and Latin American policy discourses.

OVERVIEW

Social exclusion is a philosophical construct that reinterprets the notion of poverty from economic deprivation to include social and political disadvantage. This widens the concept of deprivation to include conditions such as race and cultural exclusion, geographical exclusion, and exclusion based on age and disability. Exclusion from full citizenship rights prevents individuals and families from participating fully in mainstream society. This module introduces students to this concept as a comparison with American attitudes and policy decisions on social welfare.

Social exclusion is defined by the European Union as "[W]hen people are prevented from participating fully in economic, social, and civil life and/or when their access to income and other resources (personal, family, social and cultural) is so inadequate as to exclude them from enjoying a standard of living and quality of life that is acceptable by the society in which they live. In such situations people often are unable to access their fundamental rights. (Council, 2002, p. 15)"

Each of the European Union member countries defines social exclusion slightly differently. For example, the Blair government in the United Kingdom defines social exclusion as "a shorthand term for what can happen when people or areas suffer from a number of linked problems such as unemployment, poor skills, low incomes, poor housing, high crime, bad health and family breakdown." (Opportunity for All, 2001)

Though various member countries focus on different aspects of social exclusion, Mayes (2001) states that social exclusion represents "not just a description of the adverse consequences of disadvantage but of the process by which people become distanced from the benefits of participating in a modern society" (p. 1). Thus, it describes exclusion as a process as well as a condition and compares dramatically with the poorly defined, static notion of poverty in the United States as unemployment or inadequate monetary resources. Thus, it is integral to a through understanding of global social work and social work in the United States.

SAMPLE READINGS

- Council of the European Union. (2002). *Draft Joint Report on Social Inclusion*. Brussels, Belgium: EU.
- http://europa.eu.int/abc/index_en.htm: Provides a brief overview of the organization of the European Union
- http://www.eurunion.org: The European Union in the United States
- http:/www.Europa.eu.int/comm/employment_social (Joint Report on Social Inclusion, pp. 1–14.): Summary of the first set of national action plans. Prepared in 2002, this report summarizes the situations reported by the 15 European Union member countries in national action plans based on certain criteria.
- Sojo, C. (2001). The socio-political and cultural dynamics of social exclusion. In E. Gacitua, C. Sojo, & S. Davis (Eds.), *Social exclusion and poverty reduction in Latin American and the Caribbean*. Washington, DC: The World Bank.

SAMPLE ASSIGNMENTS

1. Find a news story on social exclusion or on a European Union topic (it may not be easy to find an article in the popular press about social exclusion, but using a search engine will help). This will demonstrate to students: (1) the European Union as a government entity, and (2) that important matters are sometimes underreported in the media.

2. Describe the European Union. List the various parts of the governance structure and their roles in governing. Compare it with the structure of the United States government.

3. Conduct an Internet search to locate a peer-reviewed article that deals with social exclusion. Briefly (1–3 pages) describe and analyze the content of the article.

4. Write a 7–10-page paper (using APA style, with at least 10 references) comparing the legislative development of social exclusion in the European Union with a U.S. policy initiative (such as one dealing with child abuse or mental health).

ANNOTATED BIBLIOGRAPHY

Mayadas, N., Watts, T., & Elliott, D. (Eds.). (1997). *International handbook on social work theory and practice*. Westport, CT: Greenword. (Summarizes social work practice in a number of countries on six continents.)

Mayes, D. (2001). Introduction. In D. Mayes (Ed.), *Social exclusion and European policy* (pp. 1–23). Cheltenham, UK: Edward Elgar. (Good introduction to social exclusion across member countries.)

Leibfried, S., & Pierson, P. (2000). Social policy, left to courts and markets? In H. Wallace & W. Wallace (Eds.), *Policy-making in the European Union* (4th ed.) (pp. 267–292). Oxford, U.K.: Oxford University Press. (Dated, but demonstrates the importance of the courts.)

McDevitt, S. (2003) Social exclusion in the European Union: An organized focus for social policy-making, *The Social Policy Journal*, 2(4). Binghamton, NY: Haworth Press. (Overview of structure of European Union and evolution of social exclusion)

Opportunity for All: www.cabinet-office.gov.uk/seu/2001 (This is the social exclusion Web page set up by the Blair administration.)

Ridge, T., & Millar, J. (2000). Excluding children: Autonomy, friendship, and the experience of the care system. *Social Policy and Administration*, *34*(2), pp. 160–175. (Reviews the perspective of children who experience social exclusion.)

Room, G. (Ed.). (1995). *Beyond the threshold: The measurement and analysis of social exclusion*. Bristol, England: The Policy Press. (Somewhat dated, but still heavily cited. Explores measurement of social exclusion.)

Wendon, B. (1998). The commission as image-entrepreneur in EU social policy. *Journal of European Public Policy*, *5*, 339–453. (Explores the issue of the European Commission as policy-entrepreneur.)

Social Policy
SPPP 470

COURSE DESCRIPTION

This MSW course infuses international content into a required foundation course. Thus, it reaches more students than the International Social Welfare and International Social Work courses offered elsewhere in the curriculum. International content is integrated into the foundation course in two ways. First, examples of policy in other countries are used to provide comparisons with social policy in the United States. This comparative analysis illuminates the strengths and weaknesses of American social policy. Second, the course examines international issues that have social policy implications for the United States. For example, American action on international human rights treaties is examined and critiqued.

The course reviews the philosophical and historical foundations of social policy and focuses on legislative policy directed at the problems of poverty and discrimination in American society. It also considers international policy issues and actions, with an emphasis on human rights. Attention is given to the linkages between social welfare policy and social work practice.

COURSE OBJECTIVES

By the end of this course, students should be able to:

1. Understand the functions and structure of American social welfare.
2. Comprehend the ideas, events, and social forces that have influenced the development of social policy.
3. Analyze and critique the policies and programs designed to address the problems of poverty and discrimination in American society.
4. Identify and utilize the linkages between social welfare policy and social work practice in a global context.
5. Appreciate and understand the international dimension of human rights and social policy.

(Objective 4 and 5 particularly relate to this module of Unit III.)

REQUIRED TEXTS

Karger, J. J., & Stoesz, D. (2002). *American social welfare policy: A pluralist approach* (4th ed.). Boston: Allyn & Bacon.

van Wormer, K. (1996). *Social welfare: A world view*. Chicago: Nelson Hall.

SUPPLEMENTAL TEXTS AND REFERENCE MATERIALS

Edwards, R. (Ed.). (1995). *Encyclopedia of social work* (19th ed.). Washington, DC: NASW Press.

- Healy, L. M. International social welfare: Organizations and activities, pp. 1499–1510.
- Hokenstad, M. C. & Kendall, K. A. International social work education, pp. 1511–1520.
- Midgley, J. International and comparative social welfare, pp. 1490–1499.

Hokenstad, M. C., & Midgley, J. (Eds.). (1997). *Issues in international social work: Global challenges for a new century*. Washington, DC: NASW Press.

McInnis-Dittrich, K. (1994). *Integrating social welfare policy and social work practice*. Pacific Grove, CA: Brooks/Cole.

COURSE OUTLINE

Unit I. Social Welfare: Contemporary Issues and Contextual Influences

A. Overview of American Social Welfare Today

B. Foundations of Social Welfare

C. Historical Stages of Development

D. Twentieth-Century Social Policy

Unit II. Policy Analysis and Social Action

A. Poverty and Income Support

B. Diversity and Discrimination: Policy Options

C. Connecting Policy and Practice

D. Policy Action

Unit III. Social Policy in an Interdependent World

A. Comparative Social Policy

B. International Organizations in Social Welfare

C. Human Rights: Issues and Responses

D. Globalization and Social Policy

COURSE READINGS FOR UNIT III

Required Reading

Karger, J. J., & Stoesz, D. (2002). *American social welfare policy: A pluralist approach* (4th ed.). Boston: Allyn & Bacon.

- chapter 18: The American Welfare State in International Perspective, pp. 489–510.

van Wormer, K. (1996). *Social welfare.*

- part 3: World Policy Issues
- chapter 10: Marginalized Populations: A Study in Oppression, pp. 503–590.
- chapter 11: Human Rights and Social Justice, pp. 591–642.
- chapter 12: Sustainable Development, pp. 643–669.

Recommended Reading

Brown, L. R., et al. (1999). *State of the world.* New York: W.W. Norton.

- chapter 9: Ending Violent Conflict, by Michael Render
- chapter 10: Building a Sustainable Society, by David Malin Roodman.

Social work and globalization. (2000, Summer). [Special Issue]. *Canadian Social Work, 2*(1).

Deacon, B. (1997). *Global social policy: International organizations and the future of welfare.* London: Sage.

Hokenstad, M. C., & Midgley, J. (1997). *Issues in international social work: Global challenges for a new century.* Washington, DC: NASW Press.

- chapter 1: Realities of Global Interdependence, by M. C. Hokenstad and James Midgley, pp. 1–10.
- chapter 6: International Social Development and Social Work: A feminist perspective, by Lena Dominelli, pp. 74–91.

Midgley, J. (1995). *Social development: The developmental perspective in social welfare.* Thousand Oaks, CA: Sage.

Prigoff, A. (2000). *Economics for social workers: Social outcomes of economic globalization with strategies for community action.* Belmont, CA: Wadsworth/Thompson Learning.

United Nations. (1994). *Human rights and social work: A manual for schools of social work and the social work profession.* New York and Geneva: United Nations Centre for Human Rights.

United Nations. (1998). *Human rights today: A United Nations priority.* New York: United Nations Department of Public Information.

United Nations Development Program. (1990–2001). Human development reports 1990 to 2002. New York: Oxford University Press.

COURSE ASSIGNMENTS

Three assignments will be required. The first assignment will be a take-home examination. It will cover Unit I of the course and can be answered from material and from knowledge provided in assigned readings and classroom lectures and discussion.

The second assignment will involve expert testimony on current social policy issues. The final assignment will be a substantive social policy analysis research paper.

Final Assignment—Comparative Social Policy Analysis

The final assignment is a research paper of 12–15 pages that compares a social security or personal social service policy/program in the United States with a similar policy/program in another country. Students from a country other than the United States may use their home country as the basis for comparison.

Cross-national comparisons can be used:

1. to identify and discuss the merits and deficiencies of specific policies and programs; and
2. to consider the implications and adaptations from different approaches to social welfare.

This paper should cover both objectives.

The comparative analysis should be guided by one of the frameworks discussed in class or the enclosed framework for policy analysis to provide a structure for your discussion and conclusions. Papers should include appropriate documentation from the literature using APA style.

Framework for Comparative Social Policy Analysis

A. Societal Context

- What national values influence the policy?
- What other social characteristics affect policy development?

B. Social Policy Examination

- What are the goals and objectives of the policy?
- What are the provisions of the policy?

  - Type of benefits (income or service)
  - Eligibility requirements (work-related, means tested, etc.)
  - Financing (level of government or charity)
  - Administration (public, nongovernmental, or mixed)

- Who benefits from the policy?

C. Social Policy Analysis

- What are the strengths and weaknesses of the policy?

- How adequate is the policy program?
- How effective is the policy program?
- What are the costs and benefits of the policy?
- What policy issue or issues need to be addressed?

D. Social Policy Comparison

- What are the cross-national similarities and differences in the formulation and implementation of the policy?
- What is the differential impact of the policy across countries?

Sustainable Development: Module II—National and International Efforts Toward Sustainable Development
SoWo 238

A. DESCRIPTION

This module addresses national and international efforts toward sustainable development. As taught at the University of North Carolina, it is part of an MSW course that examines perspectives and models of sustainable development. Students propose a project and present a participatory plan for engaging in sustainable development work.

B. COURSE OBJECTIVES

At the termination of the course, students should be able to:

1. Demonstrate an understanding of the effect that their personal social and cultural background (including personal and professional values) has on their own thinking and views about sustainable development. This understanding should be reflected in a plan for the student's growth and work.

2. Articulate a working definition of sustainable development that incorporates information from the past as well as current thinking about the term and provides some practical, ethically based direction for the student's work in development.

3. Identify and describe some aspects of sustainable development initiatives in the United States and throughout the world, in indigenous as well as modern social groups.*

4. Identify and analyze some social, cultural, political, and economic aspects of communities, both external and intrinsic, that may influence sustainable development, positively or negatively.*

5. Employ the knowledge and skills necessary to (a) assess the knowledge people in a community already have about their sustainability; and (b) to help communities engage in building inclusive, nondiscriminatory life-enhancing structures and practices.

6. Develop and present a detailed participatory plan indicating how they would propose to learn about the knowledge, values, practices, and structures in a specific community in preparation for development facilitation.

*Objectives 3 and 4 are emphasized in this module.

C. REQUIRED TEXTS

Bernard, T., & Young, J. (1997). *The ecology of hope: Communities collaborate for sustainability.* Gabriola Island, British Columbia: New Society Publishers.

Hawken, P., Lovins, A., & Lovins, L. H. (1999). *Natural capitalism: Creating the next industrial revolution.* Boston: Little, Brown.

United Nations Development Program. (2002). *Human development report 2002.* New York: Oxford University Press.

United Nations Commission on Sustainable Development. (2000). *Sustainable development success stories* (Vol. 4). New York: United Nations.

The readings in the syllabus beginning with an asterisk (*) should be completed for the date indicated. Additional readings are listed for your interest and further exploration. Some materials will be given to you as handouts. Please feel free to share literature you find useful for this content as we progress through the semester.

D. EXPANDED DESCRIPTION AND TEACHING/LEARNING METHODS

The course will focus on the social and cultural aspects of communities that are relevant for sustainable development facilitators. Facilitators are teachers, trainers, and organizers who serve as "cultivators" and "midwives" for community change. They may be social workers, planners, administrators, public health workers, or educators. The course will draw upon literature reflecting patterns of environmental racism and the exclusion of women and indigenous peoples from development planning and projects. Throughout the semester, students will be introduced to a variety of perspectives on the meaning of sustainable development and models of sustainable development from Asia, Africa, Latin America, and the United States. Students will analyze their own strengths for this work and the strengths of a community for which they plan to develop a real or hypothetical sustainable development project. Near the end of the semester, students will present a participatory plan for engaging with the community for sustainable development work.

The course is divided into three major areas of inquiry: Module I—current perspectives on sustainable development, Module II—examples of sustainable development projects from the United States and abroad, and Module III—training ourselves and others in sustainable development practice. Module II, included here, focuses on examples of sustainable development projects from the United States and abroad. The class will include readings, lectures, discussions, participatory exercises, and student presentations. We will draw upon speakers from the community and faculty from other departments to help us understand concepts and processes.

We will work together to foster a supportive learning environment that encourages critical thinking by being able to appreciate points of view different from our own, working to clearly articulate our own views, and linking experiences to readings and assignments.

Students with disabilities that affect their participation in the course may notify the instructor if they wish to have special accommodations considered.

E. ASSIGNMENTS AND WRITING GUIDELINES

Four written assignments and two presentations are required for this class. There are no exams. You are expected to apply concepts from the literature listed in this syllabus or from literature you have explored beyond this syllabus in your final definition of sustainable development, in both your presentations, and in the final paper. Application of the literature should demonstrate your ability to analyze and critique theories and concepts that help us understand and explain sustainable development work.

The assignments are described below.

1. **Meaning of Sustainable Development:** Students will write a paragraph that defines sustainable development, once at the beginning of the semester and once at the end. You can think about this assignment as describing to others how you will know sustainable development when you see it. Your definition at the end of the course will be part of your final paper. This first assignment is a reflection of your thoughts now, before you do a lot of reading and reflection about the meaning of sustainable development. When you define sustainable development again as part of your final paper, you should show how your definition compares with the definitions of at least two other authors. (First definition due January 27. Last definition will be incorporated into your final paper, due at the last class period, April 21.)

2. **Knowledge and Skills Growth Plan:** One-page document, prepared once at the beginning, and again at the end of the semester. The top half of the page will list what you know and can do to facilitate sustainable development. The bottom half will list what you need to know and be able to do to facilitate sustainable development. (The first version of this assignment is due January 27. The second is due at the last class period, April 21.)

3. **Conceptual Sharing:** Each student selects one class period to provide a 15-minute discussion/presentation of her (or his) critical thinking about a concept relevant to sustainable development (see suggested list at the end of this syllabus). Presentations begin January 27.

   The presentation should:

   - identify the concept(s) and its meaning (4 points);
   - discuss the usefulness of the concept for work toward sustainable development, and pros and cons (7 points); and
   - describe in what directions we could explore this concept for greater understanding/usefulness (4 points).

4. **Application of Knowledge and Skills to a Sustainable Development Project:** Students will propose a real or hypothetical sustainable development project/initiative of their choice (e.g., ecotourism, sustainable agriculture, urban micro enterprise, the education of women and girls, experiential environmental programs for

young people, indigenous/natural wellness promotion, integrated health and development projects, bioregional community project, etc.). The initiative must have goals that help community groups move toward sustainable development. Use a place where you have lived and worked, a place identified from our readings, or a place where you would like to work as the hypothetical site for your proposed project. It can be a project that has already started or that is planned for a specific community/regional location anywhere in the world. The project must have a specific location so that local social, cultural, geographic, environmental, economic, and political characteristics are incorporated in the analysis. The analysis must describe how these characteristics potentially support or prevent a community's maintenance or initiation of a sustainable development project. (This paper is due the last day of class.)

5. **Plan for Understanding Community Knowledge:** Students will develop and present to the class a detailed plan indicating how they propose to learn about the knowledge, values, practices, and structures in a specific community/region. The plan will cover the student's (facilitator's) first three to five months in a project site. It will provide detailed information about how the facilitator will come to understand all the systems of knowledge and experience already in the community. It will describe how the facilitator will build the necessary relationships with a range of community members to work toward maintaining or initiating a sustainable development project. The plan may draw upon any participatory tools or methods that facilitate the active participation and learning of the community members and help the facilitator to become a colearner.

SPRING SEMESTER PLAN

Module I—Current Perspectives, Definitions, and Historical References for Sustainable Development (not available in this publication. Contact D. Gamble if you want a copy of the complete course outline.)

Module II—National and International Efforts Toward Sustainable Development

Session I

Unit 4: Examples of Sustainable Development from across the globe.

- What are some identifiable projects/efforts from our region, from elsewhere in the United States, and from other parts of the world that are working toward sustainable development?

- Who are the facilitators and what methods are they using for participatory involvement?

- What are some of the differences and similarities in projects being initiated in our own region and in the developing world?

- Why and how do human rights influence human development?

- How does the "technology divide" influence development?

Readings

- United Nations Commission on Sustainable Development (2000). *Sustainable development success stories* (Vol. 4).

- United Nations Development Program. (2002). chapter 2: Democratic governance for human development, and chapter 3: Deepening democracy by tackling democratic deficits (pp. 51–61 and 63–83) in *Human Development Report 2002*.

Video

- *Community—focus on women's involvement in economic development in Bangladesh* (1995). Oxfam America, 26 West St. Boston, MA 02111.

Readings for additional insight

- Berry, T. (1988). *The dream of the earth.* San Francisco, CA: Sierra Club Books. (chapter 10: The New Story, pp. 123–137, and chapter 13: The Hudson River valley, a bioregional story, pp. 171–179.)

- Durning, A. B. (1989). *Poverty and the environment: Reversing the downward spiral* (World Watch Paper 92). Washington DC: World Watch Institute.

- Henderson, H. (1996). *Building a win-win world.* San Francisco, CA: Berrett-Koehler Publishers. (chapters 6, 7, and 8: Grassroots globalism, Rethinking human development and Cultural DNA codes and biodiversity, pp. 131–193.)
- Hinsdale, M. A., Lewis, H., & Waller, S. M. (1995). *It comes from the people: Community development and local theology.* Philadelphia, PA: Temple University Press. (chapter 3: Confronting and Using Power, pp. 65–78.)
- United Nations Development Program. (1999). *Human development report 1999.* New York/Oxford, England: Oxford University Press. (chapter 4: National responses to make globalization work for human development, pp. 84–96.)
- United Nations Development Program. (2000). *Human development report 2000.* New York/Oxford, England: Oxford University Press. (chapter 3: Inclusive democracy secures rights, pp. 56–72.)
- United Nations Development Program. (2001). *Human development report, 2001.* New York/Oxford, England: Oxford University Press. (chapter 4: Unleashing human creativity: national strategies, pp. 79–93.)

Session II

Unit 4, continued

- How do we define wealth and poverty in efforts toward development?
- What are some specific projects in North Carolina (or your state) that are moving us toward sustainable development?

Readings

- Bernard & Young, *The ecology of hope: Communities collaborate for sustainability,* Part 2, pp. 43–180.
- Hawken, Lovins, & Lovins, *Natural capitalism: Creating the next industrial revolution,* chapter 5, pp. 82–110.

Teaching Note

For Session II, use of a guest speaker involved with local sustainable development is recommended to help students see the local-global connections. I used a speaker from the Conservation Fund's Resourceful Communities Program who has worked with Tyrrell County down east as well as with communities in the western part of North Carolina to develop local, participatory, racially integrated community development efforts that are environmentally and culturally sensitive and economically viable. Current work is with eastern counties to help them rethink frameworks for rebuilding after hurricane Floyd by taking into account the bioregions of the eastern half of our state.

Readings for additional insight

- Henderson, *Building a win-win world,* chapters 9 and 10: Information and redefining wealth and progress, pp. 196–246.
- Peña, D., & Gallegos, J. (1997). Local knowledge and collaborative environmental action research. In P. Nyden, A. Figert, M. Shibley, & D. Burrows (Eds.), *Building community: Social science in action,* pp. 85–91, with references pp. 250–256.
- Sarin, M. (1995). Wasteland development and the empowerment of women: The SARTHI experience. In A. Leonard (Ed.), *SEEDS 2: Supporting women's work around the world* (pp. 110–133). New York: The Feminist Press. (This book contains other case studies from the United States, Zambia, Mozambique, Sudan, and Thailand that may be helpful in selecting a sustainable development project.)
- United Nations Development Program. (2000). chapter 4: Rights empowering people in the fight against poverty, in *Human Development Report 2000* (pp. 73–88).

Session III

Unit 4, continued

- What can we learn from sustainable agriculture?
- How do we interpret the balance between technological advances in plant development, environmental protection, and food security?

- What are the differences between the world's research agenda and the world's research needs?

Readings

- Adriance, J. (1995). Living with the land in Central America. *Grassroots Development*, *19*(1), pp. 3–17. (Other examples of sustainable development projects in Latin America can be found in the journal *Grassroots Development*.)
- Hawken, Lovins, & Lovins, *Natural capitalism: Creating the next industrial revolution*, chapter 10, pp. 190–212.
- United Nations Development Program, chapter 5: Global initiatives to create technologies for human development, in *Human Development Report 2001* (pp. 95–117).

Video

- *Saving their Corner of the Planet: Local conservationists in Honduras.* Kumarian Press, Inc., West Hartford, CT.

Reading for additional insight

- Bunch, R. (1982). *Two ears of corn: A guide to people-centered agricultural improvement.* Oklahoma City, OK: World Neighbors
- Henderson, H. *Building a win-win world*, chapters 11 and 12: Perfecting democracy's tools and new markets and new commons, pp. 247–292.
- Hoff, M. D. (1998). *Sustainable community development: Studies in economic, environmental, and cultural revitalization.* Boca Raton, FL: Lewis Publishers.
- Wilson, L. (1995). Fighting toxic waste dumping in Kentucky. In B. Bradford & M. Gwynne (Eds.), *Down to earth: Community perspectives on health, development, and the environment* (pp. 107–112). West Hartford, CT: Kumarin Press. (This books contains other case studies from the United States, Colombia, Honduras, Ecuador, Bolivia, Armenia, Mali, Kenya, Uganda, and Sri Lanka that may be helpful in selecting a sustainable development project.)
- World Resources Institute. (Annual). *World resources: A guide to the global environment.* New York: Oxford University Press.
- chapter 14: National and Local Policies and Institutions, pp. 235–252, in *World Resources, 1994-95*.
- Critical Trends: The global commons; Resources at risk, pp. 170–199, in *World Resources, 1998-99*.
- chapter 3: Improving health through environmental action, pp. 73–126, in *World Resources, 1998-99*.

We also have available for review case study material from World Neighbors (Oklahoma City, OK) projects in Honduras, Peru, India, and Nepal. Some case study material is also available through EcoGen: Ecology, Community Organization, and Gender, a joint project of Clark University and Virginia Polytechnic Institute and State University established to examine the role of gender in rural livelihood systems.

Chapters 3 and 4 of the *Human Development Report 1996* also has a variety of brief examples of development and growth initiatives, some of which are representative of sustainable development efforts.

Some Web sites that provide information about sustainable development projects are:

- www.netaid.org (the UNDP sustainable development Web site)
- www.wri.org (World Resources Institute)
- www.wn.org (World Neighbors)
- www.iied.org (International Institute for Environment and Development)
- caster.ssw.upenn.edu/ (Richard Estes Web site)
- www.rprogress.org (Redefining Progress, an opportunity to calculate your own ecological footprint)
- www.iisd.org (International Institute for Sustainable Development)

Module III—Training/Educating Ourselves and Others for Sustainable Development
(Contact D. Gamble for the complete course syllabus.)

DETAILS FOR ASSIGNMENT ON CONCEPTUAL SHARING

Conceptual Sharing: Each student selects one class period to provide a 15-minute discussion/presentation of his (or her) critical thinking about a concept relevant to sustainable development. The presentation should:

- identify the concept(s) and discuss its meaning (4 points);
- discuss the usefulness of the concept for work toward sustainable development, and pros and cons (7 points); and
- describe in what directions we could explore this concept for greater understanding/usefulness (4 points).

Suggested concepts include perspectives on:

1. how to think about the term "development" and development models
2. indigenous people that help us understand "the integrity of the universe"
3. the role of women in development paradigms
4. colonialism and racism in development paradigms
5. bioregionalism and its usefulness, or not, for sustainable development work
6. the meaning of community for sustainable development work
7. biodiversity and its relationship to sustainable development
8. the "Green Movement" or "Green Party" and its role in politics, local or global
9. sustainable agriculture (local or elsewhere) and food security
10. how to measure human development/progress
11. how to measure economic development/progress (economic well-being)
12. the gap between the richest 20% and the poorest 20% of the population and its relationship to sustainable development (national or global)
13. access to resources and resource exploitation when comparing the global North and South.
14. how to measure social development/progress (social indicators)
15. how to measure cultural development/progress (cultural diversity, cultural oppression, cultural preservation)
16. the best ways we can learn about sustainable development
17. the best ways we can teach about sustainable development
18. the role of the media and paths toward sustainable development
19. consumption and its relationship to sustainable development
20. the comparison of consumption between the global North and the global South
21. international conventions and their role in working toward sustainable development
22. national and/or international organizations and their role in working toward sustainable development

Global Perspectives on Women's Rights
Module

International social welfare is a field of increasing importance. Social workers, both within and outside the United States, are often forced to address issues with global implications in the context of their jobs and in the conduct of their daily lives. As advocates for economic and social justice, social workers must be familiar with issues of global human rights and must acquire the tools needed to become actively involved in campaigns for human rights throughout the world. This module focuses on women as an oppressed population and employs a global perspective to examine their struggles to secure basic human rights. It explores the similarities and differences between issues women face in the United States and other parts of the world. The role of culture in defining human rights and rights violations is highlighted.

The module focuses on selected issues relating to women's human rights in different regions of the world. Through discussion, guest lectures, field trips, videos, and class projects, students will explore the scope of women's human rights, ways these rights are ignored or violated, and some of the strategies proposed and/or implemented to further the rights of women globally. Attention will also be given to media coverage of women's rights issues and the effect of the media in highlighting women's human rights topics. Instructors may select some or all of the module topics for inclusion. As taught at the College of New Rochelle, it is an undergraduate course.

OBJECTIVES

1. To familiarize students with the concept of human rights and its multiple meanings as interpreted by national and international laws and conventions.
2. To acquaint students with the field of women's human rights and the specific categories of rights contained within this general field.
3. To identify prominent organizations dedicated to promoting women's human rights globally and discuss their goals, objectives, and programs of action.
4. To explore strategies used by national governments, citizen groups, and nongovernmental organizations to promote awareness of women's human rights issues; stop violations of women's civil, political, economic, and social rights; and advocate to protect and further rights in these arenas.
5. To acquaint students with selected women's rights struggles around the world.
6. To cultivate students' ability to collect, analyze, interpret, and communicate information about violations of women's human rights in selected countries.
7. To explore the role played by cultural values in influencing behavior and the extent to which human rights standards should be universal or relative.
8. To encourage students to view themselves as members of a global community of women and explore the similarities and differences between their struggles and those of other women throughout the world.
9. To encourage students' creativity and promote their research and problem-solving skills.
10. To explore the influence of gender as a determinant of human rights abuses and as a factor in the readiness of governments and other bodies to address these abuses.

ANTICIPATED LEARNING OUTCOMES

At the conclusion of this course, students should be able to:

1. Define human rights and list and describe selected national and international conventions that address these rights.
2. Identify at least three international organizations that promote women's human rights worldwide and describe their philosophies, goals, constituencies, and activities.

3. List categories of women's human rights, give examples of areas of the world where these rights have been violated, and describe interventions used to draw attention to and challenge these abuses.

4. Present and explain alternative perspectives relating to international human rights issues.

5. Use research and problem-solving skills to investigate specific women's human rights issues and positions held by those involved. Articulate and defend their own positions in relation to these issues and suggest interventions appropriate for women's rights advocates.

6. Identify personal experiences of victimization and violation and discuss the similarities and differences between these experiences and those of women from other cultures.

7. Discuss the influence of media in the portrayal of women's human rights issues and the positions assumed by the various publics.

8. Explain the influence of personal and societal values in defining perspectives on women's human rights issues.

9. Discuss the role of gender in human rights abuses and as a factor in their resolution.

REQUIRED MATERIALS

- Otto, D. (1998). *Rights of women*. New York: Women's International Tribune Center.
- Mertus, J. (1999). *Local action/global change. Learning about the human rights of women and girls.* UNIFEM & The Center for Women's Global Leadership.
- Bouvard, M.G. (1996). *Women reshaping human rights*. Wilmington, DE: SR Books. (Part 4, "Upholding Women's Rights as Human Rights.")
- Links related to women's human rights (http://www.cwgl.rutgers.edu/globalcenter/partlinks.html): A list of Web sites focusing on women's human rights issues; 4-page handout can be downloaded from Web. Students are expected to become familiar with all of the sites listed.

ASSIGNMENTS

- Media campaign project: Students will develop a media campaign focusing on one of the women's human rights issues discussed in the course and relating it to a particular area of the world (e.g., child prostitution in the Philippines; female genital mutilation in Africa). Instructions are appended to this module outline.
- Classroom and take-home exercises based on *Local Action Global Change* text/workbook.
- Mock tribunal: Students will work in groups. In each group, a student will prepare "personal" testimony assuming the role of a woman who is the victim of a human rights abuse for presentation at a mock tribunal or hearing. Other students will assume the roles of judges or arbiters and will react to the evidence presented.
- Study of a global women's rights organization: Students will select one organization for analysis. Through field visits, interviews, Web site study, and review of printed materials and press coverage, they will prepare an organizational analysis of the group selected. The analysis will include organizational attributes, philosophy, staffing, campaigns or activities undertaken, affiliations, and other variables, to be enumerated through written instructions distributed in class. Instructions are appended to this module outline.
- Reaction papers for videos (using outline appended to this module).

TOPICAL OUTLINE

I. Introduction of basic human rights concepts and, more specifically, the human rights of women and girls (1 week).

Introductory Exercises

- "Standing Together, Sitting Alone" (*Local Action/Global Change*, exercise No. 2)
- "Wheel of Equality" (*Local Action/Global Change*, exercise No. 9)
- "From Analysis to Action" (*Local Action/Global Change*, exercise No. 10)

II. Discussion of international laws, platforms, and covenants applicable to women's human rights (1 week).

Viewing of 42-minute video

- Heerah, S. (1996). "Beyond Beijing." Available from New York: Women Make Movies.

Reading

- *Rights of Women*, "Understanding Conventions," pp. 5–17, 137-145

III. The Universal Declaration of Human Rights; the principles of equality and nondiscrimination (1 week).

- A controversial principle: The universality of human rights
- Discussion of the concept of cultural relativism

Readings

- *Local Action/Global Change*, pp. 217–220; chapter 2 (pp. 19–37) (excluding exercises)
- *Rights of Women*, "Women and Human Rights," pp. 20–23

IV. Women's human rights in the family (2 weeks).

- Women and religious fundamentalism
- Women and marriage
- Property ownership

Readings

- *Local Action/Global Change*, chapter 3 (excluding exercises)
- *Rights of Women*, "Women and Marriage" and "Housing, Land, and Property," pp. 38–41; 60– 61.
- Exercise No. 3: "Women, Culture and the Family" (*Local Action/Global Change*)

Viewing of two 24-minute videos

- Metcalf, C., TVE International & BBC Worldwide (2000). The right to choose. Oley, PA: Bullfrog Films.
- Tatham, D., TVE International & BBC Worldwide (2000). All different, all equal. Oley, PA: Bullfrog Films.

V. Women's human right to reproduction and sexuality (1 week).

- Abortion
- Population control
- Sexual preference
- Female genital mutilation

Readings

- *Local Action/Global Change*, chapter 5 (excluding exercises, pp. 74–80)
- *Rights of Women*, "Reproductive Rights," pp. 67–69; "Sexual Orientations Rights," p. 76

Viewing of 45-minute video

- Mayer-Hohdahl, M. (1998). *Female Circumcision: Human Rites*. Princeton, NJ: Journeyman Pictures Production.

VI. Women's human right to freedom from violence (2 weeks).

- UN Declaration on the Elimination of Violence Against Women

- Women and conflict situations
- Women in prison
- Domestic violence
- Tribunals: their purposes and outcomes

Readings

- *Rights of Women*, "Sexual Exploitation and Trafficking," pp. 46–54, "Violence Against Women," 62–66
- *Local Action/Global Change*, chapter 7, exercises No. 2, 4, and 5, "A Tribunal," pp. 92–102, note especially, "Some Points to Consider in Telling Your Story"

Viewing of 48-minute Video

- Augusta Production in coproduction with the National Film Board of Canada and the Atlantic Centre (1994). *The Vienna Tribunal.* New York: Women Make Movies.

Tribunal Assignment—see appended description

VII. Women's human rights in the economy and world of work (2 weeks).

- Women and poverty
- Women and development
- Globalization and its effect on women
- Women and the informal sector
- Women, credit, and income generation
- Discrimination against women in the workplace
- Sexual harassment

Readings

- *Local Action/Global Change*, chapters 10 and 11 (excluding exercises)
- *Rights of Women*, "Women and Employment," pp. 33—37
- Exercises 3 and 4, *Local Action/Global Change*

VIII. Organizations Promoting Global Women's Human Rights (2 weeks).

- Goals and philosophy
- Strategies
- Activities
- "Track records"
- Field trip to nongovernmental organization (NGO): for example, Equality Now, Madre

Readings

- *Rights of Women*, "Resources," pp. 146–147
- *Local Action/Global Change*, pp. 214–216; *Women Reshaping Human Rights*, Selections from Part 4, "Upholding Women's Rights as Human Rights;"

Links related to women's human rights

- http://www.cwgl.rutgers.edu/globalcenter/partlinks.html

Organizational analysis assignment due (see appended description)

ASSIGNMENT DESCRIPTIONS

Mock Tribunal

Each student will prepare "personal" testimony assuming the role of a woman who is the victim of a human rights abuse. Testimony must be original, based on factual material and personal stories and accounts of incidents you read about. This testimony should be written out and will be presented orally at a mock tribunal or hearing and handed in to the instructor. Other students and/or guests will assume the roles of judges or arbiters and will react to the evidence presented.

The text describes a somewhat more elaborate process than we will be using but includes good discussion of the nature and purpose of tribunals and guidelines for those testifying.

In preparing your testimony, you should review the following guidelines:

- Pick a country you will be from.

- Pick an issue prevalent, historically significant, or recently important in that country—sex trafficking of women; rape during civil war; economic exploitation of women working in factories; killing of girl children; stoning of women for relationships out of wedlock; female genital mutilation; refusal of amnesty to women fleeing their home countries due to domestic violence, "comfort women," forced migration, and so forth.

- Be prepared to explain something about your country and the conditions that have led up to, encouraged, or facilitated the continuation of the human rights abuse you are targeting

- Discuss your imaginary family and their possible role in this abuse; discuss your community in relation to the abuse

- Discuss the incident(s) that occurred and how you felt at the time and how you feel now recalling what happened

- If relevant, mention what actions were or were not taken by authorities; mention the reactions of the international community

- State what you would have hoped would happen, how you would have wanted the matter addressed; what should/can be done now to address this issue for you and/or other women who experience similar incidents

- You need not speak as the "victim" or individual affected by the incident. You can be speaking as a representative of or on behalf of someone who died, or was too traumatized to appear herself, or couldn't make the trip to the tribunal to testify herself

Your testimony should be typed—one to two pages long. You should be prepared to read it and to answer questions the audience (those attending the tribunal) raise. It's OK to say "I don't remember" or "I was so shaken up, I don't recall all of the details."

Media Campaign Project

Select a women's human rights issue and a country or area of the world (e.g., child prostitution in the Philippines; female genital mutilation in Africa)

Develop a press kit including:

- Backgrounder
- Fact sheet
- Press release
- Ancillary photos, drawings, charts, Q and A sheet
- Brochure/booklet
- Speech
- Other (items you wish to add)

Formulate a plan of action and describe it, including sequencing, schedule, anticipated resource needs (e.g., press conference), media contacts (include list), grassroots strategies, letters to elected officials and/or foreign governments (include samples), and other methods of outreach.

Include a bibliography including all sources used, written and other.

Note: There will be a special class with a guest speaker who will teach you about media campaigns and the components of press kits.

Organizational Study

This assignment will involve your selecting and preparing an organizational analysis of a women's rights organization. Your analysis will include a comparison of the selected organization with Equality Now, the organization we will be visiting on our class trip.

To select your organization for study, you may refer to the 7-page printout "Links related to women's human rights." Once you have selected an organization, find out about it. For your research, you should conduct a phone or e-mail interview as well as Web-based research. Your organizational analysis should include the following categories:

- Purpose
- Philosophy
- Geographic location
- Auspice/sponsorship
- Membership (if applicable)
- Strategies
- Accomplishments: List and discuss several exemplary projects/campaigns
- History
- Means of communication (Web site, mailings, publications)
- Staffing/volunteers
- Other information you may wish to include
- Your own assessment of this organization

Indicate whom you interviewed, when, what was discussed, and how the interview was carried out. In addition, include a section comparing your selected organization with Equality Now.

This section need not be purely factual. It can be based on your own observations and judgment.

The paper should be 6–8 pages long, double-spaced. Include a bibliography and citations as appropriate.

Video Reactions

In no more than two typed pages:

1. Summarize the key points in the video in 8–10 sentences
2. How did you think the video related to what you have read and discussed in class? To the topic of "Global Perspectives on Women's Rights" in general?
3. What did you find most interesting, challenging, or encouraging about the video?
4. How might you use the information you gained from watching the video?
5. Would you recommend this video to other people? For what audiences do you think it is most suitable?
6. What is the point of view or perspective of the filmmakers? Do they seem like promoters of women's rights? Explain.

International Perspectives on Social Work Ethics
Module

DESCRIPTION

International and cross-cultural perspectives are important dimensions in the teaching of social work ethics. Now that 11.8% of the U.S. population is foreign born and more than 1 in 5 U.S. residents lives in a family with foreign-born members, social workers increasingly work with populations whose value perspectives may differ from their own due to differences in national culture. This module consists of readings that address international perspectives on social work ethics and a set of exercises that can be used in ethics and/or practice courses. Relevant concepts from human rights treaties are integrated into the exercises. The content in this module is supplementary to coverage of the National Association of Social Workers (NASW) Code of Ethics and general readings on ethical decision-making in social work.

OBJECTIVES

Students will:

- be able to define the universalist and relativist perspectives on social work ethics;
- gain familiarity with the International Federation of Social Workers Code of Ethics (IFSW);
- gain experience in applying cultural analysis and ethical principles to social work situations through exercises; and
- identify ways in which national culture has shaped their own values and the NASW Code of Ethics.

READINGS

Donnelly, J. (1984). Cultural relativism and universal human rights. *Human Rights Quarterly*, 6, 400–419.

Ejaz, F. K. (1991). Self-determination: Lessons to be learned from social work practice in India. *British Journal of Social Work*, 21, 127–142.

Healy, L. M. (2001). *International social work: Professional action in an interdependent world*. New York: Oxford University Press. (chapter 7: Values and Ethics for International Professional Action, pp. 151–169).

International Federation of Social Workers. (2004). *Ethics in Social Work: Statement of Principles*. Available at www.ifsw.org

Link, R. (1999). Infusing global perspectives into social work values and ethics. In C. S. Ramanathan & R. J. Link (Eds.), *All our futures: Principles and resources for social work practice in a global era* (pp. 69–93). Belmont, CA: Wadsworth.

Mayer, A. E. (1995). Cultural particularism as a bar to women's rights. In J. Peters & A. Wolper (Eds.), *Women's rights, human rights: International feminist perspectives* (pp. 176–188). New York: Routledge.

Silvawe, G. (1995). The need for a new social work perspective in an African setting: The case of social work in Zambia. *British Journal of Social Work*, 25, 71–84.

United Nations. (1979). *Convention on the elimination of all forms of discrimination against women* (especially Article 5). Available at www.ohchr.org

QUESTIONS FOR CLASS EXPLORATION AND DISCUSSION

1. To what extent are social work values universally applicable? What are areas of tension in attempting to define universal social work values? Identify values that are common to all social work and some that may be culturally determined.

2. The opposing philosophical positions of universalism and cultural relativism in the field of human rights are important for social workers to consider. Briefly stated, the universalist view is that "all members of the human family share the same inalienable rights" (Mayer, 1995, p. 176); at the extreme end of the relativist view, there are no common standards and culture determines the validity or applicability of rights. Discuss how issues in social work practice relate to these two opposing philosophies of rights. In case interventions, should social workers adopt a universalist or relativist stance?

3. Some scholars assert that social work values are heavily biased in favor of individualistic values. Are there alternative values that would inform social work practice in contexts that differ along the key dimension of emphasis on collectivity in contrast to emphasis on individuals?

4. Examine the NASW Code of Ethics and the IFSW International Code of Ethics. To what extent would they assist social workers in considering whether ethical principles are to be universally applied or adapted to context?

(Mayer, A. (1995). Cultural particularism as a bar to women's rights: Reflections on the Middle Eastern experience. In J. Peters & A. Wolper (Eds.), *Women's rights, human rights: International feminist perspectives* (pp. 176–188). New York: Routledge).

CLASS EXERCISES

1. Applying CEDAW to Practice

    The United Nations Convention on the Elimination of All Forms of Discrimination Against Women (CEDAW), adopted in 1979, is a comprehensive international treaty aimed at eliminating gender discrimination. The treaty takes a strong universalist stance in Article 5. Article 5(a) reads:

    "States parties"* shall take all appropriate measures:

    a. to modify the social and cultural patterns of conduct of men and women, with a view to achieving the elimination of prejudices and customary and all other practices which are based either on the idea of the inferiority or superiority of either of the sexes or on stereotyped roles for men and women."

    *"States parties" refers to those nations that have ratified the convention and are bound by its provisions; the United States has not ratified the convention.

    Questions for discussion or written assignment:

    What implications does Article 5(a) have for the practice of social work with diverse cultural groups? Apply Article 5(a) and the NASW Code of Ethics to the two case scenarios below:

    1. A Cambodian refugee woman living in a U.S. City asks for help at a shelter for battered women. The social worker works with the woman to help her consider her options, including marital separation, relocation, and application for public assistance. The local Cambodian Mutual Assistance Association criticizes the social worker and the shelter, charging that the focus on counseling women on their rights and on preparation for independence destroy the fabric of Cambodian family and community life. What is the social worker's role in balancing individual and community values in practice?

    2. Community change efforts may meet with charges of cultural insensitivity, both in the United States and in other countries. Two international examples come from Iran and Bangladesh. Social work educators were instrumental in bringing family planning services to Iran in the 1970s. Some were arrested during the Islamic revolution and charged by the clerics with introducing a fundamental threat to the Islamic way of life. In Bangladesh, community development workers sponsoring micro-enterprise lending and literacy programs for women have been attacked for destroying family roles. How should social work change agents proceed when their work is perceived as threatening local values?

2. Child Welfare: What Values Take Precedence?

    A school social worker has cause to suspect child abuse. A 10-year-old has come to school more than once with welts on his legs. He says that his mother hits him with a belt when he is bad. According to state law, the social worker is obligated to report the case to the state child welfare authorities. The social worker is concerned about the possible far-reaching implications of reporting in this case. The family consists of an immigrant (noncitizen) mother and three children. The father is no longer in contact with the family. The oldest child is 13 and immigrated from the Caribbean with the mother. The 10-year-old and an 8-year-old sibling were born in the United States and are therefore citizens. The social worker knows from working with other Caribbean immigrant families that corporal punishment is commonly practiced; in fact, parents may insist that it is necessary to raise well-disciplined children. The worker has seen no other signs of family disorganization; children come to school regularly and do their school work. The social worker knows that it is possible that reporting might lead to arrest; if so, the mother might be subject to deportation. This would obviously cause enormous problems; the children would be left parentless, with no opportunity for family reunification.

In deciding how to intervene, which of the following factors are relevant and how should they be prioritized?

- legal obligation to report
- social work duty to protect the child from harm
- differing cultural beliefs about parenting (cultural relativism)
- right of all children to be free from abuse (universalism of rights)
- risk of deportation of the mother
- the concept of least harm for the family and/or child
- obligations to the employing agency
- other

Use the following documents to prioritize the factors:

- NASW Code of Ethics
- United Nations Convention on the Rights of the Child
- International Federation of Social Workers Ethics Principles and Standards
- NASW Standards on Cultural Competence (optional)

Do the two ethical codes and the UN Convention lead you to different priority lists? Identify areas of conflicting perspectives, if any.

3. Values and Cultural Conflict: A Case of Misplaced Confidentiality

A young social worker, recently returned to Zambia after completing his MSW in the United States, was assigned by his agency to take an adolescent boy back to his home village. The boy, a runaway, had committed several minor thefts and had been arrested by the police in Lusaka (the capital city). As the social worker and the boy neared the end of the 10-hour drive into the rural area, they approached the village. The official car was spotted pulling into the village, and the village headman and several other elders came rushing toward the car. As the social worker slowed the car to a stop, the headman cried out: "How's our boy? What has happened to our boy?"

The social worker answered quickly: "I cannot tell you. It's confidential. I must see his parents and discuss it with them." Looking up, he saw a look on the older man's face that was at once both stunned and bemused. The young social worker was suddenly overcome with a feeling of estrangement. How removed he felt from his culture; his remarks suddenly seemed foolish in the face of the older men's obvious concern for the boy.

As the social worker relayed the story, that moment in the rural village marked the beginning of his journey to indigenize his practice and to adapt his recently gained professional knowledge. He knew that he would have to search for ways to blend the principles of social work with the strengths of Zambian society.

(Personal story told to author; anonymity requested. Also published in L. Healy, *International Social Work: Professional Action in an Interdependent World*.)

Discussion questions:

- What is the meaning of confidentiality in the context of the story?
- What is the purpose of the social work value of confidentiality?
- In what ways and in what types of cases can the lessons from this case inform domestic practice, especially in child welfare cases?

4. Distributive Justice: A Case Scenario for Discussion

AIDS Intervention Projects

An international development agency has funding available for an AIDS program in the target country in Africa (or India). Only one project can be funded at this time. The possibilities are:

- A media campaign to make high-school-age youth aware of the dangers of AIDS and the modes of transmission.
- An outreach education and intervention program for prostitutes and long-distance truck drivers who frequent prostitutes. These are the two groups with the country's highest incidence of HIV infection.
- A community residential program for persons suffering from AIDS; those affected with AIDS are typically shunned by family and society and die homeless and without treatment.

In using this as a teaching case, present a brief lecture on the principles of distributive justice and alternative approaches to distribution of scarce resources. Examine such principles as merit, greatest good for the greatest number, and aid to the most disadvantaged.

In this case, how should choices be made:

- Between preventive and palliative care for those who are suffering most acutely?
- Between reaching large numbers of youth or reaching groups at highest present risk?
- Between serving the "innocent" or groups who are stigmatized by society?

In the role of social worker, your values may conflict with those of the local population.

In the case outlined above, suppose that the agency and the social worker prefer the second option, the outreach education and prevention program for prostitutes and truck drivers, because these groups are at highest risk and are a major factor in the spread of HIV. This decision is opposed by the government of the target country. In its view, money should not be spent on the "undeserving," but should instead be directed to the country's youth.

How would you address this values conflict in making this distributive justice decision?

Using Human Rights Documents to Teach About Racism in the United States

Module

PURPOSE

Racism is a concern worldwide. The many ways that racism is institutionalized in laws and institutions are specifically identified and outlawed in one of the major United Nations human rights treaties: the International Convention on the Elimination of All Forms of Racial Discrimination. The purpose of this module is to introduce social work students to global-level concerns about eliminating racism. First, through reading the treaty, students will gain an overview of the global antiracism efforts. Then, through examination of the self-assessment prepared by the United States government on its efforts to eliminate racism, an alternative report prepared by a nongovernmental organization, and the comments to the United States by the UN Committee on Elimination of Racism, students will gain both an overview of the current state of racism in the United States and a beginning understanding of how the United States relates to the United Nations' efforts on racism.

The module is designed to be used in courses on racism and oppression or courses on social policy.

OBJECTIVES

1. To introduce students to international human rights law and United Nations human rights machinery to address racism
2. To examine the current status of racism in the United States within the global context

OUTCOMES

Students will:

*   Be able to explain the provisions of the United Nations International Convention on the Elimination of All Forms of Racial Discrimination.
*   Gain insight into the U.S. government's self-assessment of legal and societal progress toward the elimination of racism.
*   Be able to apply the United Nations treaty to one or more local problems related to racism.

Readings

National Association of Social Workers. (2000). International policy on human rights. In National Association of Social Workers, *Social work speaks: National Association of Social Workers policy statements 2000–2003*. Washington, DC: Author.

Tang, K. (2003). Combating racial discrimination: The effectiveness of an international legal regime. *British Journal of Social Work, 33*(1), 17–29.

United Nations. (1966). *International Convention on the Elimination of All Forms of Racial Discrimination*. Available at: www.unhchr.ch/

United Nations. (2001). *Concluding observations on the U.S. report by the Committee on Elimination of Racial Discrimination*. Available at www.unhchr.ch (Go to: Treaty bodies; Committee on the Elimination of Racial Discrimination; Session 59; United States).

United States, Department of State. (2000). State party report on CERD (Report of U.S. Compliance with the International Convention on the Elimination of Racial Discrimination). Access from www.unhchr.ch (Go to: Treaty bodies; select Committee on the Elimination of Racial Discrimination; Session 59, United States).

World Organization for Human Rights USA. (2000). Executive summary, Alternative report on U.S. compliance with CERD. Available at www.woatusa.org/uscomp.html

Wronka, J. (1995). Human rights. In R. Edwards (Ed.), *Encyclopedia of social work* (19th ed.) (pp. 1405–1418). Washington, DC: NASW Press.

WRITTEN OR DISCUSSION ASSIGNMENTS

1. Select one of the substantive articles in the International Convention on the Elimination of All Forms of Racial Discrimination. Discuss the relevance of the article to social work practice in your community/state and to broader issues of public policy. Discuss how the protections in the convention relate to social work ethics and values.

2. The United States report to the United Nations says that the United States has done a good job of eliminating racism from public laws and policies, although it admits that some racism remains due to entrenched attitudes. Do you agree with the U.S. report? Discuss in what ways you agree and disagree. Cite examples to back your position.

3. The World Organization Against Torture, U.S.A., a human rights advocacy group, wrote an alternate report contesting some of the assertions in the official State Department report. Select ONE major issue covered by the convention. Write your own alternative report on U.S. compliance with that treaty provision. How does your assessment compare with that of the WOAT/USA?

TEACHING NOTE

This module and set of assignments can be adapted to a comparative assignment by asking students to also read the self-report and concluding observations for another ratifying country. All documents are available on the Web site of the United Nations High Commission for Human Rights.

The module and assignments can also be adapted to the issues addressed by the Convention on the Elimination of All Forms of Discrimination Against Women, and the Convention on the Rights of the Child. These treaties and relevant country reports are also on the UNHCHR Web site. However, the United States has not ratified these treaties.

The Migration Experience: Understanding Immigrants and Refugees
Module

INTRODUCTION

This module, designed for approximately three two-hour sessions, can be used in courses on Human Behavior and the Social Environment or Social Work Practice. It could also be adapted for social policy courses with the addition of a policy component to the written assignment.

As taught at the University of Connecticut, the module is a segment of a specialized MSW-elective course entitled Services to Immigrants and Refugees and Cross Cultural Helping. The module and the course are organized around a conceptual framework of stages of migration. The framework enables students to examine the interrelationship between the sending and receiving countries and to examine the experiences of individuals in their home countries with their experiences in the new country. As explained below, the framework outlines stages in the migration experience: premigration/departure, transit, and resettlement. Since stages in migration are common to all immigrant populations, the framework can be applied to many immigrant groups. It is also applied to the individual immigrant as it facilitates understanding the individual in the circumstance of migration.

The course draws on concepts from multiple disciplines and connects them to social work knowledge and practice. Knowledge from political science and history, for example, facilitates an understanding of the influence of immigration policy on the lives of immigrants. Concepts drawn from psychology, sociology, and psychiatry, such as stress, life transitions, social networks, trans-nationalism, resilience, post-traumatic stress disorder, explain (in part) aspects of the migration experience. Using concepts from anthropology, different cultural views of health, mental health, help-seeking behavior, family, and child-rearing practice, and gender role behavior are examined.

The full course covers the following topics:

I. The Migration Process

II. Relevant Social Work and Social Science Concepts

III. Immigration Policy and Impact on Service Delivery

IV. Cultural and Cross-cultural issues

V. Social Services to Different Immigrant Groups

VI. The Impact of September 11 and Resulting Policy Shifts

OBJECTIVES/OUTCOMES FOR THE MODULE ON THE MIGRATION EXPERIENCE

Students will:

1. Be able to describe the stages of migration experienced by immigrants and refugees.

2. Be able to apply the stage of migration framework to different immigrant groups.

3. Use knowledge of premigration and transit phases to assist immigrants in their resettlement and efforts to access social and mental health services.

REQUIRED TEXTS

Potocky-Tripodi, M. (2002). *Best practices for social work with refugees and immigrants*. New York: Columbia University Press.

Edmonston, B., & Passel, J. (1994). *Immigration and ethnicity*. Washington, DC: Urban Institute Press.

MODULE ON THE MIGRATION EXPERIENCE (3 SESSIONS)

Conceptual Framework: Stages of Migration. The sessions address the premigration/departure, transit, and resettlement stages of migration. The "stage of migration framework" is applied to individuals, families, groups, and communities. It is specifically applied to diverse groups, which include Southeast Asians, Koreans, Haitians, Dominicans, Central Americans, and persons from the republics of the former Soviet Union. The migration experiences are further illustrated through viewing and discussion of the film *El Norte*.

Video: Use of the Film *El Norte*

El Norte, 1983. Cinecom International Films, Independent Productions.

* *El Norte* portrays the Guatemalan migration experience. It illustrates the issues of undocumented migration as well as the migration stages outlined in the conceptual framework presented below. The film and class discussions are covered in three segments (three classes). The segments of the film also correspond with the stages of migration framework.

Stages of Migration Framework

Stage of Migration	Critical Variables	Factors That Influence Each Migration Stage
Premigration	• Social, political, economic and educational factors • Separation from family and friends • Decisions re: who leaves and who is left behind • Long wait and living in limbo prior to departure • Leaving a familiar environment • Life-threatening circumstances • Experiences of violence and/or persecution • Loss of significant others	• Age • Family composition • Urban/rural background • Education • Culture • Socioeconomic background • Occupation • Belief system • Social support
Transit/Intermediate	• Perilous or safe journey of short or long duration • Refugee camp or detention center stay of short or long duration • Awaiting a foreign country's decision re: final relocation • Loss of significant others	
Resettlement	• Cultural issues • Reception from host country • Opportunity structure of host country • Discrepancy between expectations and reality • Degree of cumulative stress throughout migration process • Different levels of acculturation among family members	

Sources

Drachman, D. (1992). A stage of migration framework for service to immigrant populations. *Social Work*, 37, 68–72.

Drachman, D., & Halberstadt, A. (1992). Stage of migration framework as applied to recent Soviet émigrés. In A. S. Ryan (Ed.), *Social work with immigrants & refugees* (pp. 63–75). New York: Haworth Press.

Drachman, D., Kwon-Ahn, Y. H., & Paulino, A. (1996). Migration & resettlement experiences of Dominican and Korean families. *Families in Society*, 77(10), 626–638.

Drachman, D., & Ryan, A. S. (2001). Immigrants and refugees. In A. Gitterman (Ed.), *Handbook of social work practice with vulnerable and resilient populations* (pp. 651–686). New York: Columbia University Press.

The following teaching/learning issues are covered in the three segments.

SEGMENT I

Premigration (Guatemala)

- Political and economic forces that generate the migration of members of a family
- Experiences of violence
- Losses: family members, village, friends
- Expectations for a better life in a new country
- Decisions regarding who should migrate
- Social supports
- Nature of rural environment in home country
- Cultural issues (their influence on parent/child, sibling, and community relationships; and worldview)
- Religious issues
- Age of family members who migrate (its influence on the migration experience)

SEGMENT II

Transit (Mexico)

- Experiences of violence, trauma, stress (their cumulative effect)
- Losses (their cumulative effect)
- Language issues
- Cultural issues (different culture despite same language)
- Nature of social supports
- Reception in the country of transit (Mexico)

SEGMENT III

Resettlement (United States)

- Dissonance between expectations and reality of life in new country (U.S. poverty, differences in living conditions between U.S. wealthy and U.S. poor)
- Reception in the United States (limited rights of undocumented immigrants; workplace issues; contacts with institutions: hospitals, Immigration and Naturalization Service)
- Language
- Shift from rural to urban/technological society
- Cumulative effect of stress

- Social supports

- Cultural issues (differences in help-seeking behavior)

READINGS

Devore, W., & Schlesinger, E. (1998). *Ethnic-sensitive social work practice* (5th ed.). Boston: Allyn & Bacon. (chapter 10: Ethnic-sensitive practice with refugees and new immigrants)

DeWind, J. (1990). Haitian boat people in the United States: Background for social service providers. In D. Drachman (Ed.), *Social services to refugee populations*. Washington, DC: National Institute of Mental Health.

Drachman, D. (1992). A stage of migration framework for service to immigrant populations. *Social Work, 37*, 68–72.

Drachman, D., Kwon-Ahn, Y. H., & Paulino, A. (1996). Migration and resettlement experiences of Dominican and Korean families. *Families in Society, 77*(10), 626–638.

Dugger, C. (1996, April 15). Woman's plea for asylum puts tribal ritual on trial: Flight into detention. *New York Times*, p. A1.

Gil, R. (1990). Cuban refugees: Implications for clinical social work practice. In D. Drachman (Ed.), *Social services to refugee populations* (pp. 57–72). Washington, DC: National Institute of Mental Health.

Luong, O. S., & Porr, P. (1990). Social work practice with Indochinese refugees. In D. Drachman (Ed.), *Social services to refugee populations* (pp. 91–121). Washington, DC: National Institute of Mental Health.

Mandel, Y. (1990). Soviet refugees. In D. Drachman (Ed.), *Social services to refugee populations* (pp. 73–90). Washington, DC: National Institute of Mental Health.

Pierre-Pierre, G. (1993, July 16). A long wait for a new life is not quite over. *New York Times*, p. B1.

Potocky-Tripodi, M. (2002). *Best practices for social work with refugees and immigrants*. New York: Columbia University Press. (pp. 3–52)

WRITTEN ASSIGNMENT: THE IMMIGRATION EXPERIENCE

Choose either an individual, a family, or a population that has immigrated to the United States. Discuss and analyze the immigration experience:

I. In your introduction, provide information on émigré's country of origin, age, race, ethnicity, occupation, socioeconomic class, religion, gender, urban/rural background. The questions and factors listed below are aimed to guide your thinking and should be addressed. The paper, however, should be presented so that a picture emerges of the human experience in the context of immigration.

II. Consider the following when describing and analyzing the émigré's departure experiences:

   a. Why did the individual, family, or population leave the native country? Discuss the larger societal and personal forces that propelled the move.

   b. How old were the individuals when they left their home country?

   c. Who made the decision to leave?

   d. Who left? Who was left behind? What was left behind?

   e. Discuss the circumstances, events, plans, and procedures involved in departing.

   f. Analyze the effect of time on departure (long wait prior to departure; abrupt departure).

   g. Describe and analyze the response of others regarding the departure (response from country-at-large, response from émigré's community and family).

   h. Describe the hopes and expectations of those leaving.

   i. Were there plans for arrival in the new country (plans for housing, school, employment, whom one might contact after arrival)?

III. Was there an interim country, institution, or place where immigrants stayed following departure and prior to resettlement in the country of destination? If so, discuss experiences in the interim place (length of time, circumstances, and events).

IV. Analyze the resettlement experiences and consider the following factors:

- Language
- Culture
- Race
- Developmental life stage
- Opportunity structure
- Employment
- School
- Expectations regarding life in the United States and reality of U.S. life
- Reception in the United States (immigrants' rights, entitlement to benefits and services, level of social and economic integration into U.S. society)
- Nature and degree of stresses
- Nature and degree of acculturation among family members
- Support networks
- Contact with others remaining in the home country

Cite and discuss the literature throughout the paper. Incorporate concepts from social work knowledge, migration studies, and literature on the immigrant group.

War and Peace in Bosnia
(a three week in-country course plus extensive orientation the prior semester)
Social Work 301, History 301, or Political Science 301

COURSE DESCRIPTION

A three-week immersion in the history, politics, and social welfare structure of Bosnia before, during, and after the recent war. This study abroad course provides an opportunity to travel abroad, meet and interact with Bosnians and the international community in Bosnia helping to stabilize and rebuild the country, to experience being the "foreigner," to discover different ways of thinking, and to view the world through the prism of another culture.

PHILOSOPHY AND RATIONALE

Since its first appearance in the historical records of the Early Middle Ages, Bosnia has always been a multireligious and multiethnic state and society. It has been a place where different peoples and churches mingled, where the great empires of the East and West met. And throughout that long history, while there has often been conflict and hostility, there have often been long periods of flourishing culture and constructive coexistence and interaction. Despite the facile representations of the war by the U.S. media, the recent conflict in Bosnia was not so much a war between various ethnic groups as it was a war by radical nationalists, of several ethnic groups, against that tolerant, multiethnic society and those who supported it—a war of power and economics. A careful study of Bosnia in both peace and war will offer much to students as we continue in the United States to struggle to increase the level of tolerance and multiculturalism.

This course is grounded in the recognition that American students in general have very little contact with other nations and cultures, despite, or very possibly because of, "globalization." This unique interdisciplinary perspective focuses on social justice, human rights, and civil development in a historical and cultural context. The experience of actually going to Bosnia, seeing firsthand the devastation wrought by the war, and investigating the nature and causes of the conflict are clearly the most effective means of countering the simplistic, one-dimensional, sound-bite news most people in this country received about the Bosnian crisis. There is simply no better way to learn than to go there and investigate firsthand.

COURSE OBJECTIVES

By the end of this course students should be:

1. Familiar with Bosnia, a "normal European" country with a tremendously rich culture and history that was torn apart by war, but is not some strange and perpetually violent place.
2. Clearer about the war itself: its roots, causes, and consequences.
3. Developing a sophisticated understanding through firsthand experiences and observations of the:

   - methods and problems of peacemaking and international intervention;
   - the reconstruction of a state and civil society;
   - the role of social workers in the humanitarian response to refugees and repatriation, displaced persons, and resettlement;
   - the origins and resolution of ethnic conflicts; and
   - the problem of landmines and de-landmining.

4. Thinking critically about their own society and especially the ways their society thinks about and portrays other societies and conflicts.
5. Identifying the effects of the war in Bosnia on The Northland community:

- changes in relationships among local residents from former Yugoslavia; and
- development of local social service programs responding to the refugees from Bosnia and participation in humanitarian and peacemaking activities in Bosnia.

COURSE TOPICS AND STRUCTURE

The course comprises three disciplinary perspectives: history (Bosnia's history of peace and cooperation, as well as the origins of ethnic conflict), political science (landmines, international intervention, and peacekeeping), and social work (refugees and repatriation, the humanitarian role of UN agencies and nongovernmental organizations [NGOs] in a war and its aftermath). Students will register for the course in one (or more) of these disciplines, but all students will participate in the same activities. These three focuses will be integrated into one course. Looking through the lenses of these disciplines will be a more realistic and holistic encounter with the nature of war and peacemaking for all students rather than any exclusively focused approach.

The course will be divided into two phases: an orientation course during the spring semester and the course in Bosnia during the Maymester. Successful completion of the orientation will be a prerequisite for being allowed to accompany the course to Bosnia. This orientation course will meet roughly once every other week and will include background readings, films, and discussions on the war and Bosnian culture, history, and geography. It will also address basic issues of safety, culture shock, how to pack, and other nuts-and-bolts issues important for students who have had little experience abroad.

The main part of the course in Bosnia will consist of meetings with government and NGO officials and visits to sites of historical importance, as well as to locations where landmine clearing and housing reconstruction/repatriation are taking place. The main site of the course will be Sarajevo, the capital of the Republic of Bosnia, Herzegovina, and the scene of the longest military siege in modern history. Extended visits will also be made to Tuzla, an important refugee city during the war; to Mostar, the unofficial "capital" of Croatian-Bosnia and the scene of horrific three-way fighting during the war; to Banja Luka, now the official capital of the "Serb Republic" of Bosnia; and to either Šrebrenica or Gorazde, cities that, despite "Protected Area" status by the UN for Bosnia Muslims, were subjected to vicious sieges. (Srebrenica finally fell to the Bosnian Serb nationalists while UN troops were stationed there and watched as all of the city's several thousand men and boys were taken away and massacred.)

To ensure that the daily meetings and trips will be as meaningful as possible, and also to monitor the students' learning and processing of the experience, 30–60 minute orientation and debriefing meetings will be held on a more or less daily basis, either before the day's first activity or at the end of the day. At these meetings, students and faculty will have an opportunity to discuss what they have experienced on that or the previous day, to discuss the readings for that or the next day's activities, and, finally, to talk over any problems or conflicts that may arise from time to time in this situation of constant living together in small spaces. In addition, students will also be required at various appropriate intervals during the trip to write short, 1–2-page reaction and analysis papers based on our interviews, visits, and readings.

EVALUATION PROCEDURES

Evaluation of students' performance in this course will be based on a variety of instruments. All students are expected to take an active part in the meetings and interviews that form the bulk of our activity in Bosnia; this is indeed the primary reason why the enrollment in the course will be kept relatively low. Through our readings and discussions in preparation for each meeting, students will be expected to develop their own questions for the individuals with whom we meet and essentially to conduct interviews with them. Students will also be required to keep a journal of their impressions, thoughts, and experiences. They will be asked to begin these journals during the spring semester orientation class to force them to begin reflecting on what they know of Bosnia, what they expect, and, perhaps, what they fear, even before their arrival in the country. The journals will be collected and read by the faculty several times during the orientation and at least a couple of times during the sojourn in Bosnia to give them insight into the students' feelings and experiences and also to afford them the opportunity to comment on them while the experience is still ongoing. Finally, students will be writing several short reaction and analysis papers during the course that will be collected, read, and graded by the faculty while in-country, so as to stimulate student thought and give them timely feedback on their academic development during the course. The journals, essays, and active participation will together make up roughly one-half of the course's final grade.

The remainder of the grade will be based on the student's completion of a major research paper, to be completed after our return from Bosnia. This assignment will be discipline-specific; the only part of the course where requirements will vary depending on whether the student is registered for the course as history, political science, or social work. In all three cases, however, the student will be asked to reflect on and apply what she/he learned during the course in a manner that conforms to the concerns and standards of her/his particular discipline.

Finally, every student is required to participate in the development and carrying out of some kind of project to "give something back" to Bosnia. The idea is to avoid encouraging "war tourism," in which we come to Bosnia, observe the ruins left from the war, take the peoples' testimonies about what happened to them, and then go away. We intend, instead, to make some kind of small but concrete and constructive contribution to some part of Bosnian society, to leave it, in some small way, better off than before we came. If it can be arranged, these projects will take place over a day or two as a group project while in-country; it could take the form of cleaning up rubble, helping to repair housing or public areas, and so forth. Alternatively, if no group project can be arranged during the course, students will develop their own projects to be completed once they return; examples could include collecting money for an orphanage, for a school, or for an NGO that provides prostheses for children maimed by landmines (an actual project from the pilot year). It is our belief that these projects are a crucial element, not only for contributing something to the country that will be hosting our educational course, but also for rounding out the students' understanding of what it means for a country and a society to experience war, how much there is that needs to be done to recover from such a war, and how much can be, and is done, by different groups of people. These projects will not be graded *per se*, but they are required for passing the course. (The spring orientation course will be based on a pass-fail format.)

REQUIRED MATERIALS FOR ORIENTATION

There is a very large literature, from many different perspectives, on the recent war in Bosnia. While much of it is of dubious value, much of it is excellent. Students are required to read several books/view several videos providing basic background on Bosnian history and the war during the orientation phase.

- American Refugee Committee, Minneapolis, Minnesota, Grant Proposals for 2002 Refugee Resettlement Programs. (e.g., to the Dutch Government, to UNHCR)

- Andric, I. (1984). *The bridge on the Drina*. Chicago, IL: University of Chicago Press. (A Pulitzer Prize-winning novel tracing Bosnian history from the fifteenth century to the outbreak of the First World War.)

- Donia, R., J., & Fine, V. A. (1995). *Bosnia and Herzegovina: A tradition betrayed*. New York, NY: Columbia University Press. (One of the best, concise overviews of Bosnian history, emphasizing its unique multicultural traditions and identities.)

- Education Services. (1975). *Serbo-Croatian Language/30*. Washington, DC: Educational Services. (A phrase dictionary and study guide.)

- UNHCR, Information Notes on Former Yugoslavia (1993–1995) Zagreb, Croatia: United Nations High Commission on Refugees. (A monthly review of the war and assistance to refugees and displaced persons) United Nations High Commissioner on Refugees (UNHCR) was the lead agency for humanitarian assistance to the republics of former Yugoslavia.

In addition to these readings to be completed during the orientation before departure for Bosnia, the course will utilize in-country a number of other primary documents, for example, from the UNHCR, from The American Refuge Committee's projects and a collection of articles, memoirs, and documents, *Why Bosnia?* edited by Rabia Ali and Lawrence Lifschultz.

There are also, finally, a number of excellent films available on the Bosnian war. Full-length feature films like "Pretty Village, Pretty Flame" (a Bosnian film) or a documentary on the history of Sarajevo could be very usefully viewed and discussed during the orientation course before departure, while several short documentaries, such as on the international war-crimes trial of Bosnian Serb Duško Tadic, the fall of "UNPA" Šrebrenica, or the war in Mostar, would be most effectively viewed and discussed while in-country, as preparation for a particular visit or interview.

ADDITIONAL MATERIALS

- Ali, R., and Lifschultz, L. (1993). *Why Bosnia?* Writings on the Balkan War. Stoney Creek, CT: Pamphleteer's Press. (A collection of articles, memoirs and documents by people directly affected by the war.)

- Burg, S., & Shoup, P. S. (2000). *The war in Bosnia-Herzegovina: Ethnic conflict and international intervention*. Armonk, NY: M. E. Sharpe. (A detailed, somewhat less angry, but still critical, overview of the various phases in that response.)

- Center for Investigation and Documentation of the Association of Former Prison Camp Inmates of Bosnia-Herzegovina. (2000). *I begged them to kill me: Crime against the women of Bosnia-Herzegovina*. Sarajevo, Bosnia-Herzegovina: Bosnia Press. (A horrifying collection of firsthand accounts of the victimization of women as a tool of war.)

- Daalder, I. (1999). *Getting to Dayton: The making of America's Bosnia policy*. Washington, DC: Brookings Institution. (An equally detailed, but more dispassionate, conservative account focusing specifically on the United States' role.)

- Gow, J. (1997). *Triumph of the lack of will: International diplomacy and the Yugoslav war*. New York: Columbia University Press. (A scathing indictment of the "international community's" responses to the Bosnian crisis.)

- Judah, T. (2000). *The Serbs: History, myth, and the destruction of Yugoslav*. New Haven, CT: Yale University Press. (An excellent examination of the history of the Serb nation and its national ideology and how they found themselves in the role of international "bad guys" in Bosnia.)

- Maas, P. (1997). *Love thy neighbor: A story of war*. New York: Vintage Books. (A compelling account of a *Washington Post* war correspondent's shattering experiences traveling in Bosnia during the war, which gives ordinary victims of this war a voice.)

- Mojzes, P. (1995). *Yugoslavian inferno: Ethnoreligious warfare in the Balkans*. New York, NY: Continuum. (A Yugoslavian American professor focuses on the role of religion, religious-cultural identity, and the "mytho-history" of the nationalities in aggravating the conflict and whether it can be properly understood as a religious war.)

- Rohde, D. (1998). *Endgame: The betrayal and fall of Srebrenica, Europe's worst massacre since WWII*. Boulder, CO: Westview Press. (A superb, thoughtful, and disturbing account by a journalist awarded the Pulitzer Prize in 1996 for his reporting on the city. He chronicles the evolution of a war crime and the outside world's complicity in it—a microcosmic study of the entire conflict in former Yugoslavia.)

- Sacco, J. (2000). *Safe Area Gorazde*. Seattle, WA: Fantagraphics Books. (A "commix" work [similar to Art Spiegelman's *Maus*] describing from firsthand experience the horrors of the siege of the Gorazde, one of the so-called "United Nations Protected Areas.")

- Sells, A. M. (1998). *The bridge betrayed: Religion and genocide in Bosnia*. Berkeley, CA: University of California Press. (President Clinton's favorite Balkans book, by a Haverford College religion professor, which argues that the various ethnic groups actually had gotten along well for centuries. Sells, of Serbian-American descent, writes that strife in the Balkans can be blamed not on historic enmity but on more recent anti-Muslim and Serbian nationalist rantings. He begins his preface with, "The story told here is not one I wish to believe or to tell.")

- Silber, L., & Little, A. (1997). *Yugoslavia: Death of a nation*. New York: Penguin USA. (An excellent nuts-and-bolts account, published as a companion to a BBC documentary, which draws on hundreds of interviews with politicians, soldiers, and citizens to bring readers behind the scenes of Europe's bloodiest conflict since World War II.)

- Sudetic, C. (1998). *Blood and vengeance: One family's story of the war in Bosnia*. New York: W.W. Norton. (A review of Bosnian history through the experiences of one family in Srebrenica from before the Second World War to the most recent war.)

LIST OF POTENTIAL MEETINGS AND ACTIVITIES

The following is a list of the meetings and activities that made up the syllabus for the 2002 pilot program. It should provide a general idea of how the course operated and what it focused on. The meetings are not listed chronologically, but are organized roughly according to the type of meeting. The precise makeup of the list of activities will naturally change slightly as contacts evolve and expand. Most particularly, we are anxious to develop more contacts in the "Republika Srpska" for the "other" side in the conflict.

- Interview with vice-mayor of Sarajevo
- Interview with Minister for Refugees, Federation of Bosnia and Herzegovina
- Interview with Minister for Missing Persons, Federation of Bosnia and Herzegovina
- Interview with Minister for Women's and Gender Affairs, Federation of Bosnia and Herzegovina

- Interview with staff and director for repatriation at headquarters of United Nations High Commissioner for Refugees in Sarajevo
- Interview with UNHCR field staff in Banja Luka, Republika Srpska
- Interview with main office of American Refugee Committee in Sarajevo
- Meetings with field staff American Refugee Committee in Banja Luka
- Interview with Bošniak family repatriated to a village in predominantly Serb area
- Meeting with field staff American Refugee Committee in Mostar and visit with repatriated family in Serbian village
- Visit to orphanage in Sarajevo and interview with director
- Meetings with principal, counselor, teachers, and students at Meša Selimovic Gymnasium (high school) in Tuzla
- Meeting with principal, teachers and students of Gymnasium No. 5, Sarajevo, including attendance of school's annual sports exhibition and awards ceremony
- Meeting with vice-principal, teachers, and students of Gymnasium No. 2, Sarajevo
- Interview with dean for International Relations, University of Sarajevo
- Interview with professors and students, faculty of Social Work, University of Sarajevo
- Interview with professors and students, faculty of Political Science, University of Sarajevo
- Interview with professor of Islamic Theology, Islamic Institute, University of Sarajevo
- Interview with historian and director of Institute for the Study of Genocide, University of Sarajevo
- Visit to Bošniak Cultural Institute and Museum, Sarajevo
- Visit to National Museum, Sarajevo
- Visit to headquarters of United Nations landmine clearing operation, Sarajevo
- Interview with staff of Norwegian People's Aid and extensive tour of NPA's training and landmine-clearing operations in and around Sarajevo
- Visit to Prosthetics Manufacturing and Fitting Clinic in Tuzla
- Visit to Landmine Victims Association in Tuzla
- Interviews with several individuals who participated in the war (on both the government and Serbian-nationalist sides)
- Interview with a Bošniak young man who was trapped in the besieged town of Gorazde and is now an "Internally Displaced Person"
- Visit to "Tunnel Museum" documenting the Bosnian and Herzegovinan Army's attempts to keep Sarajevo alive during the war through a tunnel underneath the airport, connecting the besieged town to free territory
- Tours of war-devastated regions in Sarajevo and Mostar
- Tour of former Olympic site, the scene of some of fiercest fighting near Sarajevo, and vantage point for Serb-nationalist assault on Sarajevo
- Visit to former soccer stadium turned into mass cemetery in Sarajevo, and to other cemeteries
- Short visit to Pale, Radovan Karadzic's "capital" of the Republika Srpska during the war
- Tours of cultural and historical landmarks in Sarajevo, Mostar, Banja Luka, and Jablanica
- Visit to service in Serbian Orthodox church in Sarajevo
- Visit to service in Roman Catholic church in Sarajevo
- Visit to service in Islamic mosque in Sarajevo
- Visit to Shabbat (or Sabbath) service in Jewish synagogue in Sarajevo (included participation in Shabbat meal and lengthy visit with members of congregation)
- Attendance at local championship soccer game between FC Sarajevo and FC Zeleznica

POSTSCRIPT

The "pilot" program of this course in May 2002 proved to be a life-changing experience for several of our students. The course was in all respects an overwhelming success. Based on the students' reactions during the trip, their responses in their journals, and their research papers and community service projects that they completed after our return, it is obvious that each student learned a tremendous amount. They learned not only in the factual sense about the Bosnian war, but also in a much more general and difficult to quantify sense about other cultures, about their own society, and about the nature of the world. Our group's reception by the Bosnian people with whom we came into contact was quite moving. From our translator-drivers to the UN and NGO staff with whom we met, to the teachers and shop people we encountered, everyone welcomed us enthusiastically and made us feel that our presence in their country and our inquiry to the causes and consequences of the recent war were very much appreciated by them. It was impressed on us constantly how isolated and abandoned the Bosnians feel and how very much they want contact with our country and want people outside their country to really understand what happened to them.

TIME LINE FOR PRESTUDY ABROAD COURSE/ORIENTATION IN SPRING SEMESTER 2004 AND STUDY ABROAD EXPERIENCE MAY–JUNE 2004:

September 2002

Submit proposals to University Study Abroad Office about 15 months preceding the term in which students will register for the study abroad.

Spring Semester 2003

Advertise program, recruit students by sponsoring several information sessions on course, creating a Web site, and so forth.

Fall Semester 2003

October 15:   deadline for applications
October 15–30:   interview prospective students
November 1–15: notify students of their acceptance so they can register for the orientation course in the spring semester
December 1: $200 nonrefundable registration fee due

Spring Semester 2004

January 15: $800 payment due.
February: Students pay for airline tickets from travel agency
February–April: Orientation course (approximately 12 hrs.) for background on the geography, culture, history, social welfare, and political systems of the country; language study and practice; discussions of the assigned readings and video; trip preparations.
March 1: $1,100 final payment due

The International Environment of Social Welfare: Web Sites on International Development for Student and Faculty Research and Learning
SOCW6392

COURSE DESCRIPTION

This doctoral-level course requires students to engage in critical thinking regarding social welfare issues. It analyzes theories of causation and alternative models for national or international interventions. The course also explores how political, economic, cultural, religious, and historical factors may affect social welfare policies and the delivery of human services in low-income, developing, industrial, and postindustrial societies. The course focuses primarily on the countries of North, Central, and South America.

Space prevents publishing the full course outline here, but interested readers may contact Professor Díaz.

The following Web links are included in the syllabus for this course. They provide invaluable sources of further learning and information for faculty members, as well as students.

INTERNATIONAL DEVELOPMENT RESOURCES

Links to Degree Programs in International Development Studies

Degree programs' Web sites from North America, Europe, Asia/Oceania and Africa, divided geographically.

International Development Resources

- http://www.pvo.net/usaid/index_intl.html

  This page provides a search system for locating private voluntary organizations worldwide. It enables interested individuals to obtain a list of PVOs as well as descriptions of those organizations in the area of socioeconomic development.

- http://www.blds.ids.ac.uk/blds/

  British Library for Development Studies online catalog at the International Development Institute, including Europe's largest and most comprehensive research collection on development and the largest collection of development-related journals in Europe.

- http://www.eldis.org

  ELDIS, a free search engine from the Institute of Development Studies, Sussex, U.K., offering an easy route to the latest information on development and environmental issues.

- http://nt1.ids.ac.uk/oxfam/index.htm

  Online Oxfam Great Britain library catalogue. Oxfam is one of the best-known nongovernmental development, relief, and campaigning organizations in the world.

- http://www.idrc.ca/books/reports

  The online reports of the International Development Resource Centre. The International Development Research Centre is a public corporation created by the Parliament of Canada to help researchers and communities in the developing world find solutions to their social, economic, and environmental problems.

- http://www.bl.uk

  The Web site of the home page for the British Library. Look for the Social Policy Information Service (SPIS).

- http://bellanet.org

  Free development resources from Bellanet, including software and publications. The Web site includes practical advice and discussion of approaches to the use of information and communication technologies (ICTs) for knowledge sharing and collaboration; research studies on management and evaluation, collaboration, and policy papers on the use of ICTs in international development; open source software applications; free Internet and computer training materials; and a number of e-mail discussion lists on development topics.

- http://www.elsevier.nl

  A comprehensive digital library in numerous topic areas from Elsevier Science. Includes online journals, books, electronic products, bibliographies, and many other resources.

- http://www.oneworld.net

  Comprehensive worldwide news and situation analyses from Oneworld.net, the Internet community of 679 organizations in the area of human rights and sustainable development. In addition to information about Oneworld.net partners, you can receive free news and editorial updates on your area of interest.

- http://www.itdg.org

  Intermediate Technology (IT) Publications Web site. IT Publications is the world's largest publisher and supplier of books and journals on appropriate technology.

- http://www.cid.harvard.edu/caer2/; and http://www.cid.harvard.edu/hiid/index

  The Harvard Institute for International Development has been dissolved, but extensive publications from the institute are available through the Web sites above.

- http://www.un.org/esa/research.htm

  United Nations international development research and analysis site.

Development Organizations

- http://www.worldbank.org/html/extdr/toc.html

  Resources from the World Bank Group.

- http://www.un.org/

  United Nations general Web site.

- http://www.undp.org/

  The Web site of the United Nations Development Program.

- http://www.unicef.org

  The home page of UNICEF, the United Nations children's agency.

- http://www.ohchr.org

  The home page of the United Nations High Commission on Human Rights. Extensive materials on human rights treaties, including country reports on compliance.

- http://www.wfp.org/index.htm

  World Food Programme, the food organization of the United Nations.

- http://www.wfp.org/links/

  International development (organization) links provided by the United Nations World Food Programme.

- http://www.unsystem.org

  United Nations site locator for the international organizations that are not part of the UN system.

- http://www.interaction.org/

  The Web site of InterAction, a diverse coalition of more than 160 U.S.-based relief, development, environmental, and refugee agencies working in more than 100 countries around the world. It is the leading U.S. advocate for sustainable development, refugee, and disaster assistance, and humanitarian aid. Offers internship and employment opportunities.

- http://www.sidint.org

  The Web site of SID, the Society for International Development, one of the largest membership-based civil society organizations working in the field of development.

International Social Development Journals

- *International Journal of Social Welfare*
- *International Social Security Review*
- *International Social Science Journal*
- *International Social Work*
- *Social Development Issues*
- *Social Policy & Administration*

Disaster Management Links

- http://www.colorado.edu/hazards/

  Natural hazards page at the University of Colorado–Boulder, featuring an online library, periodicals, other online publications, information on upcoming conferences and training in emergency/disaster management, disaster-related organizations, institutions offering emergency management courses, and other disaster-related links.

- http://www.paho.org/english/ped/pedinet.htm

  Links to disaster management sites from Pan American Health Organization, an international public health agency with more than 90 years of experience in working to improve health and living standards of the countries of the Americas.

- http://www.fema.gov/library

  Virtual library and electronic reading room of FEMA, the Federal Emergency Management Agency.

- http://www.interaction.org/disaster

  The disaster response page of the InterAction (see above): disaster news, reports, and other resources.

Free Disaster-Related Periodicals

- http://www.colorado.edu/hazards/resources/periodicals.html

Contributors

EDITORS

Lynne M. Healy is Professor at the University of Connecticut School of Social Work in West Hartford, Connecticut and Director of the School's Center for International Social Work Studies. She teaches courses in international social work, ethics, and social work/non-profit management. At the School of Social Work, she initiated the International Center, approved by the faculty in 1993, and developed an elective specialization in International Issues. Dr. Healy is currently President of the North-American and Caribbean Association of Schools of Social Work and a Vice-President of the International Association of Schools of Social Work (IASSW). She served a previous term on the IASSW Board of Directors as an at-large member, and was Program Chair for the 1992 IASSW Congress held in Washington, DC. Also active in national associations, she served as Chair of the International Commission of the Council on Social Work Education (CSWE) for 5 years and is a member of the CSWE International Commission and the NASW International Committee. Dr. Healy has published numerous articles and several books on international social work, including: *International Social Work: Professional Action in an Interdependent World* (Oxford, 2001) and *Models of International Collaboration in Social Work Education* (with Y. Asamoah and M. C. Hokenstad, CSWE 2003) and has assisted CSWE in compiling two collections of course materials on international social work (1997 and forthcoming). She serves on the editorial boards of *The Caribbean Journal of Social Work, The Asia-Pacific Journal of Social Work, Administration in Social Work, The Journal of Immigrant and Refugee Services*, and *The Journal of Social Development in Africa*. Dr. Healy has taught and consulted in Jamaica and Mauritius and has conducted many workshops on internationalizing social work curriculum.

Rosemary J. Link is a Professor teaching in the Department of Social Work and the Peace Studies Program and Chair of the Professional Studies Division at Augsburg College in Minneapolis, Minnesota. Dr. Link is currently involved in a State Department Grant to increase international and inter-cultural dialogue in classrooms and is building a video/internet 'world cultures' module into her coursework. Currently the partners in the 'world cultures' curriculum project are: the School of Social Work at the University of Ljubljana, Slovenia, Augsburg College USA, and the Department of Social Work and Psychology at the National University of Singapore. Dr. Link has a long-term interest in bringing world issues into social work and peace studies curriculum in order to increase students' global awareness and peaceful cooperation. Active in international organizations, including as a writer for the Child Poverty Action Group in London, UK, Dr. Link is also former chair of the NASW, Minnesota International Committee, and a member of the CSWE International Commission. She is Chair of the Board of Southside Family Nurturing Center in Minneapolis which implements the objectives of the United Nations Convention on the Rights of the Child and former Chair of the Department of Social Work, Augsburg College. Dr. Link has a number of publications relating to global issues and social work curriculum, including the book co-authored with Dr. Chathapuram Ramanathan, *All Our Futures: Principles and Resources for Social Work Practice in a Global Era* and *When Children Pay* co-authored with Dr. Anthony Bibus. Dr. Cacinovic Vogrincic and Dr. Link also co-authored a chapter "Learning Together Through Faculty and Student Exchange: Augsburg College and the University of Ljubljana, Slovenia" in the CSWE publication, *Models of International Collaboration*.

AUTHORS

Frederick L. Ahearn, Jr.	*Catholic University of America*
Karl Bahm	*University of Wisconsin–Superior*
Maria Bartlett	*Humboldt State University*
Katharine Briar-Lawson	*University at Albany*
Diane S. Falk	*Richard Stockton College of New Jersey*
Beth Cagan	*Cleveland State University*
Héctor Luis Díaz	*University of Texas at Arlington*
Haji Dokhanchi	*University of Wisconsin–Superior*
Diane Drachman	*University of Connecticut*
Judy Anne Dwyer	*University of Wisconsin–Superior*
David Engstrom	*San Deigo State University*
Richard Estes	*University of Pennsylvania*
Dorothy Gamble	*University of North Carolina at Chapel Hill*
Judith Gordon	*College of New Rochelle*
Charles Guzzetta	*Hunter College–CUNY*
Vanmala Hiranandani	*University of Northern Iowa*
M. C. "Terry" Hokenstad	*Case Western Reserve University*
Robin Mama	*Monmouth University*
Golam M. Mathbor	*Monmouth University*
Suzanne McDevitt	*Edinboro University of Pennsylvania*
Shirley Porterfield	*Washington University*
Willam Roth	*University at Albany*
Margaret Sherraden	*University of St. Louis*
Barbara F. Turnage	*University of Central Florida*
Robin R. Wingo	*Minnesota State University–Mankato*
Joseph Wronka	*Springfield College*